Digital futures

living in a dot-com world

edited by James Wilsdon

Forum for the **Future**

Earthscan Publications Ltd, London and Sterling, VA

First published in the UK and USA in 2001 by
Earthscan Publications Ltd

ISBN: 1 85383 789 X

Typesetting by PCS Mapping & DTP, Newcastle upon Tyne
Printed and bound by Creative Print and Design (Wales), Ebbw Vale
Cover design by Susanne Harris
Index prepared by Indexing Specialists, Hove, East Sussex

For a full list of publications please contact:
Earthscan Publications Ltd
120 Pentonville Road
London, N1 9JN, UK
Tel: +44 (0)20 7278 0433
Fax: +44 (0)20 7278 1142
Email: earthinfo@earthscan.co.uk
http://www.earthscan.co.uk

22883 Quicksilver Drive, Sterling, VA 20166–2012, USA

Earthscan is an editorially independent subsidiary of Kogan Page Ltd and publishes in association with WWF-UK and the International Institute for Environment and Development

A catalogue record for this book is available from the British Library

Library of Congress Cataloging-in-Publication Data

Digital futures : living in a dot-com world / edited by James Wilsdon.
     p. cm.
  "Forum for the Future."
  A product of the Digital Futures project set up by Forum for the Future.
  Includes bibliographical references and index.
  ISBN 1-85383-789-X (hardcover)
   1. Electronic commerce—Great Britain. I. Title: Living in a dot-com world.
II. Title: dot-com world. III. Wilsdon, James, 1973– IV. Forum for the Future
(Organization) V. Digital Futures (Project)

HF5548.325.G7 D54 2001
306.3'4—dc21

                                            2001023220

Digital Futures partners

DEM⊙S

Forum for the **Future**

"green alliance...

local futures

new economics foundation

**CABINET
OFFICE**

𝒮DETR
*ENVIRONMENT
TRANSPORT
REGIONS*

dtı
Department of Trade and Industry

SPRU
Science and Technology
Policy Research

TCPA

UK CEED

▪▪ UNIVERSITY OF
▪▪ BRADFORD

Fore*sight*
Making the future work for you

South West *of* **England**
Regional Development Agency

Smart South West

Unilever

THE POST OFFICE

Contents

Contributors

Tom Bentley is the Director of Demos, an independent think-tank. (tom@demos.co.uk)

Frans Berkhout is a Senior Fellow and leader of the Environment and Energy Programme at SPRU (Science and Technology Policy Research) at the University of Sussex. (f.berkhout@sussex.ac.uk)

David Boyle is Senior Associate at the New Economics Foundation, and the author of *Funny Money* (HarperCollins, 1999) and *The Tyranny of Numbers* (HarperCollins, 2001). (dcboyle@compuserve.com)

John Browning is co-founder of First Tuesday, a global network dedicated to helping entrepreneurs achieve success. He is also co-editor of *New Economy Watch* and a contributing editor of *Wired*. (jb@poplar.com)

Madeleine Bunting is a columnist and leader writer for *The Guardian*. (madeleine.bunting@guardian.co.uk)

Kevin Carey is the Founding Director of humanITy, the world's first digital charity, which focuses on IT and social exclusion. He is also an adviser to the Cabinet Office. (humanity@atlas.co.uk)

Ian Christie is an Associate Director of the Local Futures Group and a writer on sustainable development issues. He is the co-author of *Managing Sustainable Development* (Earthscan, 2000) and *From Here to Sustainability* (Earthscan, 2001). (ian.christie@localfutures.com)

Evan Davis is the Economics Editor of the BBC's Newsnight programme, and the author of *Public Spending*. (Penguin, 1998). (evan.davis@bbc.co.uk)

Malcolm Eames is a Fellow in the Environment and Energy Programme at SPRU (Science and Technology Policy Research) at the University of Sussex. (m.eames@sussex.ac.uk)

Tara Garnett has worked on sustainable development issues for Sustain, the London School of Economics and, most recently, Transport 2000. (tara@transport2000.demon.co.uk)

Andrew Gillespie is Professor of Communications Geography and Executive Director of the Centre for Urban and Regional Development Studies at the University of Newcastle. (andy.gillespie@ncl.ac.uk)

Nick Green was previously Policy Officer at the Town and Country Planning Association, and now teaches at the Bartlett School of Planning, University College London. (ucftcng@ucl.ac.uk)

Sir Peter Hall is Professor of Planning at the Bartlett School of Planning, University College London. From 1998–99, he was a member of the Deputy Prime Minister's Urban Task Force. (p.hall@ucl.ac.uk)

Richard Hawkins was a Senior Fellow at SPRU (Science and Technology Policy Research) at the University of Sussex, and now works as a senior advisor at TNO in the Netherlands. (Hawkins@stb.tno.nl)

Mark Hepworth is Director of the Local Futures Group, and Visiting Professor of Economic Geography at Birkbeck College, University of London. (mark.hepworth@localfutures.com)

Julia Hertin is Research Officer in the Environment and Energy Programme at SPRU (Science and Technology Policy Research) at the University of Sussex. (j.hertin@sussex.ac.uk)

Peter Hopkinson is Senior Lecturer in Environmental Management at the University of Bradford and course director of the university's MSc in Business Strategy and the Environment. (p.g.hopkinson@bradford.ac.uk)

Peter James is part-time Professor of Environmental Management at the University of Bradford, and a senior research associate of UK CEED. His publications include *Sustainable Measures* (Greenleaf, 2001) and *Driving Eco-innovation* (Pitman, 1996). (peterjames2000@cs.com)

Stephen Joseph is Executive Director of Transport 2000, and a member of the Commission for Integrated Transport. (stephen@transport2000.demon.co.uk)

Ben Jupp is a Research Associate of the think-tank Demos. (ben.jupp@nof.org.uk)

Charles Leadbeater is an independent writer, Demos Research Associate, and an adviser to Atlas Venture, the US–European venture capital fund. He is the author of *Living on Thin Air: The New Economy* (Viking, 1999). (charlie@malvernrd.demon.co.uk)

Amory B Lovins is Chief Executive Officer (Research) at the Rocky Mountain Institute, Director of The Hypercar Centre, and co-author of *Natural Capitalism: The Next Industrial Revolution* (Earthscan, 1999). (ablovins@rmi.org)

Alex MacGillivray is Deputy Director of the New Economics Foundation, and has researched and published widely on new technology, social inclusion and sustainable communities. (alex.macgillivray@neweconomics.org)

Gordon Mackerron was a Senior Fellow at SPRU (Science and Technology Policy Research) at the University of Sussex, and now works for the energy consultancy NERA. (gordon.mackerron@nera.com)

Simon Marvin is Professor of Sustainable Urban and Regional Development at Salford University and Co-director of the Centre for Sustainable Urban and Regional Futures. (s.marvin@salford.ac.uk)

Paul Miller is a researcher at Forum for the Future, where his work focuses on the sustainability of the new economy. (p.miller@forumforthefuture.org.uk)

Professor Jim Norton is Head of e-Business Policy at the Institute of Directors. Prior to joining the IoD, he led the Cabinet Office team which produced the report *e-commerce@its.best.uk*. (j.norton@iod.co.uk).

Jonathon Porritt is a Programme Director of Forum for the Future and Chairman of the UK Sustainable Development Commission. (a.paintin@forumforthefuture.org.uk)

Rebecca Willis is Policy Coordinator at Green Alliance. (rebecca@green-alliance.org.uk)

James Wilsdon is Senior Policy Adviser at Forum for the Future and coordinator of the Digital Futures project. (j.wilsdon@forumforthefuture.org.uk)

Acknowledgements

True to the spirit of the network society, this book stems from a collaboration between a diverse web of individuals and organizations. Above all, we are grateful to the Digital Futures partners for making this research possible through their generous contributions of time, money and expertise.

Particular thanks to the members of the project steering group: John Adams (DETR); Terry Beal (South West RDA); Tom Bentley (Demos); Frans Berkhout (SPRU); Colin Bluck (Smart South West); Gary Boswell (Nationwide Building Society); David Boyle (New Economics Foundation); Ian Christie (Local Futures Group); Tim Cradock (WH Smith); Malcolm Eames (SPRU); Alan George (Unilever); Katrina Giles (AOL); Hark Gill (Royal Bank of Scotland); Andy Gillespie (University of Newcastle); Colin Gomm (BP); Nick Green (Town and Country Planning Association); Vernice Halligan (Ericsson); Mary Heathcote (Foresight); Mark Hepworth (Local Futures Group); Julia Hertin (SPRU); Anna Hilton (Fishburn Hedges); Charlotte Hines (MORI); Peter Hopkinson (UK CEED/ University of Bradford); Mike Hughes (BT); Peter James (UK CEED/ University of Bradford); Alan Jelly (Unilever); Rachel Jones (Fishburn Hedges); Ben Jupp (Demos); Charles Leadbeater; Martin LeJeune (Fishburn Hedges); Alan Knight (Kingfisher); Alex MacGillivray (New Economics Foundation); Giles Mackey (BP); Peter Madden (DETR); John Magill (MORI); Paul Miller (Forum for the Future); George Martin (Forum for the Future); Simon Marvin (University of Salford); Russell Moss (Foresight); Kate Murphy (Foresight); Chris O'Connor (Ericsson); Paul Pritchard (Royal and Sun Alliance); Jonathon Porritt (Forum for the Future); Lisa Ramshaw (Amazon.co.uk); Douglas Robinson (DTI); James Sergeant (Cabinet Office); Christine Smedley (Amazon.co.uk); Charles Tucker (Post Office); Chris Tuppen (BT); Jon Tutcher (Sun Microsystems); April Vesey (DTI); Andrew Ward (Nationwide); Rebecca Willis (Green Alliance); Ian Wood (BT).

Thanks also to everyone at Earthscan, particularly Jonathan Sinclair Wilson, Akan Leander, Frances MacDermott and Nim Moorthy. Finally, many thanks to Rowan Davies for her skilful and sensitive editing.

The authors of each chapter would like to add the following acknowledgments.

Chapter 1

Grateful thanks to the many people who contributed time and ideas to this work, particularly James Wilsdon, Peter Madden, Paul Jefferiss, Tom Bentley, Keith Collins, Ian Christie, Stephen Tindale, Robin Murray, Roger Levett, Paul Ekins, Evan Davis, Andy Arnold, Chris Tuppen, John Adams, Jon Tutcher, Douglas Robinson and Nick Butler. Many thanks, too, to BP and the Imagination Gallery, for their support.

Chapter 2

We would like to acknowledge the support and assistance of our partners in the Digital Futures project, and especially to the Post Office and Royal and SunAlliance for hosting two theme seminars. We would like to extend particular thanks to Perry Walker (New Economics Foundation), Andy Bush (Sun Microsystems) and Martin Wright (*Green Futures* magazine) for their contributions to these seminars.

Chapter 3

Thanks to everyone who contributed to this chapter, in particular Rebecca Willis (Green Alliance), Jonathon Porritt, Paul Miller and Halima Khan (Forum), Ian Christie and Kate Oakley (LFG), Alex MacGillivray (NEF), Christina Smedley and Lisa Ramshaw (Amazon.co.uk), Katrina Giles (AOL) Chris Godwin (IBM), Martin LeJeune and Rachel Jones (Fishburn Hedges), and to all those who attended the dot-com ethics seminar held in October 2000, which was generously hosted by Amazon.co.uk. Thanks also to all those companies and individuals who participated in the survey.

Chapter 4

We are grateful to a number of people whose ideas helped shape this chapter. Anne George undertook some of the research at Demos. Jon Tutcher at Sun Microsystems hosted a seminar to discuss the findings. Other useful contributions came from Katrina Giles (AOL), Gary

Boswell (Nationwide), Daniel Miller (UCL), Damien Tambini (IPPR), Ed Mayo (New Economics Foundation), Anne Power (LSE), Gabriel Chanon (Community Development Foundation), Ken Warpole (Comedia), Cathy Pharaoh (Charities Aid Foundation), Fiona Halton (Pilotlight), Penelope Harvey (University of Manchester), Lizzie Jackson (BBC), Sonia Liff (University of Warwick) and David Wilcox.

Chapter 5

We would like to thank everyone who contributed to this chapter, and especially Ian Wood (BT), Wingham Rowan (GEMS), Hark Gill (NatWest), June Bowman (ONS), Katrina Giles (AOL), James Wilsdon (Forum), Adrian Harvey (Fabian Society), Chris O'Connor (Ericsson), James Sargeant (Cabinet Office), Charles Tucker and Annette Hutchinson (The Post Office), Stephen Leman (DfEE), Alan Wyle (National Association of Village Shops), Bernie Ward (NEF), Kevin Carey (HumanITy), Felicity Ussher (silicon.com), Danny Miller (UCL), Sonia Liff (Warwick) and David Lascelles (Centre for the Study of Financial Innovation).

Chapter 6

Thanks to all those who took part in interviews and the theme workshop, and particular thanks to South-West RDA for organizing and hosting the e-regions workshop.

Chapter 7

Thanks to Deirdre Hopkinson and Sue James for their encouragement and support, members of the Digital Futures consortium for information and feedback, and Charles Tucker of The Post Office for organizing a seminar to discuss the first draft.

Chapter 8

We are grateful to a number of people whose ideas helped to shape this chapter: Joe Ravetz (University of Manchester); Gary Boswell, (Nationwide Building Society); Tim Craddock, Muriel Stirling and Rick Latham (WH Smith); Graham Bell and Gideon Amos (successive directors of the TCPA); members of the TCPA Policy Council; participants in a TCPA seminar in October 2000; and last but no means least, James Wilsdon (Forum for the Future)

Glossary

ACCPE	UK government Advisory Committee on Consumer Products and the Environment
avatar	three-dimensional virtual personality
B2B	business-to-business
B2C	business-to-consumer
BAT	best available technology
broadband	high speed data connection
C2B	consumer-to-business
C2C	consumer-to-consumer
CEO	chief executive officer
CO_2	carbon dioxide
DETR	Department of the Environment, Transport and the Regions
digital divide	the gap between information 'haves' and 'have nots'
DTI	Department of Trade and Industry
DTV	digital TV
ecobots	a search engine facility which uses environmental criteria
EDI	electronic data exchange
EIA	Energy Information Administration (US)
e-materialization	reducing material and energy inputs through information technologies
EU	European Union
G2C	government-to-consumer
GDP	Gross Domestic Product
GEM	guaranteed electronic markets
GHG	greenhouse gas(es)
GPS	global positioning satellites
GRI	Global Reporting Initiative
HGV	heavy goods vehicle
IAQ	infrequently asked question
ICT	information and communication technology
infomediary	intermediaries who exchange information online

inter-operability	ability to operate on a range of systems
intranet	internal computer network inaccessible from the internet
IPR	intellectual property rights
ISP	internet service provider
IT	information technology
LCA	life-cycle assessment
legacy system	out-of-date computer hardware still in use
LETS	local exchange and trading schemes
LGV	light goods vehicle
MtC	million tonnes of carbon
m-commerce	mobile commerce
MP3	digital music format
natural capital	stocks or flows of environmental and natural resources
NEF	New Economics Foundation
NGO	non-governmental organizations
NIMBY	not in my back yard
OECD	Organisation for Economic Co-operation and Development
open source	software with a publicly available programming code
PC	personal computer
PDA	personal digital assistant
RDA	regional development agency
RDC	regional distribution centre
rebound effect	a negative second-order effect
REEP	Regional Electronic Economy Programme
RPG	regional planning guidance
R&D	research and development
SME	small- to medium-sized enterprise
SPRU	Science and Technology Policy Research Unit (Sussex University)
STB	set-top box
t-commerce	commerce using time as a currency
TCPA	Town and Country Planning Association
telematics	transportation aids using internet and telecommunication technologies
UN	United Nations
virtualization	the provision of goods or services in a virtual format
walled garden	a closed internet environment with access only to certain websites
WTO	World Trade Organization

Figures, tables and boxes

Figures

Tables

Boxes

Foreword

Jonathon Porritt

If we're to believe the hype from the dot-coms, the internet is changing everything for the better. Reduced prices, increased convenience, wider choice and at the same time it's all great for the environment because everything is going 'virtual'.

But here's one tiny slice of a countervailing reality. A friend of ours in London has become an extremely enthusiastic user of e-shopping services, and buys all her 'bulk stuff' (the washing powder, loo paper and industrial quantities of breakfast cereals for the kids) over the internet. Yet she also regularly nips down (in the car) to her nearest store for all the fresh produce and to check out any new bargains. So when you add the emissions from the delivery van to the emissions from a loyal shopper, you actually end up with a net increase, rather than any decrease.

We can't of course generalize from one small example. In fact, as this collection of fascinating research papers and provocative think pieces makes clear, almost any generalization about the environmental and social consequences of the new economy is hard to substantiate. Businesses and consumers are using the new technologies in all sorts of different ways to suit all sorts of different purposes.

And that is exactly why Forum for the Future set up the Digital Futures project in the first place – to get a snapshot of where we are as the new economy really begins to bite, and to explore how we make the most of the opportunities that this brave new world offers. To do this, we brought together a quite unique consortium of Government departments, private sector interests (from both the 'old' and the 'new' economies) and some of the UK's leading think-tanks and NGOs.

Part of the challenge for those involved was that there's still so little hard and fast evidence. We may be witnessing the onset of the digital revolution, but until now there's been very little information for policy makers and opinion formers to go on.

Against that backdrop, it's inevitable that such a study raises as many questions as it manages to answer. But as you'll see, the relentless optimism of today's e-entrepreneurs appears to be a fair reflection of the potential for these new technologies to help deliver real social and environmental benefits.

One reason for this is the profound shift towards innovation and entrepreneurship. This capability is transforming every sector, from agriculture to aerospace, pharmaceuticals to farming. When I hear advocates of the new economy saying that we need to rethink the role of policy, regulation and traditional institutions, that we need to under-stand and value intangible assets, that we need to foster creativity and innovation, I can't help feeling the green economic agenda is strikingly similar.

But we are unlikely to reap these benefits without a lot more forward planning and anticipatory framing of the market. Inevitably, there are many discordant notes in today's electronic symphony, includ-ing a disturbing strand of digital determinism ('that's where the technologies are taking us, brother, and there's nothing anyone can do about it'), a sometimes bullying bravado ('get wired, my friend, or get bankrupt'), and more than a touch of complacent insouciance at the dark side of these bright new technologies – especially in terms of the potential loss of privacy and the growing intrusiveness in our lives.

For environmental and social justice campaigners, we've seen all this techno-determinism before. And as both Government and business now seek to retrofit policy to mitigate and repair some of the damage done through the old industrial economy, this is precisely the time for practitioners of the new economy to avoid falling into the same old trap. It would be a shame to screw up quite so badly with the digital revolution as we did with the Industrial Revolution, knowing so much more this time round about how best to avoid some of the more damag-ing social and environmental outcomes.

For me, the single most important conclusion to emerge from this early research into an extraordinarily exciting future is that the worst thing we can do is to stand back in awe or be swept unthinkingly along by the sheer pace and scale of technological change.

It's been inspiring to see the way in which both our private sector and Government partners in this project have engaged so frankly and constructively in those potential dilemmas. Many of these are reflected in the 'agenda for a sustainable digital economy', which appears in the Introduction.

E-business sits at a crossroads. Is it going to head down the old economy route of putting profit before planet and people, or can it lead the way towards more sustainable, accountable forms of capitalism? Amidst all the turmoil, there is everything to play for.

Introduction

Digital Futures: an agenda for a sustainable digital economy

James Wilsdon and Paul Miller

Living in a dot-com world

Predicting the future is a hazardous business. History is littered with prophecies that went awry. Take Charles Duell, the US Patent Commissioner, who in 1899 proposed shutting down the Patent Office on the grounds that 'Everything that can be invented has been invented.' Or Thomas Watson, the former CEO of IBM, who declared in the late 1940s that 'there is a world market for maybe five computers'.[1]

Forecasting trends in information technology is particularly tricky. Who could have anticipated the white-knuckle ride of the e-commerce sector over the course of 2000? The year opened on a wave of dot-com euphoria, as high-tech shares soared to record highs. The merger of AOL and Time-Warner in January signalled that the internet had come of age, as an old-economy giant was swallowed by a new-economy upstart. E-commerce mania hit a peak in the UK on 15 March, when lastminute.com was floated on the stock market at a value of £730 million. A month later, the market crashed, and the lengthy comedown began. A string of high-profile dot-coms collapsed and many began to wonder what all the fuss had been about. Who can say where it will all go next?

Mindful of such pitfalls, this book steers clear of glib predictions. Its authors make no claims to be cyber-soothsayers. They have no digital crystal balls. However, they do try to make sense of emerging patterns in the use and application of e-commerce, and to assess how these will affect our economy, society and environment. By mapping the present, they seek to highlight the possibilities for creating a new economy that is cleaner, greener and more socially inclusive than the old.

The book is the product of the Digital Futures project, a collaboration between government, business and the voluntary sector. Its overarching aim is to examine e-commerce through the prism of sustainable development, to better understand the relationship between its economic, social and environmental dimensions. The project was born out of a recognition that two of the most powerful drivers of change within modern economies are the explosion of digital technologies, and the shift towards sustainable development. Both require us to rethink the nature of goods and services; both have the capacity to transform the relationship between governments, companies, citizens and consumers. Yet there have been surprisingly few attempts to assess whether the digital and sustainability revolutions will complement or conflict with one another. Digital Futures has sought to build an intellectual and political bridge between the communities of e-commerce and sustainability, which have many things in common, but have not yet engaged in much dialogue.

Examining the social and environmental opportunities that are presented by e-commerce requires us to do more than simply describe the wonders of technology. If you're the sort of person who salivates at the prospect of your toaster being able to email your fridge, then this book probably isn't for you. Our interest lies not so much in the gadgets and techno-wizardry of the digital future, as in the potential that technology offers us to tackle the social and environmental challenges that we face.

An agenda for a sustainable digital economy

The central theme of this book is that there are more 'e's than you might think in e-commerce. E is for electronic – the internet revolution that is transforming the way we live, work and do business. It is also for enterprise – the dynamism and creativity that drives the new economy. E is for environment – the scope to use new technology to reduce our impact on the natural world. And e is for equity – the possibilities that the net presents for new forms of social inclusion and interaction. Add all these together and you get the final e – the explosion of new opportunities to tackle the challenges of sustainability.

In this introduction, our research findings are summarized in the form of ten headline principles – what we might call our 'ten dot-

Definitions

Sustainable development

Sustainable development is all about achieving a balance between the economic, social and environmental dimensions of a society or an organization's activities. The UK government defines it in terms of four objectives:

- social progress which recognizes the needs of everyone;
- effective protection of the environment;
- prudent use of natural resources;
- maintenance of high and stable levels of economic growth and employment.[2]

E-commerce

There are ongoing debates about the best way of defining e-commerce. Within Digital Futures, we have followed the broad definition used by the Cabinet Office in its report 'e-commerce@its.best.uk':[3]

> 'Electronic commerce is the exchange of information across electronic networks, at any stage in the supply chain, whether within an organization, between businesses, between businesses and consumers, or between the public and private sectors, whether paid or unpaid.'

Ten principles for sustainable e-commerce

1 Beyond the hype, there's hope.
2 The new economy can access all areas.
3 Community is alive and clicking.
4 E is for environment.
5 HTML = heavy traffic made lighter?
6 Trust me, I'm a dot-com.
7 Right now, matter matters more (not less).
8 Smart technology needs smart institutions.
9 We need to join the dots.
10 It's about time.

commandments' – for sustainable e-commerce. Within the chapters that follow there are more detailed suggestions as to what government, business and the voluntary sector can do to take this agenda forward.

Digital Futures: the project

Digital Futures was launched in February 2000 as a one-year inquiry into the social and environmental impacts and opportunities of e-commerce. A consortium of 28 organizations participated in the project, including think-tanks, NGOs, companies and government departments. The project focuses on the UK, and so provides a case study of the relationship between e-commerce and sustainability within a particular national context, although many of its conclusions are more widely applicable.

Think-tank partners
- Demos
- Forum for the Future
- Green Alliance
- Local Futures Group
- New Economics Foundation
- SPRU – Science and Technology Policy Research
- Town and Country Planning Association
- UK CEED/University of Bradford

Government partners
- Cabinet Office
- Department of the Environment, Transport and the Regions
- Department of Trade and Industry
- Foresight
- South West of England Regional Development Agency

Corporate partners
- Amazon.co.uk
- AOL UK
- BT
- BP
- Ericsson
- Kingfisher
- The Post Office
- NatWest
- Nationwide Building Society
- Royal & SunAlliance
- Smart South West
- Sun Microsystems
- Unilever
- WH Smith

Each of the eight think-tanks led research into a particular piece of the e-commerce and sustainability jigsaw – for example, impacts on planning, transport, or community. Throughout the project, the think-tanks worked closely with the corporate and government partners, through a series of workshops and meetings, discussing and reaching conclusions on each theme. This book contains the results of that research.

At the end of each chapter, we have invited a leading thinker or practitioner to respond. Many of these support our findings, some highlight certain areas of disagreement. Our aim in inviting the responses was to include a diverse mix of voices and opinions within the book, reflecting the fact that it is still too early in this debate for consensus to emerge.

Principle 1 Beyond the hype, there's hope

E-commerce creates new opportunities for environmental and social sustainability. Despite the boom and bust of the dot-com start-ups, the underlying significance of e-commerce remains undiminished. E-tailers like Amazon and lastminute.com are the most visible tip of the e-commerce iceberg. Beneath the surface, a more profound transformation is taking place, as traditional sectors embed digital technologies within all aspects of their operations. Analysts bandy around ever-higher numbers in an attempt to convey the significance of this revolution. Take your pick: the OECD suggests that worldwide e-commerce will be worth US$1 trillion by 2005, whereas web research firm Forrester says it will be worth $3 trillion by 2003. Whichever of these statistics is closest to the mark, one thing is clear. Now, in the early stages of the e-revolution, is the right time to pose some IAQs (infrequently asked questions) about the potential of e-commerce to bring wider social and environmental benefits.

As Chapter 1 shows, the defining characteristic of the new economy is not technology but innovation. The internet helps creative minds to develop entirely new ways to deal with old problems. Combining new technologies with social and institutional innovation could mean a radical rethink of the way that companies, and governments, deal with their wider responsibilities. Unlike sectors such as oil and chemicals, which have had to retro-fit to accommodate social and environmental concerns in response to stakeholder pressure, e-business is uniquely well placed to incorporate them at the design stage. The trick is to address these issues now, before they become a burden or a challenge to the existing way of doing things. A young, fast-changing sector can adapt far more easily than one which is trapped in established mindsets. With a mixture of vision, imagination and intelligent policy, it should be possible to splice sustainability into the DNA of the new economy.

Principle 2 The e-economy can access all areas

The digital revolution could refresh the parts that other revolutions haven't reached, by spreading its benefits to all regions of the UK and all sectors of society. As the digital economy takes off, increased emphasis is being placed on the need to bridge the digital divide by ensuring that the benefits of the internet are available to all, regardless of location, age, language, disability or income. The UK government has set an ambitious target in this area with its pledge of universal internet access by 2005. Yet as our research shows, the digital divide will not be solved through access alone. The roll-out of technical access – whether via PC, mobile phone, or digital TV – is the easiest part of the problem to address. A more fundamental challenge is to overcome the underlying forms of division that contribute to the digital divide: the skills divide, the regional divide, the social divide.

Our research has looked in detail at the regional divide. As Chapter 6 shows, in the UK's new economy, place matters. When the internet recruitment company Boldly-go.com researched the location of dot-com companies in the UK, almost 80 per cent were based in the south-east, with London accounting for almost 60 per cent. Outside London, Silicon Fen (Cambridge) and Silicon Glen (Edinburgh/Glasgow) accounted for just 3 per cent and 4 per cent respectively. There is a strong south-east bias and no intrinsic dynamic towards more equitable patterns of regional development.

E-commerce could be a vehicle for revitalizing marginalized areas and communities if we can find ways to spread the benefits around. There are new regional institutions and policies that could make this happen, but regional development authorities (RDAs) and local authorities need to strengthen the links between e-commerce, sustainability and governance. At the moment, sustainability is seen as an add-on, rather than being seen as central to the development of the new economy. Without active policy to create change, the new economy is more likely to reflect, rather than transform, the social, environmental and economic maps of the UK.

Another focus of our research is on what lies over the bridge across the digital divide; what impacts will far higher levels of internet access and usage have on local economies and communities? As Chapter 5 suggests, the low-income market, which many e-tailers shun, will become increasingly significant. There are millions of people in the UK who lack bank accounts or credit, and so are excluded from shopping online. In order to bring these people into the e-marketplace, companies will have to develop novel networks of producers and consumers, and different forms of electronic currency.

We also need to find ways in which e-commerce can strengthen local economies and keep local money and resources flowing. Access to global markets can be very positive for small businesses, but there is a danger that e-commerce will give impetus to the rise of the global at the expense of the local. In order to strengthen local economies, we need to take advantage of the exciting scope for alternative currencies – such as local exchange and trading schemes (LETS) and time banks – which can be supported through the internet.

Principle 3 Community is alive and clicking

Online relationships, supported by e-commerce, can add a valuable extra dimension to real world interaction.
Despite fears that the internet and e-commerce will contribute to the erosion of social relationships and undermine local communities, our research finds that the trend is in the opposite direction, towards the creation of online relationships as an addition to, not a substitute for, existing social networks. Historically, commerce and social networks have a long tradition of mutual dependency. Friendships ease commerce, from gentlemen's clubs to Tupperware parties. Commerce provides the infrastructure for friendship, from teenagers hanging out in shopping malls to the roads, railways and airports that have grown to service business, but which also enable us to visit friends and relations.

As Chapter 4 shows, e-commerce is no exception. All sorts of networks are being strengthened by the internet, and e-commerce is supporting the development of the technology, infrastructure and software that enable these new sources of social capital to flourish. For example, many people are gaining internet access through digital TV (DTV) at relatively low cost, largely because TV companies have signed lucrative deals with retailers to sell goods and services through the same channels.

In some instances, the internet generates new forms of virtual community. More commonly, though, it strengthens existing patterns of social interaction, or enables people with shared interests to exchange ideas and coordinate activity. Even if the initial contact with an individual or organization is electronic, it usually turns into a face to face relationship. To give three examples: internet banks in the US have recently started opening branches; the CompuServe police discussion forum now has an annual barbecue; and the Scottish community on AOL's Local Life channel have regular social get-togethers.

Principle 4 E is for environment

E-commerce could help to cut energy and resource use, and improve environmental productivity.

E-commerce leads to more efficient ways of doing business, and this can have important environmental benefits. A lot has been written about these environmental gains – Joseph Romm of the US-based Center for Energy and Climate Solutions, for example, suggests that e-commerce will create year-on-year reductions of up to 2 per cent in the energy intensity of the US economy. Romm points out that despite high levels of economic growth in the US between 1997 and 1999, energy consumption hardly increased at all. This points to the potential for significant gains in resource productivity, reducing the quantities of energy and physical material that are needed to provide a certain product or service.

Our research uncovers plenty of opportunities for such gains. Firstly, there could be gains from virtualization – the spread of entirely intangible products like entertainment, information and software, which can be delivered in the form of a computer file. Although this still requires computer equipment and energy, it cuts out the environmental costs of manufacture and transport. Virtualization is happening already: banking and accounting takes place online; MP3 music files are distributed in digital form; and the *Encyclopaedia Britannica* is now only available online, with one website replacing millions of leather-bound books. The potential for virtualization is discussed in more detail in Chapters 1 and 2.

Gains could also come from more efficient business practices, made possible by business-to-business (B2B) e-commerce. Re-engineering supply chains through B2B exchanges and centralizing procurement can lead to less warehousing, less transportation and less waste overall. A further example is the internet-based energy management systems being developed, which allow businesses to fine-tune their energy requirements and, again, cut down on waste.

There could be gains, too, from the new business models enabled by internet technology. Auction sites like eBay allow trading of second-hand goods, prolonging the useful life of products and reducing waste. As Chapter 1 shows, in the longer term, we may shift to an economy based on access rather than ownership as the short-term leasing of many goods and services becomes possible online. Leasing means that producers retain ownership and ultimate responsibility for their products, and have an incentive to make them robust, long-lasting, reusable and recyclable.

E-commerce could also support green consumerism. Online, it is easier to track down ethical products, and many environmental organizations are beginning to investigate e-commerce as a way of strengthening green consumer trends. Online consumer clubs, too, could allow green consumers to aggregate their buying power and increase their influence. A green search engine, or ecobot, could be developed to trawl the web to find products that meet social or environmental standards. Chapters 1 and 2 offer more ideas.

Principle 5 HTML = heavy traffic made lighter?

Virtual traffic can replace real traffic. With the right policy framework, e-business could create more efficient logistics and distribution systems.
Few people would disagree that our transport system is under increasing stress. Just look at the way the rail network trundled along at a snail's pace for the months following the Hatfield rail disaster in the autumn of 2000, or the way the fuel protests of September 2000 left supermarket shelves empty within days. According to the DETR, 6 per cent of major roads in England are at 100 per cent stress, and the average traffic speed in central London is the same now as it was at the end of the 19th century.

Changes in freight distribution over the last decade to just-in-time delivery, and a shift towards more environmentally damaging modes such as air and heavy goods vehicles, seem to have exacerbated the problem. And now e-commerce is changing things again. Will its overall effects be positive or negative? If we look at the direct impacts of e-business on transport, there is a fair amount to be cheerful about. It seems likely to make distribution more efficient, reduce waste, and improve the utilization of vehicle capacity.

Yet there is also potential for negative effects. E-commerce tends to make greater use of air freight in order to reduce delivery lead times, and of light goods vehicles to deliver products to consumers' homes. Unless we take action now, the rise of e-commerce could lead to busier skies and residential streets jammed with half-empty white vans. E-commerce also has indirect effects on transport that are more difficult to predict. If home delivery of groceries increases rapidly, what will people do with the time freed up by not having to drive to the supermarket? Are they likely to jump into their cars, now idle on the driveway, and think of more places they want to go?

Our research finds that with the right blend of government policy and business action, e-business could help to make logistics more environmentally and socially sound. However, as we argue in Chapter 7, it's too early to give e-business transport networks the green light for sustainability. The current signal is amber, with some warning signs that the second-order effects of e-commerce may run counter to sustainability. Now is the time to take precautionary action to ensure that the digital economy contributes to wider policies for sustainable transport and distribution.

Principle 6 Trust me, I'm a dot-com

E-commerce is changing the relationship between companies and their stakeholders, and could usher in a new era of corporate transparency and accountability. E-commerce changes the balance of power between companies and consumers. The most obvious benefit of this is cheaper products and services, as consumers learn to compare prices at the click of a mouse. Yet as Chapter 3 argues, consumers aren't the only stakeholders who could benefit from e-commerce. The internet is the ideal environment for new forms of cooperative ownership and management. It is not an organization that anyone can join, it is a set of relationships, and should therefore lend itself to more inclusive, employee- and stakeholder-driven models of capitalism.

Employees are like gold dust in the knowledge economy. Their intellectual capital is vital to building successful companies, as evidenced by the financial rewards that many dot-coms originally offered their staff. Now that share prices have taken a nose-dive, some employees are turning to more traditional forms of collective bargaining. For instance, both Amazon and eTown have faced calls for union recognition.

Suppliers too are in a stronger position. Most analysts agree that B2B e-commerce is where the real growth will happen over the next five years. Its basic selling point is that it cuts costs; estimates vary, but the scope for savings in some sectors is thought to be 20 to 30 per cent. The volume of transactions that will pass through these exchanges is mind-boggling. For example, the auto-industry exchange Covisint, born from an alliance between Ford, General Motors and DaimlerChrysler, is set to bring together 35,000 component makers with an annual trading volume of US$250 billion.

If suppliers box clever, they'll build up their reputation on social and environmental issues to compete in this market. The narrow focus on price in the purchasing protocols that govern many transactions, and the speed and volume of transactions through such exchanges, may make it difficult to know who you are dealing with. To avoid supply chain PR disasters such as those that hit Nike and GAP in the 1990s, ethical audit and compliance systems will need to enter the digital age. There are already systems, such as those offered by Clicksure.com, that provide online assurance on issues of quality. Our research argues that B2B exchanges will need to develop similar protocols to ensure that trading partners meet environmental and social standards.

Currently, debates about trust on the internet are focused on privacy and the security of transactions. As e-commerce becomes more sophisticated, purchasers – whether in business-to-consumer (B2C) or B2B transactions – are likely to want assurance on a wide range of issues, including the social and environmental credentials of products and services. Companies will have to capitalize on their reputation to offer that assurance.

Principle 7 Right now, matter matters more (not less)

Potential environmental gains won't be realized without a concerted effort from government and business to align e-commerce with wider sustainability objectives. At a time when so much is changing as a result of e-commerce, the last thing we want to do is slip into a sense of complacency about the inevitability of positive environmental outcomes. The environmental benefits from virtualization, dematerialization and increased efficiency will not flow automatically; consumer preferences, and business practices, take a long time to change. The investment in capital, time and creativity needed to bring about these changes is considerable. We need to make sure that people have the information and incentives that they need to help them to shift systematically to more sustainable patterns of production and consumption.

Above all, we mustn't underestimate the rebound effect, whereby all the extra environmental 'space' created by new technology is instantly swallowed up by our insatiable appetite to consume ever more exotic products and services. Of course businesses can find more efficient ways to make their products, but if this just means that we buy more, then any environmental gains are cancelled out. Anticipating and attempting to mitigate such negative rebound effects poses a great challenge to policy makers and responsible companies. We also mustn't ignore the social and cultural factors that drive consumption; most of us enjoy shopping for reasons that have precious little to do with obtaining goods and services in the most efficient way.

Now – at this critical juncture in the development of the new economy – is precisely the time when we need to devote more effort to ensuring that technology and innovation are channelled in a direction that makes a genuine difference to sustainability. Many of the policies that the green movement has long advocated – such as environmental taxes and tighter regulation – will become more, not less, important. We need to reward those who innovate. We need to encourage businesses to break away from established models. We need a policy framework that provides incentives to business to think through, and enact, environmental gains. The scale of the challenge should not be underestimated if we are to make the most of this window of opportunity.

Principle 8 Smart technology needs smart institutions

Technology is developing at breakneck speed. Institutionally we're struggling to keep up. We need multiple forms of innovation if e-commerce is to become an ally of sustainability.

It's often the case that technology catches us by surprise. The e-commerce explosion is no exception. Governments and NGOs sometimes give the impression of being caught off-guard, without adequate tools or policy frameworks to make the most of the internet.

As Chapter 1 points out, if we look back 150 years, the extent to which the Victorians matched scientific and technological innovation with radical institutional innovation is striking. When we fast-forward to the revolution of the new economy, we appear to be timid and cautious where the Victorians were confident and innovative. We are scientific and technological revolutionaries, but political and institutional conservatives. We need to change the way our institutions are designed if we are to deliver a sustainable way of life.

The same applies to the business world. At the moment, much of the innovation in the new economy is devoted to creating faster computers, smaller gadgets or broader bandwidth. Far less effort is devoted to the kind of whole-system innovation that will be needed to move the economy onto a sustainable path. One example is the development of the car. Over the past 30 years, engines have become many times more fuel efficient, but carbon dioxide emissions from cars have still increased. While the technology has improved, we haven't managed to change the behaviour of consumers, or develop new models of ownership – such as car pooling – in order to reap the benefits for sustainability. The same applies to e-commerce; the focus needs to be on whole-system innovation that identifies how e-commerce can contribute to more complex webs of sustainable energy, transport, production and consumption.

We also need innovative social and environmental entrepreneurs from within the e-generation. Looking across the e-world, there are some encouraging signs. In the US, groups such as Silicon Valley Community Foundation have sprung up to direct entrepreneurs' time and newly-acquired wealth into social and community initiatives. In the UK, fewer people had a chance to make their millions before the downturn in the market; but a handful have started to invest in social projects – including Tim Jackson, the founder of QXL, who recently established a £70 million charitable trust. Kate Oakley, a leading writer on the new economy, suggests that e-entrepreneurs will eventually make a contribution to the social fabric of our towns and cities equivalent to that of the great 19th-century industrialists. Just as the Victorians built museums, libraries and universities, so these new Victorians will seek to 'channel their wealth into good works of all sorts, from soup kitchens to school programmes, AIDS hospices to playgrounds.'[4]

Principle 9 We need to join the dots

Partnership will be key to the creation of a sustainable digital economy. Dot-coms, dot-govs and dot-orgs will need to work together more often and in new ways. The internet blurs traditional boundaries; it brings the high street into our homes, and brings government out of its Whitehall corridors. The web is becoming a natural meeting point for new partnerships and new alliances, and the barriers to these alliances are not as great as one might imagine. Dot-coms have a surprising amount in common with dot-orgs, especially with dot-orgs from the environmental movement. Both the new economy and sustainable development are creations of the last third of the last century. Both seek to challenge the established conventions of the old economy, and are prepared to take risks and push for change. E-businesses are no strangers to partnership; web success depends on forging alliances with suppliers, technology firms and content providers.

If we are to create a sustainable digital economy we need, literally, to join the dots. Dot-coms, dot-orgs and dot-govs need to share ideas and work together to embed sustainability in every area of the new economy. In a sense, the Digital Futures project is an experiment in these new ways of working, drawing different sectors together to explore the sustainability challenges and opportunities of e-commerce in a collaborative way. We believe such models will need to be replicated throughout the new economy.

We've found that building relationships between these sectors is not just a matter of asking business to adapt. NGOs and governments can both learn from the models of cooperation and fluid alliances that sustain the dot-com world. NGOs are good at pressuring companies, but they also need to build trust, identify common ground and support companies to get things right at the design stage. Government needs to work hard to counter its image as a barrier to be leapt over, an obstacle to innovation. It needs to seek out good practice and use its influence to encourage it elsewhere.

Principle 10 It's about time

A year in cyberspace is said to be four months. As the internet pushes us faster and faster we need to think about our attitude to time and long term responsibility.
Time: no one seems to have enough of it, and with the rise of the internet it seems we have less and less. Back in 1965, Gordon Moore noted that in the previous six years the number of transistors that could be fitted on a chip had doubled every year. He predicted that this trend would continue, leading to an exponential rise in the power of computers. He was right. Although the doubling of power has taken place once every 18 months, Moore's Law means that by 2015 there will have been a 137-billionfold increase in the power of microchips in a little over half a century.

In the new economy, speed is critical to success. Technology moves fast, and because first-mover advantage is so powerful, internet companies have to move even faster. Yet slowness can also be a virtue. The e-business community does sometimes need to think in longer time-horizons, which encompass not just the next investment decision, but also the social and environmental changes that those decisions will bring about. In thinking about e-business and sustainability, we need to cope with several different time cycles: cycles of investment and innovation on the internet, which are measured in weeks and months; cycles of investment in the physical infrastructure of energy systems, roads and towns, which are measured in decades; and cycles of change in the natural environment and the biosphere, many of which are measured in centuries or millennia.

The way we view time is key to creating a sustainable digital economy. It doesn't mean abandoning the hectic pace of e-life, but it does require us to switch lanes occasionally. Things look different from the slow lane. There is time to pause, reflect, and consider the long-term issues that really matter.

Notes and references

1   Margolis, J (2000) *A Brief History of Tomorrow*, Bloomsbury, London
2   DETR (1999) *A Better Quality of Life: A Strategy for Sustainable Development in the UK*, HMSO, London
3   Performance and Innovation Unit (1999) *e-commerce@its.best.uk*, Cabinet Office, London
4   Oakley, K (2000) *The New Victorians*, unpublished article

1 Mind over matter: greening the new economy

Charles Leadbeater and Rebecca Willis

The new economy

Shawn Fanning, the 19-year-old renegade founder of Napster, is an unlikely environmental hero. Napster is an online music community, based around a technology that is simple yet powerful. It allows a computer user, armed with a modem and the Napster software, to download a piece of music – as a computer file – via the internet.

At first sight it may appear that this technology has little to do with tackling climate change or pollution. Yet, on closer examination, the environmental potential of Napster is considerable. If the entire music industry were to embrace Napster-style technology, we would be able to phase out the production of compact discs, tapes and all the materials, packaging and transport associated with these physical products. Shawn Fanning turns out to be not just a techno-entrepreneur but an environmental entrepreneur as well.

Of course, the Napster technology is not an environmental free lunch. To download a file using Napster, you first need a computer, which has to be manufactured and disposed of and which consumes electricity. The Napster story also highlights some of the difficulties this kind of innovation will face in order for its environmental potential to be realized. It will take a long time to wean consumers away from their compact disc collections. Consumers, as well as producers, will have to adapt and innovate. The mainstream media companies will not embrace the technology unless they can be sure that they will be able to charge people to listen to music and watch films – hence Napster's recent deal with Bertelsmann, the German media giant.

If the world's music industry manages to make this switch, environmental benefits will follow. Similar gains could be made in the film, television, video and even book industries if major producers and publishers shift to digital formats. The economics, technology and environmental impact of the world's entertainment and media industry could be transformed within a decade, not by new regulations or corporate research and development, but by the revolutionary ideas of a few young turks working at the margins of the law. Fanning has made it possible to imagine the world's media industry developing along entirely new lines.

In the next few years, more and more companies will face this kind of challenge as new technologies revolutionize industrial processes from top to bottom. All great entrepreneurs open up possible futures that would have remained closed off without their insight, imagination and drive. Entrepreneurship of the kind that Fanning is engaged in will be critical if we are to achieve environmental sustainability.

To explore the full environmental potential of these changes, we need to look beyond the technology. These are more than just technological breakthroughs; they open up new opportunities for our management of the entire economy. We need to look at the social and political conditions that support the Shawn Fannings of this world, and examine the environmental opportunities that emerge. In short, we need to consider the potential of the new economy.

This new economy can be defined in narrow or broad terms. At its narrowest, it is associated with the rise of information and communications technology, particularly the internet and e-commerce. A broader definition is that the new economy is not defined by any particular technology so much as the widespread capacity for innovation.

It comes in many guises: the post-industrial society, the information society, the knowledge economy. Whatever you call it, the new economy is innovation-driven. New sources of competitive advantage derived from innovation are transforming every sector, from agriculture to aerospace, pharmaceuticals to farming. As the US government's *Digital Economy 2000* report puts it,

> *'Three hundred million people now use the internet... [T]hese numbers do not tell the full story. We are witnessing an explosive increase in innovation... we are witnessing myriad new forms of business activity'.*[1]

It is crucial to adopt this much broader definition of the new economy. It makes it possible to look beneath the surface of the new technologies at the underlying economic and social changes that are taking place.

From these changes could emerge new ways of protecting and enhancing the environment.

In this chapter, we look at changes in the way we use and value capital, and at new approaches to consumption, production and ownership. We draw out the environmental potential of these shifts, and recommend ways to realize it.

To start with, it is worth examining some key aspects of the new economy that could present opportunities for environmental policy. First, the explosion in innovation; second, new links between economic and biological thinking; and third, the cultural differences between the new economy and the old.

Innovation

Information technology is having a profound effect on the way businesses are organized. The goal in the old, industrial economy was optimization: finding the most efficient way to make a product, given existing technology. The new economy is driven by innovation and adaptation: finding creative new ways to generate value. This provides the potential for whole systems of production to be rethought from the ground up, rather than undergoing incremental change. This kind of whole-system innovation is complex, however, and is often only realized within a much larger context of social, organizational and political change.

Yet it is whole-system innovation that will be needed to deal with the environmental challenges we face. Take car use as an example. New, more sustainable forms of car transport will require scientific and technological innovation, such as hydrogen fuel cells; but the true potential of this technology will not be realized without social innovations that create new patterns of car use and allow consumers to share cars through leasing schemes. Such a social shift requires regulatory innovations such as road pricing; these, in turn, may only be possible through the political innovation of enabling cities to control their own taxation. We need to imagine not just new technologies, but whole new social systems.

So far, though, we have not summoned up the will to do this. We are scientific and technological revolutionaries, but political and institutional conservatives. Compare this with the Victorians. The 19th century was revolutionary because the Victorians matched their scientific and technological innovations with radical institutional innovations: the extension of democracy; the creation of local government; the birth of modern savings and insurance schemes; the development of a professional civil service; the rise of trade unions; and the emergence of the research-based university. We are timid and cautious where the Victorians were confident and innovative.

To realize the environmental potential of the new economy we have to channel its innovative power towards the creation of social institutions that can deliver a sustainable way of life. The building societies and insurance schemes created by the Victorians had a lasting legacy, shaping the lives of millions of people over many decades. We need to design institutions that have a similar longevity and impact.

New economic insights

The new economy could change the way we think about the natural world. We are seeing the emergence of a new intellectual synthesis that applies the same principles to both the modern networked economy and to complex ecosystems. The more the economy becomes innovation-driven, the more evolutionary theory becomes relevant to our understanding of how firms succeed, and even why stock markets rise and fall.

Innovations, whether in business or ecology, are rarely the product of individual, unilateral action. Organisms evolve in their niche within the environment; a company co-evolves and declines with its customers, suppliers and partners. And as the economy becomes more networked and global, so it becomes like one of the complex adaptive systems in nature, such as a tropical forest. These complex systems are ordered without being designed. An evolutionary account of innovation and economic growth stresses the features of the economic system as a whole: the degree of experimentation and diversity; the tolerance of failure; the opportunities for co-evolution.

The US thinker Hal Varian borrows the model of 'recombinant growth' from the biological sciences to explain how innovations succeed by reacting with each other, as happens in the natural world. He writes that:

> '*in the fertile ground of research labs and startups, people are taking apart and recombining these basic elements [of internet technology] to forge new products, services, processes and business models... a willingness to pull things apart and reconstitute them in a new form underlies the genius of these inventors.*'[2]

Jane Jacobs, the US economist best known for her work on cities,[3] recommends that we learn ways of improving our economic systems from ecology, particularly the ability to self-organize and self-refuel. She suggests we learn from the fragile but complex webs spun by spiders, or from the principles by which plants capture sunlight and turn it into energy. The attraction of these biological models is that they explain not just the force that is driving the new economy, but some of its disorderly downsides as well. The new economy is prone to bubbles and slumps because dynamic self-organization can all too easily descend into chaos.

This convergence between biological and economic thinking will not, in itself, improve the environment; but a growing intellectual synthesis could make it easier to take account of the natural world in the economic sphere. As the economy becomes more innovation-driven, it will increasingly resemble the complex and adaptive systems we see in nature. Linear, hierarchical thinking – about the economy, and about our relationship with nature – could be replaced by contingent, adaptive thinking, which acknowledges the need to co-evolve rather than control.

Cultural shifts

Both the new economy and sustainable development are creations of the last third of the 20th century. Most people 30 years ago had not seen, let alone used, a computer, and nor had they heard of climate change. The new economy has emerged alongside a growing consciousness of the environmental challenges we face.

Independent, well-educated knowledge workers who want to work in a clean environment are likely to support green ideas. California, the home of the new economy, is also home to one of the world's most assertive environmental movements (although Silicon Valley itself is a growing environmental nightmare of overcrowding and congestion). Forum for the Future's 2001 survey of new economy companies reveals that dot-com senior managers are broadly sympathetic to social and environmental issues.[4] However, the survey also reveals a gulf between thought and action; only one-fifth of the companies surveyed have any systems or policies in place to measure or mitigate their environmental impacts. The spirit is willing, but the flesh is weak. This points to the need for a concerted effort to help new economy companies turn green thinking into green behaviour.

While the new economy has given rise to a new breed of entrepreneur, the environmental movement has been changing too. Environmentalism was largely a protest movement 30 years ago, providing a radical critique of modern capitalism. While protest is still an important influence, many individuals and organizations have been shifting towards a more accommodating framework, in which business is seen as a potential ally in the search for environmental solutions. This new culture of partnership was apparent in Tony Blair's recent call for

'a new coalition for the environment, a coalition that works with the grain of consumers, business and science... that harnesses consumer demand for a better environment, and encourages businesses to see the profit of the new green technologies'.[5]

Similarly, the Department of Trade and Industry's latest strategy for sustainable development was drawn up in consultation with many key players in the environmental movement. It was even launched at a Greenpeace conference – a move that would have been unthinkable a decade ago. The new economy is fertile ground for these partnerships, and these twin changes in the economy and the environmental movement could create a powerful new force for sustainability. They could place the relationship between the economy and the environment on a new footing and allow us to resolve what have seemed to be intractable problems.

Of course, the mere fact that this path to a greener future is a possibility does not mean it will become reality – far from it. We must not fall prey to the over-optimism that infects so many starry-eyed advocates of the new economy, who believe that technology and free markets can solve all our problems. The political will – and intervention – that is required to steer the new economy towards sustainability should not be underestimated. Nor should we dismiss the potential for deep conflicts over values – particularly where the commercial imperatives of the global economy are concerned, as the November 1999 protests in Seattle against the World Trade Organization (WTO) showed all too clearly.

The convergence of the new economy and environmentalism will not remove hard choices, but it may make them easier to resolve. The question to which we now turn is: how can we make the most of this potential?

New approaches to capital

In industrial and agrarian economies, the material assets of land, machinery, raw materials and labour (brute power) are of paramount importance. The new economy depends instead on intangible assets like knowledge, imagination, creativity and trust; and it takes intangible forms, like brands, services and software.

Traditional financial accounting, the foundations of which are more than 500 years old, is designed to track and record transactions involving physical property. It is not adept at measuring the value of assets that cannot be easily packaged, bought or sold. Most corporate balance sheets record the value of assets like land and buildings, but in new economy companies the most valuable wealth-creating assets go unrecorded. The difficulty inherent in valuing new economy companies is shown clearly in the volatility of their share prices. Market valuations greatly exceed the physical assets of the company, but there is no clear way of measuring the difference between physical and intellectual assets.

Innovations in accounting aim to measure these 'stealth assets'. The US Balanced Scorecard method relates financial performance to customer and employee satisfaction. The Skandia Navigator, developed by the Swedish insurance company Skandia, is one of many tools designed to measure a company's intellectual assets. There is a growing demand for such accounting practices that acknowledge and measure intangible assets. As a recent report from the US government points out, the incorporation of intangible investments into accounting methods

'could have significant effects on a range of measures central to our understanding of the economy... [it] would highlight the limitations of GDP as the almost-exclusive gauge of longer-term growth trends.'[6]

In a striking parallel, environmentalists are calling for more systematic methods of accounting for 'natural capital'. Environmentalists have long argued that traditional measures of gross domestic product (GDP) do not reflect the true environmental costs of economic activity. The environment provides vital services to industry – such as clean air, water, raw materials and waste disposal – that are generally undervalued. As Paul Ekins points out, the underpricing of environmental functions – an atmosphere that yields climate stability, biodiversity, degradation of wastes and so on – leads to their overuse, and as a result the underlying stocks of natural capital are being run down.[7] The challenge is to assess the value of these assets, and to work toward accounting for the full environmental costs of economic activity.[8]

Already, a good deal of progress has been made in developing environmental accounts at both the corporate and the national level. A good corporate example is provided by the carpet manufacturer Interface, which is working with Forum for the Future to calculate its 'sustainability cost' – the notional sum it would have to set aside to restore the environmental damage its activities cause. That calculation allows the accounts to be amended to include a figure for environmentally sustainable profits. Just as companies set money aside to modernize machinery as it wears out, Interface will set money aside to restore the environmental capital it uses. Just as profits are amended to take account of taxes and interest, Interface will amend them to take account of environmental costs.

There are similar initiatives at the national level, such as the methodology of national environmental accounting developed in The Netherlands in the 1980s. Many countries, including the UK, now have their own environmental accounts. Economists at the World Bank have gone even further, developing new tools with which to measure national wealth in terms of natural, human and manufactured capital.[9]

We could never hope, or want, to place a monetary value on all aspects of the natural environment. However, these examples show that methodologies for valuing environmental capital are well developed, and efforts continue apace. Processes such as the Global Reporting Initiative and the SIGMA Project are at the forefront of this trend.[10] The challenge now is to integrate environmental capital and other intangible assets more fully into accounting systems. As the borders of financial reporting break down, it will become far more common for companies and nations to provide more complex accounts, which combine financial and non-financial measures of performance.

New kinds of consumption

The convergence of the new economy and environmentalism could lead to far-reaching changes in what we consume and how we consume it. There are four main ingredients to the possible new consumer culture: an emphasis on services rather than physical goods, the dematerialization of some consumer products, the virtualization of other products, and changes in consumer values and ethics.

Services

The new economy will accelerate the rise of the service economy and the shift away from manufacturing, at least in developed countries. Information technologies will continue to increase productivity in old industries and, as a result, the number of jobs in manufacturing will decline as those in services rise. By the year 2050 perhaps as little as 5 per cent of the population will be employed in the traditional industrial sphere as we know it.[11]

Increasingly, people will value manufactured goods, such as mobile telephones, for the services they bring: voicemail, text-messaging, internet access. The falling costs of technology will allow more people to start service businesses using computers and communications in areas such as design, marketing, public relations and so on. Moreover, as the world becomes full of more efficient gadgets, consumers will increasingly value experiences that make them feel special and leave them with a 'warm glow'. Writers such as Joseph Pine and James Gilmore advise companies that in the 'experience economy' they must concentrate on making memories rather than goods. Car-makers, they argue, should focus on enhancing the all-round driving experience, furniture-makers the sitting experience, clothing manufacturers the wearing experience. Physical goods still matter, but only to the extent that they provide people with the experience they want.[12]

A service-based economy could be more environmentally sustainable than an industrially-based one. For example, Ireland's 1999 environmental accounts found that forestry and fishing accounted for 29 per cent of greenhouse gases while employing only 12 per cent of the labour force. The service sector, however, generated 19 per cent of greenhouse gases while employing 50 per cent of the workforce. However, a mass service economy is not without its own environmental challenges. Services are only beneficial if they are substitutes for products – and some argue that this is not happening. Jim Salzman, for example, writes that services work as *complements to* traditional production factors such as labour and resources, improving their efficiency and leading to increased environmental impacts through greater resource flow'.[13] And of course, a shift to a service economy in one country may hide the fact that the manufacturing industries have moved elsewhere – probably to developing countries – rather than disappeared.

Increased trade and international travel may exacerbate the problem. The search for new consumer experiences – the latest foods, the most exotic destinations – is rarely environmentally friendly. Take the hotel complexes which ring the Indian Ocean island of Mauritius. These vast hotels welcome hundreds of guests at a time, mainly flown in from Europe and South Africa. They manufacture an experience for their guests – not the experience of being on the island of Mauritius, but of lying on a palm-tree-lined, silver beach, bathed in a blazing sunset. Not only do these experience factories consume large quantities of energy, water and cleaning materials, but they also depend on global air travel. Tourism, the leading experience industry of the new economy, accounts for about 11 per cent of world GDP. This share is projected to rise above 20 per cent by the year 2008, when it will be worth more than $7.5 trillion.[14] Just 20 years ago, roughly 280 million people took international trips each year; today this number has doubled, and the growth shows no signs of abating.

So the service sector will itself need innovation if it is to realize its environmental potential. As a first step, hotel groups such as the Inter-Continental and the Taj Group in India have pioneered waste-saving programmes, to recycle materials and water. In the long term, innovations in aerospace, such as hydrogen-powered planes, will be needed to create more sustainable forms of long distance travel. Above all, greater innovation in policy is needed to reduce environmental impacts to a minimum. This means, for example, shifting the tax burden away from labour and services towards materials, energy and consumption.

Dematerialization: the great energy debate

The new economy generates more value than the industrial economy, and uses less energy and fewer materials per unit of output. Physical products are becoming lighter and incorporating more intelligent software. Toyota, for example, estimates that software and electronics will account for 30 per cent of the value of the average car by the year 2005. The laptop computer used to write this chapter weighs about the same as the older model it replaced; both contain similar amounts of plastic, gold, silicon and other metals. Yet this newer laptop is perhaps five times more powerful than the old one. This difference is entirely due to the way in which the same physical ingredients have been minutely rearranged according to a new recipe. The improvements in power and performance are due to human intelligence rather than additional materials.

The combination of information technology and communications has created the potential for e-commerce to reorganize physical retailing. Banks used to measure their market share by the total length of all the counters in all their branches, up and down the country. These days most banks are investing in electronic services delivered to their customers over the internet and digital television. These cost less, are less energy intensive, and do not require customers to make a physical journey to a bank. According to one study by US energy expert Joseph Romm, the ratio of energy used per book sold between a traditional bricks-and-mortar store and Amazon.com is 15:1.[15]

At this point, though, the rebound effect rears its ugly head. As computers and other electronic devices become cheaper, so we will use more of them, more of the time. The internet is set to create a 24/7 economy in which the lights and the computers are always on. In the Leadbeater family home, there are four kids, five computers, three mobile telephones, four landlines, two televisions, a microwave, an electric kettle, a washing machine, a dryer, a dishwasher, and two ovens – as well as numerous CD players, Walkmans and radios. Compare that with the Leadbeaters just two generations back; they had neither a television nor a car, their kettle went on the gas hob, and they used their single telephone as if it were a luxury.

That our use of energy and resources is becoming more efficient is not in doubt. What is questionable is our ability to turn this into environmental benefit, rather than gobbling it up through more consumption – and this takes us into the realm of politics, not technology. In the US, this political battle is being fought hard. At the extreme, there are those who reject any attempt to curb energy use for environmental ends in case it damages the digital economy. Supporters of the US coal industry, such as Mark Mills, say that coal is needed more than ever to power the computer networks that are the backbone of the new economy. In a notorious *Forbes* article, 'The Internet Begins with Coal',[16] he claims that the internet accounts for as much as 8 per cent of US electricity consumption. According to Mills, 'no energy policy, including and perhaps especially the anti-electricity aspects of the Kyoto Protocol [on climate change], should be considered without passing it first through a digital sanity test.'[17]

So for Mills the choice is stark: save the economy or the climate. However, this argument is both irresponsible and inaccurate. First, it ignores the immense potential of renewable energy to generate electricity; the internet does not have to 'begin with' coal, it could begin instead with wind turbines or solar panels. Second, it ignores the potential of new technologies to increase productivity. The internet can help to reduce waste and improve energy efficiency. As Joseph Romm observes, 'In the very near future the internet will itself be used to save energy directly... many utilities have begun exploring internet-based home energy management systems'.[18] This suggests that regulation of the energy market could make the new economy more, not less, competitive.

In direct contrast to Mills's pessimism, Romm estimates that e-commerce could reduce overall US carbon dioxide (CO_2) emissions by up to 2 per cent per annum between 2000 and 2007.[19] Yet this will not happen without a concerted effort to maximize the environmental potential of new technologies.

Virtualization

The *Encyclopaedia Britannica*, once a badge of respectability to be found on all middle class bookshelves, used to run to 30 hardback volumes, at a cost of more than £1000. Today, it is only available on the web – for free. This is an example of virtualization at work. Whereas dematerialization means doing more with less resources, virtualization describes the emergence of entirely intangible products – entertainment, information and software – that can be delivered in the form of computer files. These virtual formats involve none of the physical manufacture, storage and travel impacts of physical products, and they create different cultures of consumption. A computer file can be endlessly replicated at little cost and with few extra resources.

Again though, there is a need for some qualifications. The benefits of virtualization will not flow quickly, because consumer preferences take a long time to change. What's more, virtualization is less likely to displace the real economy of goods than to enhance and complement it. The rise of the home video industry helped to increase the number of people visiting cinemas. Newspapers that publish online editions find that sales of the physical version rise. The same is probably true of communication. The internet allows more people around the globe to communicate electronically. As a result, more want to meet face to face. Global communications will encourage global trade and travel. In addition, a proper assessment of the environmental benefits of virtual products needs to take into account the entire system used to produce and distribute them. Consumers may choose in future to download books from the internet, but if they then print them off at home onto high quality paper, the environmental gain will be negligible, or even negative.

Nonetheless, given the right policy framework, the environmental potential of virtualization is considerable. Governments could help to encourage the spread of virtual music, film, television and books by designing internet taxes carefully to reward e-commerce that reduces resource use.

Consumer values

The new economy is rich with information, including information about where and how products have been made. Increasingly, production systems will generate this information as a matter of course, and consumers could have ready access to it through the internet, providing the basis for electronic eco-labelling. Such initiatives already exist. The shop at Doncaster's Earth Centre allows customers to obtain further information about the social and environmental impact of their products by scanning a bar code into a computer. This sort of technology could one day be in place in every supermarket, giving consumers as much or as little information as they want.

The internet is creating many new ways for people to aggregate their buying power in consumer clubs. Environmental consumers could form such clubs to give their combined buying power the weight it lacks in the traditional high street. These innovations are likely to emerge from ethical internet portals like oneworld.net, which are already starting to explore e-commerce. The new economy also has the potential to forge links between local communities. If people can buy, sell and barter through a local network, this will reduce the environmental impacts of shopping, as well as promoting local regeneration. The research by Alex MacGillivray and David Boyle of the New Economics Foundation examines some of these opportunities (see Chapter 5).

However, whatever the efforts to encourage local initiatives, the new economy will also extend the reach of consumerism. The global communications revolution amounts to a globalization of desire. Consumers everywhere now have access to the internet, and through that they can be reached by advertisers and marketeers. Also, the culture of much e-commerce – epitomized by lastminute.com – is immediate, impulsive and not at all conducive to careful consideration of the implications of spending decisions for sustainability.

New kinds of production

As well as reshaping what we consume and how we consume it, the new economy will reorganize the ways in which we produce goods and services.

Local or global?

The falling cost of technology could make it economically viable for more people to work at home. This would mean fewer journeys, less commuting and less use of inefficient office space. In the same way, as MacGillivray and Boyle demonstrate, the internet could allow local, small markets to flourish.[20] However, the new economy is also propelling a process of globalization and consolidation, and the effects are far-reaching. E-commerce allows the creation of far more dispersed and opaque production networks. In the old industrial economy, it might have been possible to identify the factory that made the goods and emitted the pollution. These days, most manufactured products – shirts for example – are made by complex, elongated networks. Identifying the person who bears responsibility for pollution in these networks is difficult, especially when the basic material might be woven in one east Asian country, dyed in another, finished in another and packaged in Hong Kong, before being shipped to retailers in Europe. This can be overcome, to a certain extent, by better information flows; but the sheer volume and scale of transactions complicates things greatly.

Intelligent production

New technology should allow companies to make far more efficient use of physical capital. Better monitoring of the operation of processes – from running chemical plants to cleaning cars – should allow companies to eliminate waste and use capacity more efficiently. As a result, the yield from a fixed sum of capital should go up, replacement costs should go down, and waste should be minimized.

Manufacturing companies have long recognized that increasing the productivity of existing equipment reduces the need to invest in costly new plant. Texas Instruments, the semiconductor manufacturer, estimated back in the 1980s that small improvements to quality in its existing chip plants had increased yields to such an extent that it was the equivalent of building an additional plant. As the research by Peter James and Peter Hopkinson shows (see Chapter 7), the efficiency of freight distribution could also increase significantly. Web-enabled systems allow an increased use of existing capacity, for example by making sure that lorries are full on return journeys. An example of such a system is the US-based National Transportation Exchange (www.nte.net).

The same argument applies to the transport system as a whole. Public transport could be a major beneficiary of better information systems. One of the main disincentives affecting the use of public transport is the time it takes to transfer between trains, taxis and buses. On some estimates, up to 50 per cent of journey time can be taken up with changing between modes of transport. Better information and planning should make it easier to plan a journey from beginning to end, and so make public transport more attractive.

Simply having the information is only the first step; what policy makers and managers do with it is what counts. Real gains may only come when this flow of information is used to underpin new approaches to road and journey pricing, which in turn will require both political and social innovation.

Innovation in production

The traditional view is that regulations to improve environmental performance are bad for competitiveness. Firms make choices about their optimal production strategies and environmental regulations simply add costs to them. In the knowledge-driven economy, however, environmental regulation could have a new role. Open markets and tough environmental standards, when combined intelligently, may be the best way to spur innovation that simultaneously improves competitiveness and helps the environment. Environmentalists such as Amory Lovins argue that production processes can be made more efficient by redesigning them from scratch. This whole-system-redesign approach is one example of how we can generate win–win economic and environmental innovations.[21]

What is the realistic scope for such innovations? Take pollution as an example. Pollution is a form of waste; it is the unnecessary or inefficient use of materials. Waste is the result of poor process control and design. The best way to reduce pollution is not to treat is as it emerges from the process, but to redesign the process itself. That means making production more knowledge-intensive: by embedding knowledge in the process at the outset, improving design, and building in better information gathering so that the process can be monitored and controlled more accurately.

When the Massachusetts jewellery company Robbins was facing closure for violating waste discharge regulations, it developed a new system that purified wastewater and reused it. The water that came out was 40 times cleaner than that which had gone in through the city's pipes, and helped to improve overall water quality as well as reducing discharges to zero. As a result, Robbins saved more than US$115,000 a year in water, chemicals and disposal costs, and reduced water usage from 500,000 to 500 gallons per week. The capital cost of installing the new water recycling system was $200,000. A conventional treatment plant that enabled Robbins to comply with the waste discharge regulations would have cost $500,000.[22]

There is a role for both market competition and demanding regulation in promoting environmental innovation. This mixed approach works with the grain of the knowledge-driven economy, not against it.

New forms of ownership

The new economy allows us to think differently about ownership. In the industrial economy, ownership of physical products and assets is essential. Owning a car or a stereo is a badge of honour for young people. In the new economy, outright ownership of physical products may come to matter less, as consumers and companies start to value assets more in terms of the services and experiences they produce.

Knowledge-intensive products, like software and recipes, never cease to be the property of the owner when they are transferred to another user. A recipe does not stop being Delia Smith's when it is used by a cook at home. In the same way, computer users increasingly download software from the internet as and when they need it. The pure knowledge products of the knowledge economy are not consumed and owned in the way that physical products were; they are licensed, leased and shared.

Companies and consumers will increasingly seek to minimize the costs of owning assets that they do not need all of the time. They will want access to products as and when they need them. Take cars as an example; in the future, consumers might be more interested in how to complete a journey in the most efficient way, rather than in buying a car which might sit outside their home most of the time without being used. Rather than owning a car, people might become increasingly interested in a 'journey service', which would allow them to lease or borrow a car only when they needed it.

The environmental potential of this shift from ownership to leasing, borrowing and sharing has been highlighted both by Amory Lovins and Jeremy Rifkin.[23] Rifkin reports that in less than 18 years, non-commercial auto leasing has risen from obscurity to a point where one-third of new vehicles in the US remain the property of the car-makers or dealers who lease them to the customers. In the UK, Mercedes Benz runs a leasing scheme through which customers can lease whatever car they want, when they want it, within an agreed price range. Were a family to need a people carrier for their annual holiday, they could get one, return it after they had used it and then get a saloon for the rest of the year. According to Helmut Werner, Mercedes Benz' chairman, 'We do not want to just sell another car but rather offer a complete package of transportation services.'

The same changes in ownership patterns are underway in the corporate world. Increasingly, companies do not want to own assets that are not core to their business or which they have no particular expertise in managing. As Stan Davis and Christopher Meyer argue in their book *Blur*: 'We need to walk away from the idea that owning or even controlling capital is a necessary resource for fulfilling market need.'[24] Davis and Meyer argue that in a fast-paced economy, ownership of fixed assets and equipment can hinder a company's ability to move from one business to another. Their maxim for fixed assets like land, offices, computers and machinery is 'Use it, don't own it.' Knowledge-based companies need to own and retain their real assets: their people and the culture which binds them together. The offices, furniture, cars and machinery can be bought in from elsewhere.

This shift from outright ownership to leasing could result in significant environmental gain. Leasing means that producers retain ownership and ultimate responsibility for the product. That gives the manufacturers an incentive to make the product as robust and durable as possible, extending its life. The manufacturer has a far greater incentive to design using materials that can be easily recycled, thereby minimizing waste.

Changes in ownership structures could also have profound implications for energy use. In 1999, the companies Ocean Spray and Owens Corning decided to outsource their power needs, handing responsibility for lighting, heating, cooling and motors over to the energy company Enron. If they had retained control over their energy use, it would not have been economic for them to invest in energy efficiency measures with a long payback period. However, because Enron had ownership of the company's energy needs through a long-term contract, it could justify much longer-term investments in efficiency, to the benefit of the environment. Much the same shift is increasingly envisaged for domestic energy; an energy supplier could sell a 'warm homes' service through investment in insulation and efficient heating appliances, rather than selling extra megawatts of energy supply. This example, and many others, illustrate that when better information about yields from capital equipment is combined with the shift to leasing and outsourced ownership, it can lead to dramatic environmental improvements.

Assessing our chances

Our tour through the capital, consumption, production and ownership of the new economy shows the potential for real environmental improvement. Learning to value knowledge and innovation could go hand in hand with a better valuation of natural capital. New websites could make it easier for people to buy green. Better information could radically increase manufacturing productivity. And new forms of ownership could prompt firms to take responsibility for the full life cycle of their products, from cradle to grave. The potential is there.

At the same time, a new synthesis is emerging from the convergence of the new economy and the environmental movement. Thirty years ago, both were on the margins of the economy, politics and society. These days the new economy and the environment combined exert a huge influence on how our societies develop. This convergence will not solve our environmental problems in and of itself; it is far from being a magic bullet. However, it has created an opportunity.

The new economy will only develop along more environmentally sustainable lines if technological, social, organizational and political innovations work in combination. Governments at local, national and international levels have critical roles to play in stimulating innovation. They can help to create capabilities through investment in science and research; they can stimulate linkages between science and business that will exploit new technologies; and they can promote innovation in consumer markets by setting standards and encouraging competition. The potential will only be realized through policy that works with the grain of the economy and the environment. Policies that have hitherto been experimental and hesitant – valuing intangible assets, providing incentives for innovation, encouraging new forms of ownership – will need to become mainstream and bold. We will need creativity and determination on the scale of the Victorians. Have we got what it takes?

The opportunity

How green the new economy ultimately becomes depends on the decisions we make now. Below, we offer some suggestions as to the way forward.

Valuing the intangible

Government, working with accounting bodies, should develop and reach a consensus on new measures of economic activity, bringing assessments of the value of intangibles and assessments of environmental impact together. These new measures should operate at the national and corporate accounts level, to provide a more rounded assessment of the total costs of individual products and services.

Encouraging the virtual

Government should carry out a thorough assessment of the impacts and benefits of the shift from physical to virtual products, such as MP3 files and other computer formats. This should in turn influence tax and regulatory policies. For example, it may be that the environmental gains from a rapid uptake of virtual formats could justify differential taxation and approaches to regulation.

New green consumerism

The green movement should be at the forefront of attempts to create a green consumer culture on the internet. It should create green consumer clubs to aggregate buying power, and encourage companies to provide more online environmental information to consumers.

Promoting innovation

Government should review products and process regulations so that they better promote innovation, which is good for both competitiveness and the environment. This means shifting the basis for regulation away from best available technology (BAT) towards targets and outcomes. Governments should set ambitious targets for energy and resource productivity that can only be achieved through radical innovations in the way we work, produce and consume.

Innovation and clusters

Most innovation takes place within clusters or networks of companies, often linked to a university that provides a knowledge base. Silicon Valley in California and Silicon Fen around Cambridge are well known examples. To foster environmental innovation we need a 'green valley' initiative, aimed at creating two or three regional centres of excellence in environmental technologies.

Environmental entrepreneurship

Government should investigate how to promote new breeds of environmental entrepreneurs. These would not be confined to developing businesses around environmental technologies. Most would be like James Dyson, the household appliance innovator, who regards the environment as a vital ingredient in mainstream product and process design.

The way forward

There may be a new way forward for the economy and the environment; a way forward in which innovation can feed competitiveness, environmental efficiency and, ultimately, sustainability. We will only get there with new ways of thinking, new technologies, new approaches to regulation, and a great deal of knowledge-sharing.

It would be a mistake to naively believe that we have entered a promised land in which the interests of business can be magically reconciled with the interests of the natural world. However, it would also be a mistake to turn our backs on the territory opening up before us – territory that did not exist 30 years ago, in which the interests of the new innovation-driven economy and the environment may converge.

Notes and references

1   Economics and Statistics Administration (2000) *Digital Economy 2000*, US Department of Commerce, Washington, June
2   Varian, H (2000) 'The Law of Recombinant Growth', *The Industry Standard*, February
3   Jacobs, J (2000) *The Nature of Economies*, Modern Library, New York
4   Wilsdon, J (2001) *Dot-com Ethics: E-business and Social Responsibility*, Forum for the Future, London, January
5   Prime Minister's speech to Green Alliance/CBI, 24 October 2000; see www.green-alliance.org.uk for full text
6   Economics and Statistics Administration (2000) *Digital Economy 2000*, op cit
7   Ekins, P (2000) *Economic Growth and Environmental Sustainability: The Prospects for Green Growth*, Routledge, London
8   See, for example, Hawken, P, Lovins, A B and Lovins, L H (1999) *Natural Capitalism: The Next Industrial Revolution*, Earthscan, London; Ekins, P (2000) op cit
9   See, for example, Dixon, J and Hamilton, K (1996) *Monitoring Environmental Progress: Expanding the Measures of Wealth*, World Bank, Washington
10 The Global Reporting Initiative (www.globalreporting.org) is an international effort to create a common framework for voluntary reporting of the economic, environmental and social impact of organization-level activity. The SIGMA Project (www.bsi-global.com/sigma) is a UK-based initiative to create a sustainability management system, based around the valuation of natural, human and financial capital.
11 Rifkin, J (2000) *The Age of Access: The New Culture of Hypercapitalism, Where All of Life Is a Paid-for Experience*, Tarcher/Putnam, New York
12 Pine II, B J and Gilmore, J H (1997) *The Experience Economy*, Harvard Business School Press, Harvard
13 Salzman, J (1999) 'Facing the Challenges of an Evolving Economy', *Environment, Science and Technology*, December

14 Figures from the World Travel and Tourism Council, www.wttc.org
15 Romm, J (1999) *The Internet Economy and Global Warming: A Scenario of the Impact of E-commerce on Energy and Environment*, Center for Energy and Climate Solutions, Washington
16 UK Department of Trade and Industry (2000) *DTI Sustainable Development Strategy*, London, October
17 Mills, M and Huber, P (1999) 'The Internet Begins with Coal', *Forbes Magazine*, May
18 Statement of Mark Mills to the Subcommittee on National Economic Growth, Natural Resources, and Regulatory Affairs of the Committee on Government Reform, US House of Representatives, www.house.gov/reform/neg/hearings
19 Statement of Joseph Romm to the Subcommittee on National Economic Growth, op cit
20 Romm, J (1999) *The Internet Economy and Global Warming*, op cit
21 Hawken, P, Lovins, A B and Lovins, L H (1999) *Natural Capitalism: The Next Industrial Revolution*, Earthscan, London, op cit. See also Porter, M and van der Linde, C (1995) 'Toward a New Conception of the Environment–Competitiveness Relationship', *Journal of Economic Perspectives*, vol 9, no 41
22 Porter, M and van der Linde, C (1995) 'Toward a New Conception of the Environment–Competitiveness Relationship', op cit
23 Rifkin, J (2000) *The Age of Access*, op cit
24 Davis, S and Meyer, C (1999) *Blur: The Speed of Change in the Connected Economy*, Capstone, Oxford

Response

by Evan Davis

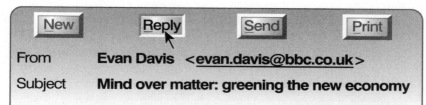

From   Evan Davis   <evan.davis@bbc.co.uk>

Subject   Mind over matter: greening the new economy

It is seductive to believe that the new economy will somehow allow us to reconcile our demand for greater consumption with the demands of environmentalists for a sustainable economy. That we will increasingly dispense with clumsy hardware, like CDs and *Encyclopaedia Britannica*, and consume greener formats, like MP3 files and online books. And it's surely true that technology and innovation – digital or otherwise – will continue to improve resource productivity, just as technology has a long and distinguished record in improving the productivity of labour and capital. Technology certainly does give us a greater material-consumption bang for a given number of resource-depleting bucks. But can we rely on that improvement to reconcile the conflict between material living standards and a sustainable economy? Alas, I suspect not.

'Can technology reduce environmental degradation?' is the wrong question. The *relevant* question is whether we will in fact choose to exploit technology for environmental gain, or whether we will simply exploit it to increase our material living standards. As far as this is concerned, there is little room for complacency. Our experience so far suggests that the benefits of technology are typically directed towards making us richer, rather than greener.

For example, although technology delivers cars that are more efficient, we have not chosen to drive cars that use less fuel. To date, the digital age has not been one of low consumption Minis obtaining 80 miles to the gallon; it is the age of the sports utility vehicle, obtaining 25.

Indeed – according to the Union of Concerned Scientists – in spite of cleaner-burn engine technology, the average new vehicle from every car manufacturer, except one, generates more greenhouse gases today than ten years ago. These early years of the digital era hardly promise a new green dawn. Nowhere is this more apparent than in the hub of the digital age, California. A state of big cars, big air-conditioners, cheap fuel, and long commuting distances.

Why does the economic system deliver this outcome? Because the price of fuel is adjusted to prevent total demand dropping too much. So, for example, if new technology improves efficiency and reduces the demand for fuel, then the price of fuel falls, which promotes an offsetting rise in demand again. Moreover, as technology increases living standards generally, it tends to make fuel more affordable. In short, technology can make it easier to consume fuel more carelessly.

Even if you do not accept this argument, it should be clear that new technology creates new demands for consumption, rather than just depressing old demands. The development of television undoubtedly reduced the number of journeys to cinemas that people took; but at the same time, it stimulated and fuelled consumption, by tantalizing us with pictures of experiences to which we had not been previously exposed. It fostered a demand for journeys that may previously not have existed. The internet will do the same. As fast as email depresses our need to travel to meet existing friends, it will empower us to make a wider circle of new friends to whom we wish to travel. It will reduce the need for us to drive three blocks to visit our near-neighbours, but increase our desire to fly to Australia to meet our newly acquired pen-friends.

This argument may sound unduly pessimistic. Perhaps it is based on a general degree of scepticism about whether the new economy is quite the shift in economic and cultural paradigms that some have suggested. But lest it appears gratuitously negative, let me stress again my agreement with one conclusion of the new-economy optimists. Technology does have the *potential* to enable us to live more comfortably and sustainably. That is not as much a new economic phenomenon as a continuation of the old economy trend towards more productive use of resources. If we are worried about resource use, let us be clear that technology is a potential ally, so long as we can find ways of effectively deploying it to that end. Thus, as Charles Leadbeater and Rebecca Willis argue ,'the mere fact that this path to a greener future might be a possibility does not mean it will become reality. Far from it... The political will – and intervention – required to steer the new economy toward sustainability should not be underestimated.'

On that, we can surely all agree. ∎

2 E-topia? Scenarios for e-commerce and sustainability

Malcolm Eames, Frans Berkhout, Julia Hertin, Richard Hawkins and Gordon Mackerron

Introduction

This chapter presents some ideas about how e-commerce could develop in the UK over the next 10 to 20 years, and the social and environmental implications that may follow. A number of alternative futures are possible – all futures depend upon the choices made now. If the right choices can be made at this early stage in the development of the digital economy, greater benefits will result and potential dangers can be avoided.

However, looking at the future is never easy. We need to be both creative and modest. Some social and economic development will continue along the traditional lines, but the unexpected will occur, especially when a radical technological innovation like the internet begins to have an effect. In this study we have been faced with two particular sources of uncertainty. The first concerns the future of e-commerce itself. With technologies, services, markets and regulation still undergoing rapid innovation, it is difficult to identify the paths of future change. The second source of uncertainty is over the impacts of e-commerce on sustainability. There is a lack of knowledge, as yet, about what the wider impacts of e-commerce on society and the environment might be.

We are faced with the difficult problem of seeking to make better decisions in the face of deep uncertainties about the course and impacts of future change. The strategy adopted here is to project pictures of future worlds, or storylines, that describe a 'possibility space' – a set of plausible futures that span a range of conceivable outcomes. These e-commerce storylines are used to deduce possible impacts, illustrated with a set of quantitative and qualitative indicators. Differing patterns of impact reflect differences in the storylines.

The storylines and indicators together make up the four scenarios: CyberSpace, DigitalIslands, CyberSociety, and NetworkedCommunities. These scenarios are designed to stimulate analysts, policy makers and strategists to question their own assumptions about how e-commerce might develop. They are conceptual vehicles for framing ideas about the future. They are expressly *not* predictions, but are designed to inform choices today that will shape future outcomes.

In building these scenarios, we have taken as a starting point the social and political make-up of possible future worlds. Technology is seen not as an autonomous force of change, but as being embedded in social, political and economic settings. These settings shape its use and diffusion. Technology makes things possible, but whether or not these new opportunities are seized depends on whether service providers and consumers see some clear benefit in doing so. The patterns of incentives and obstacles to innovation are largely determined by the way in which markets, regulations and consumer preferences develop.

The scenarios approach

Scenarios are planning and communication tools that are used to explore complex, uncertain and sometimes disputed futures. The scenarios presented in this report have three main objectives:

- to illustrate broad socio-economic contexts within which e-commerce may develop;
- to identify specific features of internet technologies and e-commerce markets under these different socio-economic contexts; and
- to provide a basis for a preliminary assessment of the social and environmental impacts of alternative e-commerce futures.

The scenarios consider the development of e-commerce and its impacts primarily in the UK, but set within a European and global context. We have adopted two time horizons: 2010 and 2020. While the 2020 horizon is highly speculative with respect to the development of information and communications technologies, it is included to take account of much slower changes in infrastructures, like roads and digital networks, on which e-commerce depends.

A recent review of futures studies identified five main dimensions of change:[1]

1 population growth and settlement patterns;
2 the rate and composition of economic growth;
3 the rate and direction of technological change;
4 the nature of governance; and
5 social and political values.

We have taken the last two dimensions as our starting point. Social and political values and the nature of governance are seen as critical determinants of future change. This means that the scenarios have been generated from a set of conceptual associations, rather than from an empirical model of the real world (see Figure 2.1). The strength of this approach is that it provides an intellectual coherence. But 'values' and 'governance' are not simple or easily definable concepts, and we have had to make a number of simplifying assumptions about what they mean. We take values to mean contemporary tastes, beliefs and norms, and governance to mean the way in which authority and control are exercised in societies – whether local, national or global. While there are obvious connections between values and governance (a democratic society can only function if democratic values prevail), we take them to be independent in this scenarios framework.

Values and governance both reflect and shape social and economic changes. Values, the horizontal dimension, captures alternative developments in core social and political values. At one end of the spectrum – 'Individualism' – values are dominated by a desire to satisfy individual aspirations for personal freedom. The rights of the individual and the present are privileged over those of the collective and the future. Resources are distributed through free and competitive markets, with the function of governance limited mainly to guaranteeing free markets. At the other end – 'Community'– values are shaped by greater concern for the common good. The individual is viewed as part of a collective, with rights and responsibilities determined by broadly defined social goals. There is greater concern about the future, equity and participation. Civil society is strong and highly valued, and resources are allocated through more managed markets.

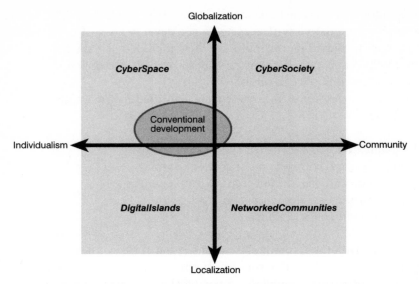

Figure 2.1   Four contextual e-commerce scenarios

The vertical governance dimension shows alternative structures of political and economic power and decision making. With the governance axis we identify different ways in which political authority may be distributed. At one end of the spectrum – 'Globalization' – the power to govern is distributed upwards, downwards and outwards away from national governments. National political and economic boundaries fade, and greater interdependence is fostered. Locally-based decision making takes place in the context of global economic, trade and environmental regimes. At the other end of the spectrum – 'Localization' – economic and political power is retained at national and regional levels. The process of globalization is weakened, and governments have greater autonomy. National and regional development is based on local capabilities and resources.

These two dimensions are used to describe a possibility space containing four alternative futures scenarios (see Figure 2.1). Through telling the scenario storylines, we trace the implications of a particular association between values and governance. Through imagination, expert judgement and, sometimes, intuition, a picture of a future world emerges.

CyberSpace

Scenario highlights

This is a world of consumerist values, a highly integrated world trading system, and significant economic expansion, with 3.5 per cent average growth in GDP year on year. Liberalized, open markets are sustained and regulated through international governance institutions. Regulatory controls at both the national and global level are weakened. Global oligopolies flourish. Sovereignty over economic policy is increasingly lost by national governments, whose function becomes the implementation of common codes and rules.

The development of a global convergent information and communication technology (ICT) environment, probably based on mobile devices, is accompanied by maximum migration of commerce to the digital domain. E-commerce makes up 25 per cent of UK GDP by 2010. Leading-edge technology is increasingly oriented towards delivering high-value consumer services. There is no formal access or content regulation for digital services, and self-regulation predominates. Growing disparities develop in the extent to which digital services become embedded in business, educational, health and leisure activities, with the benefits going mainly to the affluent.

Rapid growth is experienced around metropolitan centres, but extensive exclusion persists. This is a high-mobility, transport-intensive future. By 2010, 11 per cent of the UK road network is at 100 per cent stress. Greenhouse gas emissions increase, rising to 780 MtC equivalent in 2010 compared to 773 today. Equity declines.

Economy and e-commerce

Economy

Liberalized and open markets, an integrated world trading system, buoyant consumer demand, and the adoption of new technologies like ICT and biotechnology, bring high levels of economic growth – 3.5 per cent of GDP year on year. E-commerce is viewed as a catalyst of economic integration, which extends the scale and scope of markets, provides more transparency, and enables a reduction in the burden of regulation. Countries, firms and consumers who adapt to and exploit the new e-economy prosper. Large global businesses drive the development of global networks with structured access. As a result of an innovative and entrepreneurial culture, small businesses also flourish, servicing specialized international markets.

Digital economy

The digital economy becomes increasingly dominant across the European Union (EU), accelerating the decline of manufacturing and agriculture. Particularly high growth is seen in the ICT and logistics sectors that underpin the new economy. There is high migration to the virtual economy across all sectors, and the total volume of e-commerce is very high. As a proportion, business-to-business (B2B) transactions become less significant over time, with the growth of stable business-to-customer (B2C) e-relationships. E-money and e-banking become the norm, promoting common global currencies.

National government's ability to collect tax revenues is curtailed by the growth of the e-economy. Tax avoidance becomes easier as a result of e-banking and the elimination of import duties. Attempts to tax internet transactions fail through lack of enforcement. By 2010, the outcome of the 2005 UK referendum on joining the European currency union is seen as increasingly irrelevant, due to the emergence of global cyber-currencies.

B2C

Economic transformation is pioneered by the rapid expansion of B2C e-commerce in the finance, retailing, logistics, travel, media, education and health sectors, and in personal services offering advice, security, privacy and pleasure. Routine consumer purchases become increasingly automated as intelligent intermediaries are developed to scour the web for goods and services. This stimulates further rapid growth in global logistics and transport services. Customized marketing and strong relationships with high-income customers become increasingly critical for service providers. Retail space is transformed, with an emphasis on leisure and entertainment and high-value purchases.

B2B

Tighter supply-chain control and major efficiency gains are achieved from the automation of B2B transactions. International electronic exchanges facilitate the continued globalization of production and retailing. Integration and efficiency gains lead to substantial innovation in the logistics sector, with an emphasis on greater scale, speed and quality. However, strong anti-trust controls limit the development of purchasing and supply-chain management tools.

Government services

Administrative reform continues in government, in part enabled by the use of the internet to perform many functions. Cost savings, the continued privatization of public services, and the emergence of public-led policy making (through referendums and so on) all drive the development of e-government and electronic voting.

Regulation and governance

Policy style

There is a convergence of political cultures and policy styles. Governance becomes internationalized, multi-level, and less account-able. The role of national government shrinks. Regulation is transferred to regional and global bodies in which business interests play a key role. Social and environmental objectives are not integrated into economic policy and trade regimes. Economic instruments such as green taxes and tradeable permits are used to control acute environmental degradation. Global environmental issues are addressed only where they are recog-nized as business issues by powerful corporate interests.

Competition policy

Deregulation in all markets is underpinned by a powerful global trade regime committed to the continued removal of trade barriers and enhanced competition. A WTO e-directorate is established in 2003 to set standards for international e-commerce. Its remit expands rapidly as it takes on the role of policing global anti-trust regulation, transactional security and e-taxation. Content regulation is very limited and largely happens through service providers' self-regulation and the sale of block-ing software. Pornography, gambling and new forms of commercial e-exploitation flourish.

E-commerce technologies

Innovation

This is a consumer-driven future in which rapid economic growth and strong intellectual property rights (IPR) go hand in hand with high private investment in research and development. Innovation is driven by the provision of customized, interactive services to global markets. A convergent ICT environment is based on open global networks coexist-ing with closed private networks. Inter-operability is achieved through industry-set standards. Mobile satellite-based networks grow rapidly, although major new investments are also made in enhancing optical fibre networks. The costs of access fall, but remain high for broadband services.

User technologies

Many user devices become mobile and location-independent. By 2010, wearable computers and plug-in devices begin to replace conventional personal computers (PCs). Encryption and identification technologies become increasingly sophisticated, and user devices become personalized. Online access underlies many home-based goods and services, including health, security, leisure and education. Interactive digital television (DTV) achieves rapid market penetration and provides another entry point to e-commerce. User interfaces develop rapidly for premium markets; voice control, video and universal language translation all achieve significant market penetration between 2005 and 2015. High-capacity search engines deal with information overload. Personal digital assistants (PDAs) filter information, make routine decisions and create leisure time for the affluent.

User access and control

User access is mediated by the market, with premium services targeted at an affluent global elite. E-commerce markets are segmented through customized advertising and the price of services. The digital divide takes a new form, with near-universal access to e-commerce being achieved through DTV and PDAs by 2010, but with access to online services becoming limited by cost and capability.

Socio-economic context

This is a high-mobility scenario. Energy prices are generally low, but periodic price hikes occur due to oligopolistic behaviour and concerns over resource security. Car use grows rapidly, as does road and air freight; congestion increases. Hybrid cars are introduced from 2010 and in-car telematics improve the efficiency of road use. There is major investment in global infrastructure, including airports, ports and railways.

There is slow population growth in the UK, but a global market for many skills leads to an increasingly mobile labour force. The greater openness of borders encourages labour migration. The trend to smaller households intensifies, bringing high demand for housing near to centres of growth. A weak planning system promotes relatively unconstrained development for housing, commercial and leisure uses.

The state's role in the provision of education, welfare and health services declines, resulting in deepening inequalities of access and standards. State provision increasingly targets only the very poor and most disadvantaged. For the middle classes, private sector provision becomes the norm. There is a major increase in demand for both high-tech curative healthcare and more holistic health promotion services.

DigitalIslands

Scenario highlights

This is a world of consumerist values, with governance systems primarily located at the national level. Markets in the UK are liberalized, but the process of economic integration and globalization is constrained. The benefits of retaining some degree of economic and political independence are viewed as outweighing the benefits of further integration. There continues to be high political and economic diversity in the international system. National government structures and processes are preserved with little change. There is moderate but unstable economic growth – on average a 2 per cent growth in GDP per annum – and relatively little structural change in the economy.

There is limited technological convergence of ICTs. 'Walled gardens' are the norm. There is rapid but unstable migration of business and consumer activity to the digital domain, hampered by inadequate integration and common standards. E-commerce makes up 15 per cent of UK GDP by 2010. This growth reinforces already powerful business and commercial interests.

This is a car-dependent future, with 13 per cent of roads at 100 per cent stress by 2010. It is characterized by weak planning controls, except in wealthier areas that are able to defend their interests. Carbon emissions are high – 845 MtC equivalent in 2010. Equity declines, resulting in substantial social tension.

Economy and e-commerce

Economy

This future is defined by a combination of consumerist values, and the retention by the UK government of substantial power in key policy areas like money, tax and defence. The UK pursues an independent economic and political path, separated from the EU and the US. The more restricted scope of the UK market dampens economic growth, and limits the potential of e-commerce. The rate of decline in manufacturing slows, but export-led sectors still face lower growth rates.

Digital economy

The rate of e-enabled structural change in the economy is slower than under the CyberSpace scenario. The digital economy tends to reinforce the power of incumbent producers and service providers. Commercial 'walled gardens' and trusted brands predominate. A limited number of integrated global and regional networks compete through technical differentiation and price. There is unstable migration to e-commerce, driven by the search for efficiency gains and cost reductions rather than the rapid innovation of web-based services. The absolute volume of e-commerce is moderate, reaching a plateau as established markets become saturated and opportunities for efficiency gains dry up. 'Pirate islands' emerge as a base for hacking, e-fraud and cyber-terrorism. These continue to be a threat to the integrity and viability of e-commerce.

Tax revenues remain secure, with tax collection undergoing incremental change. E-commerce transactions are taxed effectively, and a 'byte tax' is introduced. Sterling is retained as the UK currency, mainly due to public mistrust of the euro. Financial services become mainly web-based, but there is only limited development of e-money.

B2C

After a period of experimentation, B2C e-commerce settles down and focuses on finance, entertainment, travel and some retail markets. The uptake of e-commerce remains confined primarily to the young and the affluent. For other groups, the costs of access and the lack of perceived advantages of 'clicks over bricks' subdue demand. Routine consumer purchases are increasingly automated for the affluent time-poor. High-value mobile broadband services are targeted at a narrow and slowly growing market. Buyers' clubs emerge, seeking bulk discounts for communities in less affluent areas.

B2B

In value terms, B2B remains the primary focus of e-commerce. Opportunities for greater control and cost reduction lead firms to transfer purchasing and supply chain management to the internet. Smaller-scale UK manufacturers exploit the efficiency gains offered by the greater integration of supply chains. In some sectors producers are able to use their market power to raise margins through B2B auctions.

Regulation and governance

Policy style

The Westminster model of government in the UK remains more or less intact. The process of devolution is curtailed, and there is a return to greater centralization, primarily as an attempt to improve management of the economy. Political discourse becomes more populist and fractious. Social and environmental issues remain a low priority. Environmental policy undergoes more experimentation with voluntary and market-based instruments.

Competition policy

Trade continues to grow, but the liberalization of global markets is hampered by the lack of political convergence at an international level. The WTO system is maintained more or less in its present form. National governments seek to balance the promotion of genuine competition with a desire to protect domestic capabilities in key sectors. National incumbents in the telecoms, financial services and retail sectors remain strong. Price regulation for digital services is ineffective. Transactional security and consumer redress are handled at a national level, and little progress is made in establishing an enforceable international regime. Patchy content regulation is exercised through national courts and self-regulation, though the affluent and well connected can buy their way around these controls.

E-commerce technologies

Innovation

Innovation is driven mainly by the needs of B2B transactions, except in high-value niche markets for consumer services. This is a less consumer-driven future. Moderate economic growth and weaker anti-trust regulation go hand in hand with lower private investment in research and development. Limited convergence and inter-operability are the result as the small band of global service providers and national ICT incumbents exploit technical differentiation to preserve their market share. Terrestrial cable networks continue to be the primary vehicle for digital communications, and there is limited development of broadband mobile networks. Business and private networks develop, controlled by vertically-integrated infrastructure and service providers.

User technologies

Leading edge technologies – voice recognition, language translation, and so on – are marketed primarily to businesses. Innovation and diffusion of advanced technologies are limited by market constraints. DTV and webphones achieve rapid market penetration as the cost to the user of the hardware falls. DTV dominates the entertainment market and is the major point of access to the internet.

User access and control

The 'digital divide' comes to describe the gap between those who have restricted access and are passive consumers of new web-based media, and those who actively control their cyber-interactions, and have the resources to obtain universal access. By 2010, rival service providers will give away DTVs and webphones to even relatively poor UK consumers. However, these basic units will only provide access to the franchised portals offered by the service provider, giving limited choice to consumers. More affluent and educated consumers will buy proper universal access to the web.

Socio-economic context

This is a car-dependent scenario, with steadily rising fossil fuel prices and relatively low levels of investment in infrastructure or public transport. 'Not in my back yard' (NIMBY) objections and public finance restrictions limit the building of new roads, and congestion increases. Despite this, experiments with congestion charging prove unpopular and are scrapped. Telematics begin to play a role on many major routes, as efforts are made to improve the utilization of the motorway network. Road freight predominates and grows. Air traffic increases more slowly.

The UK population grows slowly, with household numbers remaining approximately stable. There is an erosion of the green belt for new high-income housing. The planning system is weakened, but new developments attract strong protests. There is a steady shift towards the private provision of education, welfare and health services. State provision becomes more uneven, primarily because of lower economic growth and fiscal conservatism.

CyberSociety

Scenario highlights

This is a world in which social and ecological values shape global markets, and international political institutions predominate. Sovereignty over many areas of policy is relinquished by national governments in pursuit of economic stability and political convergence. Strong global and regional governance is underpinned by partnerships between governments, industry and non-governmental organizations (NGOs). Moderate-to-high economic growth – 2.75 per cent average GDP growth per annum – is maintained, with low levels of inflation. Innovation continues at high rates and is shaped by sustainable development objectives.

Convergent global ICT environments facilitate the shaping of the new economy to a 'one world' ethos. Open networks, shareware and mediated access prosper. There is selective migration to e-commerce, which rises to 20 per cent of UK GDP by 2010. Universal service obligations, transactional security, consumer redress and content regulation are all effectively policed under global regimes.

Rapid technological change coupled with high investment in public transport decouples energy and transport intensities. This is a relatively low emissions scenario, decreasing to 625 MtC equivalent by 2010. However, some road traffic congestion problems remain, with 9 per cent of the UK road network at 100 per cent stress by 2010. Issues of equity and development impact on all decision-making processes, reshaping the global distribution of environmental and technological resources.

Economy and e-commerce

Economy

This is a radical future of social, economic and technological transformation towards a more managed global economic and trading system, which aims to reconcile economic growth with equity and fairer trade. The emergent e-economy is shaped by a prevailing one-world ethos, in which e-commerce is harnessed for both economic and social goals. The internet is viewed as a means of building more sustainable economic and social networks, improving the accountability of governments and business, and encouraging access to goods and services. The UK economy is export-led, with continued growth in services and the new e-economy. Resource-intensive manufacturing and agriculture decline.

Digital economy

Commercial network infrastructures are dominated by a small number of global providers, licensed on a supra-national basis, who provide a level playing field for the international development of e-commerce. Migration to e-commerce is high, but the pace is slow due to the need to meet broad access objectives internationally. The absolute volume of e-commerce is high. Government-to-business and government-to citizen transactions are particularly important in this scenario, while B2B transactions become less significant over time.

EU monetary union is strengthened by the UK's adoption of the euro in 2003. European tax harmonization is achieved in 2005 and a complementary currency, the e-euro, is introduced in 2010. A global digital bank is established to collect and distribute taxation on global e-commerce in 2010.

B2C

With strong consumer protection regulation in place, there is rapid growth in B2C e-commerce across retailing, travel, banking and leisure. High public and private investment in sustainable transport infrastructure also boosts retail e-commerce. There is widespread utilization of common logistics services for consumer deliveries. Government support is given to consumer services that bring sustainability gains (for instance, web-controlled energy services). There is high growth in virtualized services. Trusted web intermediaries, agents and buyers' clubs flourish. Service providers develop much closer and more interactive relationships with consumers on a global scale, with a strong emphasis placed on quality and customization.

B2B

There is growing penetration of B2B e-commerce in all sectors, permitting the more efficient transmission of purchasing, legal and other information, and allowing greater transparency along supply chains; such transparency is now required under tough producer responsibility obligations. Manufacturers across all sectors are transformed into service providers selling value rather than units.

Integrated supply chain and life cycle management is adopted by business both to reduce costs and manage social and environmental impacts. Internet conferencing and virtual reality tools are widely used to reduce business travel.

Government services

The web is used extensively to develop more open and participatory policy-making processes. All public services are moved onto the web, improving the efficiency of service delivery. Active policies for universal access are implemented.

Regulation and governance

Policy style

Strong partnerships between governments, industry and NGOs aim to achieve sustainable development at a global scale. Global coordination of sustainability policy begins to take shape. New environmental treaties and regimes are formed and given real authority. Regulatory, market-based and producer responsibility instruments become more important. Global equity of access to resources becomes a significant constraint on economic policy in the industrialized world.

Competition policy

Competitive global markets are managed by powerful, but politically accountable, global regulators. Agglomeration continues in many sectors – such as auto manufacture, telecommunications and banking – and is managed by international agreements and price regulation. Collaborative self-regulation and covenants become more significant at a regional and global level. There is little formal regulation of network standards, but strong legal guarantees with respect to transactional security and consumer redress. A weak IPR regime promotes the use of open source software. Both positive and negative content regulation is established by international agreement and enforced by new agencies. However, minority activists claim a loss of cultural diversity and freedom of expression.

E-commerce technologies

Innovation

Public investment in research and development is an important driver of technological development, while social and environmental drivers play a key role in shaping innovation in companies. Fiscal, regulatory and information policies encourage the adoption of technologies with a small environmental footprint. A strongly convergent ICT environment is based on open global networks. Access from fixed broadband cable networks dominates, with mobile networks complementing these.

User technologies

There is less differentiation of user technologies, with integration of multiple functions into a limited range of standardized units. Devices are leased to the consumer to ensure wide access. A development programme sponsored by the Organisation for Economic Co-operation and Development (OECD) and the United Nations (UN) releases universal language translation shareware for both text and voice.

User access and control

Universal access provisions promote a stable and uniform environment for the development of services to mass markets. Governments require

businesses to provide access for all to networks as a condition of entry
into the market. Mass channel broadcast media grow and move onto
the web.

Socio-economic context

Major investments in transport infrastructure (road, rail, sea and air)
are made, increasing access and reducing the environmental impacts of
mobility. Much of this infrastructure involves international
public–private partnerships. There is high penetration of low- or zero-
emissions vehicles and transport telematics. Heavy freight is encouraged
to shift to rail and water through a combination of pricing mechanisms
and regulation. The substitution of virtual transactions like teleworking
and teleconferencing for mobility has some impact on transport
demand. However, the growth of tourism and global business operations results in a rapid growth of air traffic.

There is a stable population and reduced internal migration within
the UK. Household numbers increase at average rates with a higher
turnover of the housing stock. A strong planning system aims to achieve
high environmental quality and low resource use. Public expenditure
increases as a proportion of national and global income. Public education, welfare and health systems are maintained and improved.

Network communities

Scenario highlights

This is a world of communitarian values exercised through local participatory democracy. The power of global institutions is checked through
stronger accountability mechanisms, and there is greater emphasis on
community self-reliance and autonomy. As a result, there are fewer
opportunities to develop economies of scope and scale. Markets are more
fragmented and international trade is lower than in the other scenarios,
as is GDP growth, which averages 1.25 per cent. However, some locali-
ties do foster political and economic links with other regions across the
world, enabled in part by the digital economy. There is a tension
between the social and political importance attached to localization,
and the more open nature of virtual space.

Regionally-specific digital solutions emerge, often built around
legacy systems, with little technological convergence; closed networks
predominate. Management and ownership of networks is community

based, governed by rules and democratic structures. E-commerce plays a limited role, totalling 5 per cent of UK GDP by 2010, and is used primarily to encourage shorter and more efficient supply chains. Nevertheless, new forms of local electronic exchange and e-money flourish, and the use of the internet for information and public services also grows rapidly. Lower economic activity and demand for mobility make this a low-emissions scenario. Equity also improves, although tensions arise over reconciling social and environmental objectives.

Economy and e-commerce

Economy

Communitarian values coexist with governance that is increasingly exercised at a local and regional level. Global institutions play a lesser role; the local is highly valued. Local and regional markets become more important, in part enabled by the greater use of ICT. International trade and regional economic growth slow in comparison with long-term trends. This is a relatively low-investment economy, with greater reliance placed on communities' knowledge and resource base. Economic policy is dominated by the need to encourage efficient small-scale production, while also meeting ambitious social objectives of equity and participation.

Digital economy

The internet is viewed as an asset in building community self-reliance. There is local ownership of digital infrastructures and control of network standards. The web is maintained through regional collaborative agreements, underpinning new models of economic development. The smaller scope of markets and the focus on local demand brings advantages to small-scale production of goods and services. There are fewer opportunities for economies of scale, and a greater emphasis is placed on customization and a rich information environment. Stable producer–consumer relationships are managed to facilitate the growth of local markets and exchanges. There is more limited migration to e-commerce and the absolute volume of e-commerce is low. C2C, B2C and government-to-consumer (G2C) transactions are particularly important in this scenario.

A greater proportion of tax is raised at regional and local levels. Revenue collection moves onto the web. The UK does not adopt the euro, which is seen as impinging on national autonomy. However, new forms of local exchange flourish, as e-barter and e-LETS (local exchange and trading schemes) sites facilitate the electronic exchange of goods and services for B2B, B2C and C2B (consumer-to-business) transactions.

B2C

The main growth areas of B2C e-commerce are in retailing and information services. Strong trust-based relationships between local producers and consumers are highly valued, and facilitated via mobile digital devices and PCs. There is greater supply chain transparency and a revival in the home delivery of many goods. Barter and information exchange also play a role in economic relationships. Buyers' clubs emerge, aggregating demand for the benefit of producers and consumers alike. International e-tailing on the web is limited to specialist goods and services not available through local markets.

B2B

B2B e-commerce is rapidly adopted as a way of making shorter supply chains more flexible and responsive, and also as a way of driving down costs. Producers and retailers form procurement networks to purchase materials and goods not available regionally. Local web cooperatives, bringing small-scale producers together, become more common. email and internet conferencing are widely used to substitute for business travel.

Government services

The internet is widely used in the provision of public services such as welfare, health and education. Voting in elections and referendums is increasingly online, and greater participation in local decisions is encouraged through accessible web interfaces. Government becomes far more open and transparent through a network of electronic town halls.

Regulation and governance

Policy style

Government is carried out through a devolved participatory democracy. Emphasis is placed on the principle of subsidiarity, which states that policy should be enacted at the lowest level of governance. In environmental policy there is an emphasis on behavioural and structural economic changes that protect natural resources.

Competition policy

Competition policy aims to stimulate new ventures and safeguard competition within more geographically constrained markets, while also supporting well-defined sustainability goals. There is patchy regulation of network standards. International regulation of transactional security and consumer redress is relatively ineffective. Together with weaker transport links, this constrains the international potential of e-commerce. Weak IPR regimes promote the use of open source software. Mechanisms are developed for strong community-based content regulation on the web.

E-commerce technologies

Innovation
Innovation is constrained by low levels of investment in research and development, and focuses on low-cost devices and applications. Where local solutions are developed, they tend to be diffused rapidly, sometimes with public sector support. There is little convergence of network technologies, mainly due to a persistence of legacy systems and reduced availability of capital. Inter-operability remains limited and barriers between local and regional systems and networks persist. Emphasis is placed on the adaptation of existing infrastructure. This leads to the development of mixed networks – local broadband in urban communities and telephone lines in rural communities. There is also scope for local experimentation with novel technologies such as strip aerials and helium balloons. Public health concerns inhibit the development of mobile networks and technologies.

User technologies
For end consumers, PC-based systems continue to dominate access to the web and e-commerce. There is slower market penetration of DTV, and mobile devices are less significant as a vehicle of e-commerce. High-growth digital services include information and public service delivery, teleworking and virtualized leisure services.

User access and control
There is variable private access to closed networks of diverse quality, but very high access to public services on the web. Community intranets with limited access to specified services become important.

Socio-economic context

This is a low-transport-intensity scenario as a result of declining trade, lower mobility and higher energy costs. Regulation, incentives and investment in public transport reduce demands for personal mobility. By 2010, car sharing and leasing, traffic management, and home deliveries result in declining absolute car ownership. By the 2020s, zero-emission vehicles become the norm for shorter trips, and mass public transport the norm for longer journeys.

Overall, UK population is stable, although there is a slight decline in household numbers, coupled with migration from larger cities to small- and medium-sized towns. A strong planning system protects against urban sprawl and encourages denser housing and better managed commercial developments. There is a high level of public provision of education, welfare and health services, with an emphasis on equity and open access, financed primarily from taxation.

E-commerce impacts on sustainability

Research into the potential environmental and social effects of e-commerce faces a number of difficulties: the complexity of the issues, the pace of development, and a lack of reliable data. All limit the validity of current studies. Many of the decisions and investments in technologies, transport and logistics systems have not yet been made. These decisions will greatly affect whether the beneficial potentials of e-commerce can be realized.

The qualitative evaluation of the impacts presented here aims to provoke a debate rather than to provide answers. It offers a framework for analysis to enrich the current discussion, which often appears to be dominated by a controversy between e-commerce optimists and pessimists. Drawing on research carried out within and outside the Digital Futures project, the scenarios highlight at least three important aspects of e-commerce and sustainable development:

- the scope and shape of the new economy are not yet determined – diverse pathways are possible;
- the sustainability impacts are likely to be mixed and trade-offs will be necessary; and
- forward-looking and well-targeted policy measures can influence future social and environmental impacts.

Social impacts

Digital divide

In most scenarios, access is not an issue of cost, IT skills or the availability of online devices. In CyberSpace and DigitalIslands, intense competition has brought down the price of internet-enabled mobile phones and other personal devices, and many are available free of charge. Simple hand-held devices and DTV also increase online access for people with lower technical skills. However, in NetworkedCommunities most online access is still PC-based. Due to slower technological development, lack of skills, and costs, a quarter of the population remain excluded from online access.

However, other – often more subtle – obstacles to equal access arise. In CyberSpace, sophisticated systems analysing credit rating and buying records will prevent the poorer population from using many services. In DigitalIslands, the dominance of digital television gives the main service providers far greater control over content and access to certain services.

Under all scenarios, a significant percentage of less skilled or poorer people remain offline, and those who do not have a bank account are excluded from online shopping.

This is particularly problematic in CyberSpace and CyberSociety, in which online services increasingly replace traditional goods and services. For the majority of the population, however, shopping opportunities and free, advertising-funded information services improve greatly.

More broadly, participation in the knowledge-based economy is far from equal. In all scenarios, the capability to use information and communication services becomes more important in all areas of life: education, the job market, shopping and leisure. Excluded sections of the population, such as the homeless, become even more disadvantaged.

Consumer protection and security

The level of consumer protection varies greatly between the scenarios. In CyberSpace and DigitalIslands, standards are based on industry self-regulation. Large e-commerce companies are eager to ensure trust in online transactions, and so implement high voluntary standards. Many dot-com companies trade consumer data to enable the targeting of product information and marketing. In CyberSociety and NetworkedCommunities, personal and consumer information is protected through stringent laws. Enforcement of these rules is more difficult in the CyberSociety scenario because more international trans-actions are made. International privacy law is negotiated and implemented, but may be difficult to enforce.

Fraud on the supply side, for example the online sale of dubious products and services, flourishes in CyberSpace due to relatively open, globalized networks and weak regulators. This is partly offset by new encryption technologies. The commercial 'walled gardens' of the DigitalIslands scenario are less vulnerable to manipulation from outside. However, some companies intentionally exploit the weakness of consumer protection regulation to do fraudulent business, leading in turn to a drop in confidence in e-transactions. CyberSociety and NetworkedCommunities insist on strong legal guarantees and security for consumers through transaction guarantees and toughened product warranties.

Public services

The nature of public services like health, education and social services under the different scenarios is largely determined by factors other than the use of ICTs. Nevertheless, online technologies will have an effect on the quality and accessibility of these services. As the drive for cost efficiency in the public sector intensifies, online technologies play an increasing role in supporting public provision. Most public services will be online by 2010; advice is given on the internet, appointments are made via email, courses taught online. This trend is particularly strong in CyberSpace, in which the digitally excluded will have difficulties in accessing some basic services. Even if a large majority of the population is online by 2010, this does not imply that everybody knows how to make full use of the available services. This problem is much less marked in NetworkedCommunities, in which online services supplement rather than replace traditional services.

Citizenship

ICTs affect the political system, although in very different ways. In all scenarios, new technologies are used in political decision making to achieve greater transparency and accountability. In Cyberspace, online voting is introduced and increases voter turnout at elections. In NetworkedCommunities and CyberSociety, the internet is used to encourage greater participation. This is especially important in CyberSociety, in which internationalized governance structures suffer deep democratic deficits. In NetworkedCommunities, local communities experiment with ICT-supported, participatory decision-making processes.

Regional development

In CyberSpace, and to some extent in DigitalIslands, rapid growth in retail e-commerce closes down some local shops, banks and services. High streets tend to decline as banks, department stores, travel agencies, bookshops and electronics stores close less profitable branches. The impacts are much smaller in the other scenarios because the internet and other networks are dominated by non-commercial uses.

In CyberSpace and DigitalIslands, the new economy widens the gap between poorer and richer parts of the UK. The south-east of England benefits most from new dot-com business and the growth of the communications sector. In CyberSociety, regional development is more evenly distributed through public provision of ICT infrastructure, active programmes of government support, and stringent service obligations on providers. NetworkedCommunities is generally less affected by this trend. Here, ICT contributes to strengthening the identity of local communities, connected through local networks.

Environmental impacts

Resource efficiency

In all scenarios, the extended use of ICTs will improve resource efficiency. This trend will be particularly strong in CyberSpace, in which technological development is most rapid. Price signals, including the introduction of higher taxes on resource use, reinforce these effects. Increased ICT use in production reduces the use of energy and materials, as well as the generation of wastes. Similar, but less marked effects will occur in private households. More efficient energy and lighting services, which grow rapidly in the CyberSociety and Networked-Communities scenarios, bring important reductions in the energy intensity of buildings.

B2B e-commerce will lead to better-managed supply chains. Here, cost efficiency and environmental efficiency will go hand in hand. ICTs will also reduce the need for inventories of goods, reducing energy and materials use. Less space will be required for warehousing and retailing. The NetworkedCommunities scenario will benefit from these developments only to a limited extent because economic growth and investments are low and B2B e-commerce increases slowly. Equally, DigitalIslands will not be able to realize the full potential of these efficiency gains due to moderate economic growth and a lack of tax incentives. The main counter-trend will be experienced in the CyberSpace scenario, in which the scope of supply systems becomes increasingly global, and the value of physical resources tends to fall.

Virtualization

A number of products and services will be obtained in digital rather than physical form. All scenarios will see some virtualization of services like banking and billing, as well as products like music and books. Over the period to 2010, the environmental benefits of this shift will be small. In CyberSpace and CyberSociety, sales of virtual products and services grow rapidly. But as in the case of the 'paperless office', the expected environmental benefits are not met – digital products often supplement rather than replace traditional ones. In DigitalIslands and CyberSpace, the small environmental gains are offset by a steep rise in the purchase and use of internet phones, DTV sets and PCs.

Consumption patterns

The use of ICTs will lower the costs of many products and services. Impacts on resource use and pollution will depend on how consumers choose to reallocate the extra time and money. In the market-oriented scenarios, people will consume more goods, most of them tangible. The environmental outcomes of this will be diverse and difficult to assess. The current experience with the fuel consumption of cars, whereby efficiency gains are offset by the trend towards larger cars, will be repeated in other areas. In CyberSociety this effect will be avoided through strong economic incentives and regulation to use less energy and materials.

E-commerce also increases the power of consumers. Shoppers are able to choose between a large number of suppliers, compare prices, and specify requirements. In the NetworkedCommunities and CyberSociety scenarios this will promote green consumerism. New websites will link consumers with suppliers of green goods. It is likely that locally produced organic food will be sold online in the Networked-Communities scenario. Strong environmental awareness and low incomes will also lead to a boom in secondhand websites like eBay, where consumers can buy, sell and exchange a variety of goods.

Transport

In transport, the efficiency improvements of e-business tend to have positive environmental impacts under all scenarios. In the scenarios with relatively strong B2B e-commerce, ICTs will stimulate logistics to be more efficient, compress supply chains and optimize the flow of goods through the supply chain. The potential for e-commerce to dramatically reduce the number of vehicles will be fully exploited only in CyberSociety. Here, high fuel prices and planning controls encourage the emergence of sustainable distribution systems.

In all scenarios, light goods vehicle (LGV) traffic will rise, especially in residential areas. In CyberSpace, and to a lesser extent in DigitalIslands, rapid growth of competing distribution systems increases road traffic considerably. This effect is reinforced by consumers' expectations of rapid delivery. By 2010, e-commerce distribution does not yet replace individual shopping trips to a very significant degree, except in CyberSpace.

The digital economy will contribute to a rise in air transport, especially air freight and business travel, which is a major issue of environmental concern. This trend is due to the extra international trade facilitated by B2B and B2C e-commerce. In addition, more leisure time and global communications will increase the demand for long-distance travel.

Environmental governance

In all scenarios except DigitalIslands, online services increase the transparency of corporate environmental performance. Large companies are under pressure to disclose environmental information about their products and production processes. In CyberSociety and CyberSpace, NGOs use the internet to lobby for stringent and enforceable environmental laws.

Comparing scenarios and impacts – UK in 2010

The scenario storylines are matched to quantitative and qualitative indicators that illustrate the magnitude of change, allow a quick and systematic comparison, and aim to make the scenarios more accessible. Indicator values should not be interpreted as predictions or forecasts. They are based on statistics and expert judgement. No formal modelling has been undertaken, but consistency checks have been applied to ensure that different indicators are telling the same story.

Robust strategies for policy

Common themes for the development of robust policy strategies

There are different pathways to securing more sustainable outcomes for the development of the internet and e-commerce. These will be influenced profoundly by the outcomes of larger political debates and conflicts about the rights of the consumer, the role of the state, and the future of the world economy. The virtual social and economic space of the internet cannot be separated from the real socio-economic space in which governments, corporations, markets and people continue to exist and interact. The virtual is embedded in the tangible, and the tangible shapes the virtual world. As Saskia Sassen has argued,

'There is no purely digital economy and no completely virtual corporation. This means that power, contestation, inequality, in brief, hierarchy, inscribe electronic space. And although the digitized portions of these industries ... have the capacity to subvert the established hierarchies, new hierarchies are being formed, born out of the existing material conditions underlying power and the new conditions created by digital space.'[12]

Table 2.1 Summary table of the impacts of the scenarios

Indicator	Cyber-Space	Digital-Islands	Cyber-Society	Networked Communities
Scenario Characteristics				
GDP growth per year	3.5%	2%	2.75%	1.25%
Unemployment	6%	9%	5%	6%
Private car use	85%	90%	78%	75%
GHG emissions (million tonnes)	780	845	625	600
Waste (million tonnes)	250	200	175	125
Dominant device for online access	mixed	digital TV	PC/mixed	PC
Dominant use of networks	commercial	commercial	mixed	private
Dominant form of e-commerce	B2C	B2B	mixed	B2B
Potential Social Impacts of the New Economy				
Low cost access to online services	✔✔	✔	✔✔	✗
Access without IT skills	✔✔	✔	✗✗	✗
Equal access to all online services	✗	✗✗	✔	✔
Equal opportunities for offline population	✗✗	✗✗	✗	✔
Strong consumer protection	✔	✗✗	✔	✔✔
High efficiency of public services	✔✔	✔	✗	✗✗
Improved political participation	✔	✗	✔	✔✔
Balanced regional development	✗✗	✗	✔	✔
Potential Environmental Impacts of the New Economy				
Resource-efficient production	✔✔	✔	✔✔	✗✗
Resource-efficient supply chains	✔✔	✔	✔✔	✗
Dematerialization of products	✔✔	✔	✔	✗
Sustainable consumption patterns	✗✗	✗	✗	✔
Green consumerism	✗	✗	✔✔	✔✔
Less heavy goods transport	✔	✔	✔	✔✔
Less light goods transport	✗✗	✗	✗✗	✔
Fewer individual shopping trips	✔	✗	✗	✗

Key:

✔✔ progress towards objective

✔ some progress towards objective

✗ no progress towards objective

✗✗ movement away from objective

Given this basic insight, the following considerations seem vital to the construction of effective and responsive policy approaches.

Robust policy requires that e-effects are disentangled from other drivers of change

ICTs are co-evolving with social and economic changes.[3] However, this does not mean that the impacts of e-commerce on society and the environment cannot be examined. The challenge for impact assessment is to disentangle the sustainability impacts of the digital economy from the effects of broader economic, social and technological drivers of change. All the scenarios suggest that these relationships will not be linear – that is, that the causes of impacts will not be the e-commerce facilities alone, but the way in which these facilities are used by organizations and people who may or may not be motivated by sustainability objectives. E-commerce is at best only a small part of a sustainability solution, and e-commerce policy cannot substitute or compensate for lack of policy action on other fronts whose relationship to sustainability issues is already well defined.

Claims about the environmental benefits of e-commerce need to be treated cautiously

Many commentators have begun to speculate about the potential impacts of e-commerce on sustainable development.[4,5,6] On the whole, these assessments present positive accounts of the opportunities for environmental gains. They argue that the efficiency gains in production and logistics lead to a less wasteful use of resources, and that the dematerialization of goods and services allows economic development to be decoupled from environmental damage.

Yet many of these arguments seriously underestimate the close interactive relationships between material and non-material environments. Although services now command a substantial and increasing portion of the value created in industrialized economies, most service markets relate to physical products. Many of the economic indicators of e-commerce may turn out to work against the goals of environmental sustainability. For example, if online procurement were to reduce unit costs in an industry, we would expect this to lead to increased sales – a positive economic indicator. The question would still remain whether the environmental gains from making buying more efficient would instantly be swallowed up by new, additional forms of consumption.

Governments have a role to play in fostering the governance of access to the internet

Many internet pioneers saw cyberspace as a free and open space in which to exchange knowledge and ideas, unencumbered by the kinds of regulation and control applied to previous generations of communication networks. However – as the scenario analysis seeks to draw out – the internet is not one community, but a complex of communities, each with its own objectives and expectations. Stakeholder interests are likely to conflict in many areas.

There is a need for ways of governing the internet that ensure reasonable equity in the digital space for the needs of many different stakeholders. Informal systems are not always enough. Pressure is emerging for more formal protection in areas like fraud, privacy and security. The process of institution building has only just begun, and the role of government is not entirely clear. Each of the scenarios would benefit from effective and transparent governance, with clear rules and norms established for redress and consumer protection. The borderless nature of the internet makes institutional development an even greater policy challenge.

Governments should encourage network diversity

The scenarios reveal very different outcomes in the development of technologies and markets for services. A proliferation of new devices can be linked to an expanding range of services. Some services will have general applications, whereas others will be oriented to the needs of particular user groups. As internet services diversify, there is no guarantee of consensus as to what will constitute public and private spheres of network activity. A fundamental question for governments is to determine how much of this new milieu will be defined as a public network, to which equitable access and use should be guaranteed.

As the internet evolves, the distribution of access will be a key policy problem – with different outcomes possible. The social diffusion of technologies that could support broader access is not guaranteed. A major influence will be how the development of network infrastructures affects the cost of the bandwidth available to users. New standards and economic regulation are likely to be needed to prevent some consumer groups being prematurely locked into redundant technologies. The scenarios suggest that aiming for maximum network diversity is the safest policy.

A holistic approach needs to be taken to service obligations

Historically, service obligations on network providers have been a strong policy tool for ensuring wide access to network services. Most existing service obligations have operated across stable and exclusive networks with single service packages, like the Post Office and the BBC. This approach does not fit today's digital environment in which different network facilities can be used to provide many of the same services – television over telephone lines, telephony via digital television, and so on. Service obligations need to be rethought. The market provides suppliers of network infrastructure with huge incentives to get people connected, but the same is not true for traders who buy and sell commercial products and services online.

Some companies choose their customers and partners carefully. As electronic transactions generate more information about buyer and seller behaviour, exclusivity may actually increase. In an internet environment characterized more by commercial motives, the lines between the services that are open to everybody and the services that are exclusively available to a few may blur. As a result, policies that concentrate on access only – for example, putting a computer in every home, or putting all government services on the web – address only a small part of the problem. Many services, even some that are deemed 'essential', are liable to be highly unevenly distributed on the web. Access and content must be treated as part of the same policy problem, and content is where the bulk of investment – whether public or private – is likely to be required.

Dematerialization needs to be enabled by investment in modern transport and energy systems
ICTs provide opportunities for a step-change transformation in the way we consume materials and energy, but these opportunities cannot be achieved by digital networks alone. They depend on heavy investment in the built environment and the modernization of transport and energy infrastructures. Large-scale energy savings as a result of e-commerce are only achievable if market and regulatory developments keep pace. Similarly, the economic potential and environmental benefits of e-commerce under all scenarios will depend on the available transport infrastructure and logistics systems. The future success of the e-economy will depend upon progress towards a clean, efficient and integrated transport system. It will not be a substitute for it.

Greater transparency and better environmental and ethical information is critical to changing behaviour
In the knowledge economy, information plays a more central role in environmental governance. Traditional environmental regulation is

being complemented by voluntary and market-based policy instruments; the consumer is critical. All these new developments, many of which are underscored across all the scenarios, depend on greater environmental transparency and reporting. The internet can become a primary vehicle for the delivery of tailored, appropriate and authoritative environmental information to consumers, businesses and government alike. To achieve this will, in many cases, require government support, funding and regulation.

Notes and references

1   Berkhout, F, Eames, M and Skea, J (1998) *Environmental Futures Scoping Study*, SPRU, Falmer
2   Sassen, S (2000) 'Digital Networks and the State: Some Governance Questions', *Theory, Culture and Society*, vol 17, no 4, August, pp19–33
3   Mansell, R and Steinmuller, E W (2000) *Mobilizing the Information Society*, OUP, Oxford
4   Cohen, N (1999) *Greening the Internet: Ten Ways E-Commerce Could Affect the Environment and What We Can Do*, iMP at www.cisp.org/imp/october
5   Kelly, H (1999) *Information Technology and the Environment: Choices and Opportunities*, iMP at www.cisp.org/imp/october
6   Romm, J (1999) *The Internet Economy and Global Warming: A Scenario of the Impact of E-commerce on Energy and Environment*, Center for Energy and Climate Solutions, Washington

Response

by Amory B Lovins

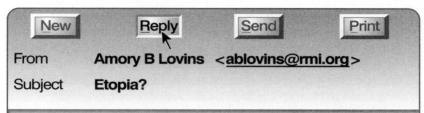

From   **Amory B Lovins   <ablovins@rmi.org>**

Subject   **Etopia?**

The SPRU team's scenario exercise is an insightful and valuable contribution. The scenario technique, pioneered by Group Planning at Royal Dutch/Shell, is a valuable vehicle for story-telling that helps us to understand the unfolding of events and to learn faster. It becomes essential when events are moving with such explosive and accelerating speed.

The Moore's Law doubling of microchip performance every 18 months is making natural-language interfaces and even virtual presence feasible. Yet this is sedate by the standards of some other technologies. Optical-fibre technology is evolving at least ten times faster, and in the US, fibre is being laid at a speed of Mach 3 – some 3200 kilometres per hour. Wireless technology is evolving faster still. Internet traffic has lately been doubling every hundred days; it won its first fifty million in four years, compared with 38 for radio and 13 for television. By the end of 1998, IT industries constituted 8 per cent of the US economy and 29 per cent of its growth. With a speed that historians will doubtless describe as breathtaking, the web is rapidly spreading round most of the world; its majority language will soon be Mandarin, not English. It is already changing many of our daily habits – though not, ironically, academic authors' citation of references only in their hard-copy form, not with online URLs!

A surprising implication of e-commerce, which I interpret less cautiously than do the SPRU authors, is that e-commerce sets in train structural changes that save much energy, and may even save net electricity. (Contrary to the US coal industry's disinformation campaign, computer equipment and the internet use at most 2 per cent of US electricity with little observable growth – not, as claimed by some, 8–13 per cent heading rapidly for 50 per cent.)[1]

At www.cool-companies.org/energy/, my colleague Dr Joe Romm, former US Acting Assistant Secretary of Energy, asks why during 1996–99 the US reduced its primary energy use per dollar of real GDP at a near-record pace, averaging 3.2 per cent per annum, despite record-low energy prices. Citing other government agencies' findings, he assembles a compelling case that as much as a quarter, perhaps even a third, of those recent US energy savings can probably be ascribed to structural changes driven by e-commerce. A simple example is the displacement of retail shops, and of a projected 5 per cent of all US office space by 2008, as a result of direct shipment from warehouses. A square metre of warehouse holds far more merchandise than a square metre of shop, yet uses 16 times less energy. A more subtle example is that better matching production to the products, qualities, and timing people want could readily trim a quarter off business inventories and free up capital to be reinvested more productively.

The argument is too rich and complex to summarize here, but one example gives the flavour. Compared to a physical book superstore, online bookseller Amazon.com carries 14 times more titles, earns treble the revenue per operating employee, turns inventory 20 times faster, and uses half the energy per square metre, cutting energy use per dollar of revenue by 15-fold. Different and possibly more transport might be employed, but with highly uncertain net effects. These would certainly tip to the favourable side if the best existing technologies and operating techniques were meanwhile introduced – as both market and technical logic would urge – to improve the energy efficiency of aircraft and automotive systems by factors of roughly three and ten respectively (for example, see www.hypercar.com).

Not surprisingly, a 60-year Shell scenario shows gross world product growing at 3 per cent a year, while world energy use rises fourfold more slowly, due to a 1.7–2.0 per cent per annum drop in energy intensity, reinforced by dematerialized production. The even more radical changes in resource productivity and business models implied by our recent book, *Natural Capitalism*, could make even that change seem conservative.[2]

The SPRU scenarios rightly emphasize that, though important, such resource savings probably matter less than social changes. These, I suspect, will emerge not from single, simple driving forces but from intricate, unpredictable, ecosystem-like co-evolution. For example, as information becomes free, privacy becomes infinitely dear; yet unbreakable encryption – a profound strengthening of the weak against the powerful – is already ubiquitous. Likewise, IT can still empower tyrants, spreading darkness with the speed of light. Yet so far at least, it is empowering civil society, so that more people have been liberated by the microchip than ever were by the sword. The web can and does spread myth, hate, noise, and merely unhelpful information; yet it is also reinforcing the sweeping social changes that are starting to give most of the world's people – women, the poor, and the politically oppressed – a voice, and with it their first opportunity to contribute to the global conversation.

This more than anything gives me hope that our species may yet pass its A-levels. The web is a bit like the nervous system that enabled multicellular organisms – symbioses of cells each made of bacteria and other bits of early life stuck together in tentative community – to start evolving into far more complex organisms with specialized organs and functions. This led to social organization and speech, then to writing and broadcasting, and perhaps soon to the beginnings of a sort of light-speed planetary nervous system. If that next step can indeed make our species smarter, better-coordinated, perhaps even wiser, it may yet help to show that this odd experiment of combining large forebrains with opposable thumbs could be rather a good idea. For as far as we know, there is nothing in the universe so powerful as six billion minds wrapping round a problem. ∎

1 Details are at http://enduse.lbl.gov/Projects/InfoTech.html and www.rmi.org/images/other/E-MMABLInternet.pdf
2 Hawken, P, Lovins, A B, and Lovins, L H (1999) *Natural Capitalism: The Next Industrial Revolution*, Earthscan, London

3 Dot-com ethics: e-business and sustainability

James Wilsdon

The myth of virtuality
or *how Harry Potter contributed to climate change*

It was like a carefully planned military operation. At strategic locations across America, a fleet of 9000 trucks revved their engines, 100 planes rolled down the runways. Their mission: to deliver *Harry Potter and the Goblet of Fire* to a nation hungry for instant fulfilment.

It sounds crazy, but it did happen. Back in July 2000, Amazon.com teamed up with Federal Express to deliver 250,000 copies of the new Harry Potter book to eager US fans. True to the spirit of 1-click™ shopping, no effort was spared in ensuring that the book hit people's doormats on the morning of publication. A press release issued the next day proudly declared it to be 'one of the largest sales and distribution events in e-commerce history'. In just 24 hours, over 300 tonnes (188 million pages) of Harry Potter magic were transported to homes across the US.[1]

We've heard a lot about the wizardry of e-commerce: how it's rewriting the rules of business; how it's shortening supply chains; how it's changing the relationship between companies and consumers. The business pages have been full of little else; one study found that between 1 March and 31 May 2000, the dot-com phenomenon generated 2800 articles in 21 newspapers.[2]

However, at least one aspect of business remains strangely untouched by the revolutionary hand of the internet. Hardly anything has been said about the relationship between e-commerce and corporate sustainability. Take Harry Potter; individually wrapping 250,000 books and express air-freighting them overnight is about the most environmentally-unfriendly method of distribution imaginable. It seems likely that it not only broke all the records for e-commerce delivery, but also for the quantity of greenhouse gases and packaging waste generated by a single novel.

The lack of attention paid by e-commerce companies to sustainability issues runs counter to larger trends in the corporate world. It is widely acknowledged that business now has to meet a much broader range of expectations than in the past: governments are introducing new regulations; consumers are requiring higher ethical standards; pressure groups are becoming more sophisticated; and communities are demanding a stake in decision making. Corporate power is under scrutiny like never before. Five years ago, Bill Gates predicted that the internet would create 'friction-free capitalism'.[3] Today, reflecting on the wave of anti-capitalist protests in Seattle, London and Prague that has coincided with the dot-com boom, 'friction-free' is not a term that springs to mind.

The e-business community's response to these trends has been one of deafening silence. This chapter is a call for greater engagement. Its central argument is that alongside the economic opportunities being created by e-commerce, there are a host of social and environmental opportunities that must be seized if the new economy is to become more sustainable than the old; opportunities that apply not just to pure-play dot-coms, but also to established 'clicks and mortar' companies now engaging in e-business.

Over the course of the year 2000, the dominant narrative about e-commerce changed from one of explosive growth and limitless opportunity to one of investor caution and company failure. Yet despite the collapse of a string of start-ups, the underlying significance of e-commerce remains undiminished. High-profile firms such as lastminute.com are the most visible tip of the e-commerce iceberg. Beneath the surface, a far more profound transformation is taking place, as traditional sectors embed digital technologies in all aspects of their operations.

Beyond the hype, even the most sceptical of commentators concede that e-commerce is changing the way we live. This means, in turn, that it will change our society, and our relationship with the natural environment. It will create new problems, but it will also open up new solutions, new ways of doing things. Now, in the early stages of the e-revolution, is the right time to pose some IAQs (infrequently asked questions) about the potential of e-commerce to bring wider benefits to society.

Three dot-com myths

So why have e-businesses failed to grapple with sustainability? In large part, they haven't felt the need – there is a widespread belief that such issues are irrelevant to your average dot-com. This is based on some powerful myths about e-commerce that need to be understood and then debunked.

The first is the myth of virtuality; the idea that because dot-coms operate in the virtual space of the internet, their impact on the physical world is negligible or non-existent. As the case of Harry Potter shows, this is often not the case. E-commerce can have as wide a range of social and environmental effects as any other economic activity, and dot-coms – whether B2C or B2B – face many of the same dilemmas over ethics, supply chains, energy use, transport and waste as their bricks and mortar counterparts. Innovative applications of internet technology could help to solve some of these problems, but only if the e-world acknowledges its impacts, and devotes some of its energies towards managing and reducing them.

The second is the myth of immaturity; the idea that e-commerce is at such an early stage that it is unfair to expect it to meet the same environmental and social standards as the rest of business. Only when the sector grows up, it is argued, will it be able to devote time and resources to what are essentially peripheral issues. This argument might hold water were it not for the constant claims that e-commerce represents the most seismic shift in business since the Industrial Revolution. Whether or not such cyberbole is justified, e-commerce is now a sufficiently established feature on the business landscape for governments, NGOs and other stakeholders to start asking questions about its environmental and social performance. E-commerce may rewrite many of the rules, but this does not give it a licence to operate with impunity. With permanence comes power, and with power comes responsibility.

The third is the myth of techno-determinism; the idea that technology has a market-led trajectory of development that is unaffected by wider social and political factors. This view was well expressed by a recent editorial in *The Economist* which, under the headline 'What the Internet cannot do', mocked the idea that IT could help to 'prevent wars, reduce pollution, and combat various forms of inequality'.[4] Such scepticism is premature. The truth is that we don't know what the long-term effects of the internet will be. The mistake is to regard it as something 'out there' that cannot be shaped to fit a political vision. The internet per se may do little to advance the cause of sustainable business, but the internet together with enlightened management and effective public policy is another story entirely.

Our focus on technology at the expense of humanity has created an impoverished notion of what the new economy could become. Say the words 'new economy' to most people, and the image conjured up is of complex gadgets and dot-com millionaires. This may be enough to arouse the party faithful, the technophile readers of new economy magazines like *Red Herring* and *Business 2.0*, but it is hardly a mobilizing vision for the future of society. As Charles Leadbeater points out, 'Knowledge about communications and computing ... is erupting all around us, and yet the gleaming new economy born by virtue of all this knowledge seems empty, lacking a soul or animating values.'[5]

Some will argue that it is not the business of business to provide such visions; that e-commerce should focus on profit and growth, and leave the politicians to deal with the bigger questions. Such a view is mistaken. It ignores some of the threats posed by the explosion in e-commerce; and more importantly, it neglects the opportunities that could be created if e-business thinks seriously about sustainability.

Firstly, the threats. As e-commerce takes off and starts to have a more visible impact on communities, jobs, transport and the environment, e-companies will need to demonstrate that they are creating more than just economic value. Although the internet has been well received during the first few years of its existence, this may not always be the case.

The social impacts of the internet may not be a pressing issue right now, but it is still only six years since the birth of the digital economy. Things may look very different 16 or 26 years on. Already, prominent voices from within the industry, such as Bill Joy, Chief Scientist at Sun Microsystems, are warning of the threat posed by the convergence of IT with other emerging technologies. In a powerful essay published last year in *Wired*, Joy argues that, 'The 21st-century technologies – genetics, nanotechnology and robotics – are so powerful that they can spawn whole new classes of accidents and abuses.' As a result, he admits to feeling 'a deepened sense of personal responsibility – not for the work I have already done, but for the work that I might yet do, at the confluence of the sciences.'[6] The biotechnology sector, with its cloned sheep and genetically modified food, has shown clearly the dangers of introducing new technologies faster than the pace of public acceptance. Without an open, honest debate about the social implications of any new technology, sooner or later there will be a backlash, a crisis of legitimacy. The IT industry should not consider itself immune.

However, there are opportunities too. Unlike sectors such as oil and chemicals, which have had to retro-fit social and environmental concerns in response to stakeholder pressure, e-business is uniquely well-placed to incorporate such concerns at the design stage. The trick is to address these issues now, before they become a burden or a challenge to the existing way of doing things. A young, fast-changing industry can adapt far more easily than one that is trapped in established mindsets. With a mixture of vision, imagination and intelligent policy, it should be possible to splice sustainability into the DNA of the new economy.

3D entrepreneurs

> 'Now that we realize e-commerce isn't a passport to untold riches, it's about time we gave some thought to something other than money'
> Tim Jackson, founder of QXL[7]

In the digital age, entrepreneurs are the new rock 'n' roll. One of the more bizarre consequences of the dot-com boom has been to make small- to medium-sized enterprises (SMEs) sexy. Teenagers who previously fantasized about becoming pop stars have swapped guitars for laptops, in a bid to become the next Jeff Bezos or Martha Lane Fox. What motivates this new breed of entrepreneurs? How do they see their business contributing to society?

In exploring these issues, a good place to start is with Louise Proddow's book *Heroes.com*, a recently-published tribute to 50 leading members of the digerati. Proddow suggests that e-entrepreneurs have a number of defining characteristics. Each of them:

- passionately embraces the dot-com era;
- recognizes that the internet changes everything and opens up new opportunities;
- rethinks how they do things, and makes dot-com central to their strategy and life;
- plays by new rules, and is more open, flexible and dynamic;
- acts in internet time and makes things happen fast;
- recognizes the value of partnerships and outsourcing; and
- lives for today and enjoys the momentum and buzz of the internet.[8]

From a sustainability perspective, this is a bit of mixed bag. Thumbs up for flexibility, dynamism and recognizing the value of partnerships; but the emphasis on speed and 'living for today' gives some cause for concern. In fact, despite their much-vaunted creativity, what actually comes across from reading *Heroes.com* is a striking narrowness of vision. Few of the entrepreneurs profiled seem willing to raise their sights above the economic bottom line to say anything about the wider responsibilities of business. There is a lack of what we might call '3D entrepreneurship', which uses technology to create environmental and social – as well as economic – benefits.

Perhaps this is to be expected. Several commentators have drawn attention to the free-market, individualistic ethos of the e-business world. For example, former *Wired* columnist Paulina Borsook has attacked the 'scary, psychologically brittle, prepolitical autism' that she frequently encountered in high-tech circles in the US.[9] Similarly, the sociologist Manuel Castells has denounced 'The illusion of a world made of Silicon Valley-like societies driven by technological ingenuity, financial adventurism and cultural individualism' which is promoted by many cyber-gurus. Such a world 'is not only ethically questionable but, more important for our purpose, politically and socially unsustainable.'[10]

Dot-com ethics survey

Rather than relying on these second-hand accounts, Forum for the Future decided to carry out some research of its own. Between July and November 2000, we conducted a survey of the attitudes of IT and dot-com companies to social and environmental issues.

From an original sample of 150 companies, we received responses from 103. Just under half of these were completed by the CEO, and the rest by senior managers. Companies were selected to represent a cross-section of the e-commerce marketplace. They ranged from large multinationals to small start-ups, and included a mixture of B2C, B2B, internet service providers (ISPs), software and hardware companies. The main criterion for inclusion was a business model based primarily around the internet. For this reason, we did not include traditional companies that are now involved in e-commerce.

Contrary to some of the negative stereotypes about dot-com entrepreneurs, the results were overwhelmingly positive:

- 65 per cent said that social and environmental issues are important or very important to their company (28 per cent said they were slightly important, 7 per cent unimportant);
- 92 per cent said that environmental and social issues are important or very important to them personally;

- 53 per cent thought these issues would be more important three years from now;
- 79 per cent agreed that the positive effects of e-commerce on society would outweigh the negative (21 per cent neither agreed nor disagreed);
- 58 per cent agreed that e-commerce will have a positive effect on the environment (29 per cent neither agreed nor disagreed, and 13 per cent disagreed);
- 62 per cent agreed that e-commerce will enable companies to be more responsive to consumers' ethical and environmental concerns (17 per cent neither agreed nor disagreed, 21 per cent disagreed); and
- 57 per cent agreed that companies with good environmental and social reputations are likely to benefit from improved financial performance (30 per cent neither agreed nor disagreed, 13 per cent disagreed).

It appears then that dot-com managers are broadly supportive of the sustainability agenda, even if they do not articulate their concerns in precisely these terms. In some ways this is unsurprising; the majority of the companies we surveyed are run by highly educated, creative people aged 35 or under, who are likely to have a reasonable level of environmental and social literacy.

However, the survey also highlights a sharp gulf between theory and practice. On asking whether companies have any systems or policies in place to address these issues, we found that:

- 79 per cent of companies do nothing to measure or manage their environmental impacts;
- 66 per cent do nothing to measure or manage their social impacts;
- 82 per cent do nothing to measure or manage their transport impacts; and
- 83 per cent offer no staff training on environmental or social issues.

This suggests that IT and e-commerce companies have a lot to learn about the basic principles of environmental and social management. Other research supports this view. For example, a recent survey by consultants PIRC of 674 listed companies found that the IT sector performed worst in terms of environmental policies and reporting.[11]

When we asked why companies had no policies and systems in place, three reasons stood out, as shown in the table below:

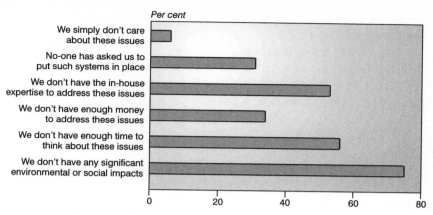

Per cent

We simply don't care about these issues

No-one has asked us to put such systems in place

We don't have the in-house expertise to address these issues

We don't have enough money to address these issues

We don't have enough time to think about these issues

We don't have any significant environmental or social impacts

0   20   40   60   80

Figure 3.1   Why don't you have any policies or systems in place?

- Lack of perceived impacts. The myth of virtuality is very powerful, and the survey shows that many companies do not recognize that they have any significant impacts.
- Lack of time. The e-world operates at breakneck speed, leaving little time to reflect or act upon these issues.
- Lack of expertise and resources. Many e-commerce companies operate under considerable financial pressure, and cannot devote resources to these issues. Often there is also insufficient staff expertise to develop policies and put systems in place.

These obstacles are not to be underestimated, but with commitment from senior managers and effective systems, they can be overcome. Closing the gap between ideals and action is a priority for any e-business seeking to establish a reputation for good corporate citizenship.

The rise of the 3D entrepreneur

The trend is already starting to move in the right direction. Looking across the e-world, there are encouraging signs of a growing interest in social responsibility. In the US, groups such as the Seattle-based Digital Partners and the Silicon Valley Community Foundation have sprung up to direct entrepreneurs' time and newly-acquired wealth into social and community initiatives.[12] Several IT and e-commerce companies have set up charitable trusts, including eBay, which allocated 1 per cent of its shares to the eBay Foundation at the time of flotation. Individuals such as Bill Gates and Jim Clark, the founder of Netscape, have donated millions to health and education initiatives, with a particular focus on the developing world.

In the UK, fewer people had a chance to make their millions before the downturn in the market, but a handful have started to invest in social projects. In March 2000, Tim Jackson, the founder of QXL, established a UK£70 million charitable trust, saying that 'it is important that entrepreneurs who have made a lot of money very quickly put some of that money back into the community'.[13] More recently, under the banner 'because innovation is about more than money', the First Tuesday entrepreneurs' network devoted one of its meetings to social ventures. Kate Oakley, a leading writer on the new economy, suggests that e-entrepreneurs will eventually make a contribution to the social fabric of our towns and cities equivalent to that of the great 19th century industrialists. Just as the Victorians built museums, libraries and universities, so these 'new Victorians' will seek to 'channel their wealth into good works of all sorts, from soup kitchens to school programmes, AIDS hospices to playgrounds.'[14]

Nonetheless, the bulk of this activity still takes place in the realm of philanthropy, and it is less common to find e-businesses that deliver social and environmental benefits through their core activities. There are exceptions – mostly small start-ups – some pioneering examples of which are listed below. A handful of larger companies are now tackling the digital divide as a strategic business issue, for example Hewlett-Packard, which has announced a US$1 billion 'e-inclusion' programme designed to bring tele-medicine, e-learning, e-commerce and microcredit schemes to 1000 villages in the developing world.[15]

These examples illustrate some of the diverse ways in which e-commerce can achieve a successful blend of economic, social and environmental innovation. A lot more, though, could be done to foster 3D entrepreneurship:

- There is a need for support networks for 3D entrepreneurs – perhaps as offshoots of existing ones such as First Tuesday – to assist with finance, advice and business development, and ensure that innovative ideas succeed.
- Government and NGOs should join forces with progressive IT, telecom and e-commerce companies to establish a 'sustainability incubator', able to provide advice and start-up capital to 3D entrepreneurs.
- New companies aiming for a stock market flotation should follow the example of eBay in allocating at least 1 per cent of their shares to a charitable trust.

Box 3.1 Top ten ethical dot-coms

- www.greenstar.org – supports communities in the developing world through a network of internet-enabled community centres, which offer a combination of web access, education, tele-medicine, renewable energy and microfinance.
- www.viatru.com – promotes fair trade and enables artisans and producers in the developing world to access global markets through e-commerce.
- www.ethical-junction.org – a B2C portal for organic and fair trade products, with its own virtual 'ethical high street'.
- www.greenorder.com – a B2B site enabling public and private sector organizations to purchase environmentally-friendly products, ranging from building materials to office supplies.
- www.flametree.co.uk – supports companies and employees seeking a better work–life balance, with web-based advice and consultancy on sustainable work patterns.
- www.drparsley.com – an ethical incubator working to bring sustainable dot-com businesses to market. Currently working on projects with the *Big Issue* and a network of organic food producers.
- www.publicsector.org – a news and consumer site for UK public sector workers that promotes green lifestyles, products and services.
- www.goodcorporation.com – encourages companies to meet a set of social and ethical standards set out in the online GoodCorporation Charter.
- www.ushopugive.com – enables consumers to donate a small proportion of the profits from online purchases to a charity of their choice.
- www.youreable.com – a community and commerce site for disabled people, carers and healthcare professionals which scooped first prize in Channel 4's 'Who Wants to Be an E-millionaire' show. Its vision is to become the first website that the disabled community turns to for information and services.

- Government and NGOs need to engage the venture capital industry in a more active dialogue on social and environmental issues, and give it incentives it to support sustainable ventures.

eBay environmentalism

It is often said that in the new economy, matter matters less. Ideas, creativity and innovation are replacing physical assets as the key to competitive success. This shift will go hand in hand with energy and resource efficiency. E-commerce and teleworking will reduce traffic congestion, and consumerism will evolve in an increasingly 'weightless' direction, as we come to value services and experiences more than the ownership of physical products.[16]

One influential report by the Washington-based Center for Energy and Climate Solutions suggests that e-commerce will create year-on-year reductions of up to 2 per cent in the energy intensity of the US economy. Joseph Romm, the report's author, is bullish about the potential for what he calls 'e-materialization'. 'The internet economy', he argues, 'can turn buildings into websites and replace warehouses with supply chain software. It can turn paper and CDs into electrons and replace trucks with fibre optic cable. That means significant energy savings.'[17]

At first sight, such arguments have a compelling logic. Shopping on the web should, with efficient logistics, mean that one truck can replace dozens of separate car journeys. B2B exchanges should improve the efficiency of the supply chain. There are some sectors – for example books, records and banking – in which e-materialization is already taking effect. Yet many remain unconvinced. *The Economist* has tackled Joseph Romm head-on, arguing that 'doing things on-line is more energy efficient only if it genuinely displaces real-world activities.'[18] So far, there are few signs of that happening, not least because most of us enjoy shopping for reasons that have precious little to do with obtaining goods and services in the most environmentally efficient way.

And as our Harry Potter example illustrates, e-commerce could create new forms of highly unsustainable consumption, as instant fulfilment becomes the norm. The worst case scenario is that we end up with hundreds of grocery delivery vans jamming up residential neighbourhoods, increasing congestion and pollution, while consumers, freed up from the time they would have spent in the supermarket, drive off in their cars to do, you guessed it, yet more shopping.

Other research themes in the Digital Futures project have looked in detail at the macro effects of e-commerce on energy use, transport and planning policy. The central issue for this chapter is how e-commerce companies can create environmental benefits through their core business activities.

Part of the solution lies in adapting existing tools and systems. As our survey results show, most dot-coms have a lot to learn about the basics of environmental management. Also, traditional companies involved in e-commerce need to ensure that the systems and policies they have in place elsewhere are carried over into their internet operations. It may be that in the rush to get online, some companies are cutting corners and treating their e-commerce activities as though they are exempt from wider environmental and social policies.

Beyond this, there are some simple steps that e-businesses could take to reduce their impacts. For example, one way to improve the environmental efficiency of e-fulfilment would be the inclusion of a 'green delivery' button alongside the 'express delivery' option on B2C sites, so that consumers could choose the greenest, as opposed to the fastest, mode of delivery.

Whole system innovation

However, as Leadbeater points out, wealth in the new economy flows from innovation, not optimization; from imperfectly seizing the unknown, rather than simply perfecting the known.[19] The lesson here for dot-coms may be to not concentrate too heavily on conventional management systems such as ISO 14001– important as these may be – but to come up with creative ways of leapfrogging traditional sectors onto a higher plane of sustainability performance. The focus needs to be on whole-system innovation; identifying how e-commerce can contribute to more complex webs of sustainable innovation around energy, transport, production and consumption.

Perhaps the greatest potential for such innovation lies in the new technologies and market models emerging on the internet. To give just three examples:

1   Auction sites such as eBay, which allow consumer-to-consumer (C2C) trading of secondhand goods can prolong the useful life of products and reduce waste. The US$3 billion-worth of stuff that's been traded on eBay since it launched is $3 billion-worth less stuff in landfill. In the longer term, writers such as Jeremy Rifkin suggest that we may shift to an economy based on access rather than ownership, as the short-term leasing of many goods and services becomes possible online.[20]

2   New technologies such as MP3 will allow certain sectors such as music and software to be almost entirely dematerialized. While it is wrong to exaggerate the significance of this in environmental terms (a wholesale shift in the UK music industry towards MP3 would create carbon savings equivalent to just 0.1 per cent of national

carbon emissions), improved access and broadband technologies are likely to encourage similar trends in sectors such as publishing and banking.

3   Ecobots. There are already many sites that use search engines or 'bots' to search the web for the cheapest product in a given category (for example, shopsmart.com). The ease with which the internet enables the searching and filtering of information should eventually lead to the development of 'ecobots' – green search engines capable of selecting products on the basis of environmental performance. The main obstacle to this at present is the same as for conventional shopping – a lack of comparable environmental data. Yet there are some sectors in which it should already be possible – for example fridges and washing machines, which are energy-rated; cars, which can be compared on the basis of fuel efficiency; and financial services, in which pensions and bank accounts can be compared according to ethical criteria.

What can be done to stimulate the wider uptake of these sustainable models of e-business? Many of the solutions require more of the same in terms of environmental policy; an accelerated shift towards green taxation, measures to promote greener transport and distribution, incentives for recycling, and increased responsibilities of manufacturers and retailers for products throughout their life cycle. However, there are other things that government and business can do. A recent report from the government's Advisory Committee on Consumer Products and the Environment (ACCPE) calls for the establishment of a dedicated website to help consumers find out more about the environmental effects of different products.[21] This is an excellent idea, which should be expanded to include the development of the world's first ecobot, as the result of a partnership between the UK government and a consortium of software developers, e-tailers and NGOs.

The Department of the Environment, Transport and the Regions (DETR) and Department of Trade and Industry (DTI) – together with businesses and NGOs – also need to revisit the existing tools and frameworks for environmental management, and ensure that these are made more relevant and accessible to new economy companies. As the leading department in this area, DETR should make a particular effort to 'bring the Valley in'; to better understand dot-com culture and the opportunities that e-commerce creates to advance sustainability.

Stakeholders.com

'In the dot-com era, trust – the direct result of integrity and reputation – remains critical... The only difference now is that reputations, which still take time to build, can be tarnished more quickly.'
Scott McNealy, CEO, Sun Microsystems[22]

How will e-commerce affect the relationship between a company and its stakeholders? Will it usher in a new era of transparency and accountability? One of the best descriptions of the changing nature of corporate power in the new economy can be found in *The Cluetrain Manifesto* (www.clutrain.com). Written by four web aficionados, this consists of a set of 95 theses designed to show how the internet has radically altered the rules of business. The first of these run as follows.

1   Markets are conversations.
2   Markets consist of human beings, not demographic sectors.
3   Conversations between human beings sound human. They are conducted in a human voice.
4   Whether delivering information, opinions, perspectives, dissenting arguments or humorous asides, the human voice is typically open, natural, uncontrived.
5   People recognize each other as such from the sound of this voice.
6   The internet is enabling conversations between human beings that were simply not possible in the era of mass media.
7   Hyperlinks subvert hierarchy.[23]

E-commerce enables these conversations to take place more easily. The internet is a perfect medium for promoting inclusivity; '[It] invites participation. It is genuinely empowering.'[24] Traditional boundaries are dissolved, and companies can become more responsive to stakeholder needs.

Are all stakeholders getting a piece of the online action? A lot is said about the relationships between companies and consumers, far less about other groups. As part of our survey, we asked e-businesses to rank their stakeholders according to importance. The results are revealing. As Figure 3.2 illustrates, customers, employees and investors are regarded as critical; the media, online communities and suppliers as important; government, geographical communities and NGOs as fairly unimportant; and trade unions as totally irrelevant.

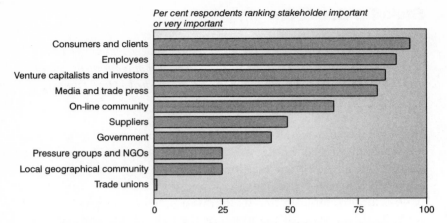

Figure 3.2   How important are the following stakeholder
groups to your company?

Consumers

As *The Cluetrain Manifesto* suggests, the internet changes the balance of power between companies and consumers. The most obvious benefit of this is cheaper products and services, as consumers learn to compare prices at the click of a mouse. Yet this new wave of empowerment also offers the tantalizing prospect of an upsurge in ethical consumerism.

In the B2C market, as prices are driven ever lower, companies will need to find new ways to add value and differentiate themselves from their competitors. Focusing on ethical and environmental performance is one route to a rapidly expanding market. In recent years, ethical investment has grown at a phenomenal rate, and is now worth £3.3 billion in the UK. Sales of organic food are predicted to be worth £1.5 billion by 2003. Opinion polls show that 30 per cent of people take some account of ethical issues when shopping.[25]

Traditionally, the barriers to ethical consumerism have been the difficulty of accessing products and the limited availability of reliable information. The internet can overcome both of these problems, and it can only be a matter of time before a large retailer launches a green or ethical shopping site. At the moment, this market has been left to a handful of small players, such as ethical-junction.org, who lack the scale to move it closer to the mainstream.

For e-tailers, there is a strong business rationale for investing time and money in improving their ethical performance. As well as opening up new markets, it can help to build more meaningful bonds of trust and loyalty with consumers. Currently, debates about trust on the internet are focused on privacy and the security of transactions. As e-commerce becomes more sophisticated, consumers are likely to want assurance on a wide range of issues – including the social and environmental credentials of products and services – and companies will have to capitalize on their reputation to offer that assurance.

Employees

In the knowledge economy, human capital is a company's greatest asset. The importance of recruiting and retaining high-quality staff underpins many of the benefits – particularly stock options – that IT and dot-com companies offer their employees. Across the sector as a whole, employment practices and management structures are reasonably progressive. Yet in the e-commerce gold rush, some companies have taken advantage of their employees' dreams of getting rich, and failed to apply the same kind of innovation and creativity to ownership structures and career development that they apply in other parts of their business. Andy Law, the founder of the advertising agency St Luke's, has drawn attention to this problem: 'Dot-coms are terribly traditional. They're owned and managed absolutely conventionally and rather than redefine business, they exist to enrich a tiny few... You see the fallout every day. Employees are burned out, alienated and disillusioned.'[26]

It doesn't have to be this way. As Bill Thompson points out in a recent pamphlet on e-mutualism, the internet is the ideal environment for new forms of cooperative ownership and management.[27] It is not an organization that anyone can join; it is a set of relationships, and should therefore lend itself to a more inclusive, stakeholder-driven model of capitalism.

Community

In its 95 theses, *The Cluetrain Manifesto* goes on to discuss the importance of community. 'To speak with a human voice, companies must share the concerns of their communities. But first, they must belong to a community.' As our survey shows, for many e-businesses, community is understood first and foremost in a virtual sense. This shift requires us to revisit traditional stakeholder models and tools for corporate accountability, and update them so that they remain relevant in the new economy.

This emphasis on the virtual can be very positive. As Chapter 5 shows, despite fears that the internet will erode social relationships, the trend is in the opposite direction, towards the creation of online communities as an addition to existing social networks. Yet it is still important to reflect on the lack of connection that many dot-coms feel with their local geography. Writers such as Richard Sennett have drawn attention to the corrosive effects of a wired workforce that fails to engage with its local community. Sennett describes how his home area of Clerkenwell, once home to printers and small manufacturers, 'is now becoming a neighbourhood of lofts, sold to the young financiers working nearby in the City, or to the officer class in the army of graphic design, fashion and advertising which has occupied London.'[28] These people use the city as a backdrop to their lives, rather than actively involving themselves in the community. They have few links to local people, local politics, and no understanding of the social capital that was ploughed into the parks, the cinema, the bookshop.

Suppliers

Most analysts agree that B2B e-commerce is where the real growth will happen over the next five years. Web research company Forrester predicts that while consumer spending on the internet will increase from US$7.8 billion in 1998 to $108 billion in 2003, B2B transactions will rocket from $43 billion to at least $1 trillion. The basic selling point of B2B e-commerce is that it cuts costs. Estimates vary, but the scope for savings in some sectors is thought to be 20–30 per cent.

Online trading exchanges are seen as a way of achieving these efficiency gains. In every sector, companies are joining forces with competitors to build huge trading hubs, in which all procurement can take place under one virtual roof. The volume of transactions that will pass through these exchanges is mind-boggling. For example, the auto-industry exchange Covisint, born from an alliance between Ford, General Motors and DaimlerChrysler, will bring together 35,000 component makers with an annual trading volume of $250 billion.

In sustainability terms, it is not yet clear whether B2B e-commerce will have positive or negative effects. Taking the supply chain as a whole, B2B undoubtedly has the potential to deliver gains in environmental productivity alongside economic efficiency. But the narrow focus on price in the purchasing protocols that govern many automatic transactions, particularly through online exchanges, creates the real possibility that environmental and ethical considerations will be downgraded or ignored altogether. The speed and volume of transactions through such exchanges may make it difficult to know who you are dealing with, and this creates risks to reputation that might have been avoided in traditional supply-chain relationships. There is a danger that what some have dubbed 'stealth corporations' use the anonymity of exchanges to sell low-cost, environmentally or socially destructive products.[29]

Currently, many e-businesses are flying blind, with few of the safety checks and systems that are required. Sooner or later, a dot-com will be hit by a high-profile sourcing scandal, similar to those faced by Nike and Gap in recent years. Dot-coms should be conscious that companies that live by the web can also die by the web. In recent years, NGOs have become extremely adept at using the internet to orchestrate campaigns against companies with poor track records (examples include shameon-nike.com and mcspotlight.com). Dot-coms are more vulnerable than most to new forms of online campaigning.

To cope with these challenges, ethical audit and compliance systems need to enter the digital age. There are already several systems, such as Clicksure.com, which provide online assurance on issues of quality, and these should be extended to cover environmental and social issues. B2B exchanges will also need to require their trading partners to meet certain environmental and social standards. It will take time for these systems to develop, but eventually, as Chris Babcock suggests in a recent paper, it should become possible to click through from a supplier's website to review the quality, environment or social standards which that supplier holds. Another click should take you to the website of the auditing agency, and even allow you to exchange emails with the individual auditor.[30]

Trade unions

For every well-paid knowledge worker reaping the benefits of his or her intellectual capital, there is likely to be someone else working long hours for modest pay in a technical support centre or fulfilment depot. When dot-com share prices were riding high, employees accepted poor conditions and a lack of job security in return for stock options. Now that share prices have slumped, workers are turning to traditional forms of collective bargaining to prevent redundancies, and companies such as Amazon.com and eTown are facing calls for union recognition. The fact that only 1 per cent of our survey respondents consider unions to be an important stakeholder shows that there is still a long way to go before good employment practices are established across the sector.

Conclusion

'We've been called everything – Amazon.con, Amazon.toast, Amazon.bomb – and my favourite, Amazon.org, because clearly we are a not-for-profit corporation.' Jeff Bezos, CEO, Amazon.com[31]

After the roller coaster ride of 2000, it's time to take stock. It is not inevitable that the new economy will see the emergence of more ethical and sustainable models of business. However, amid the turmoil and change, there is everything to play for. We could use the opportunities we have in front of us – opportunities to combine technological and economic innovation with social and environmental innovation – to take a major leap forward in the pursuit of sustainability.

Our survey shows that e-entrepreneurs have a clear sense of their responsibility to society and to the environment. The challenge is to act on this, so that in future, e-commerce is about more than just 'the soundless scrape of coins over the wire'.[32] New economy business leaders need to take stock of their impacts, and of their potential to make a difference. As the social and environmental reach of a company extends, so does the opportunity for new, interesting and profitable ways of doing business.

Internet technology provides us with ample opportunity for e-materialization – replacing the real with the virtual, reducing energy use and increasing the efficiency of supply chains. The technology provides the potential, but nothing more. It will need to be realized through new business models; through channelling innovation toward environmental goals; and through rethinking whole systems of production and consumption.

As The Cluetrain Manifesto tells us, the internet also changes the way we relate to each other, and provides the potential for new forms of accountability. The responsible company can use the internet to let everyone know how well it is doing; the irresponsible company can be easily named and shamed. The web makes it easier to reach out to your stakeholders, and to source products and services that meet ethical standards. It also makes it easier to point out when companies have gone wrong.

How will all these opportunities be realized? In part through policies and systems – through measuring, managing and reporting on environmental and social impacts. In part through learning from others in networks which allow ideas and experience to change hands; and in part through the leadership of the most committed and the most influential, who set a standard for others to follow. Beyond these specifics, there are perhaps two principles we can apply in developing a richer sense of e-business ethics: 'joining the dots' and 'taking time'.

Joining the dots

Dot-coms are no strangers to partnership. Web success depends on forging alliances – with suppliers, technology firms and content providers. But as e-business begins to tackle sustainability, these networks must expand to include meaningful partnerships with government and NGOs. We need, literally, to join the dots. Dot-coms, dot-orgs and dot-govs need to share ideas and work together to embed sustainability in every area of the new economy.

The barriers to these alliances are not as great as one might imagine. Dot-coms and dot-orgs have a surprising amount in common. Both seek to challenge the established conventions of the old economy, and are prepared to take risks and push for change. E-commerce blurs the old boundaries: it brings the high street into our homes, and brings government out of its Whitehall corridors. The web is a neutral meeting point for new partnerships and new alliances.

It's not just a matter of asking business to adapt. NGOs are good at pressuring companies, but they also need to build trust, identify common ground and support companies to get things right at the design stage. Government needs to work hard to counter its image as a barrier to be leapt over, an obstacle to innovation. It needs to seek out good practice and use its influence to encourage it elsewhere. It should not shy away from intervention, but should intervene creatively, to foster innovation, not stifle it. Both NGOs and government can learn from the models of cooperation and fluid alliances that sustain the dot-com world. In a sense, the Digital Futures project is an experiment in these new ways of working; it draws different sectors together to explore the sustainability challenges and opportunities of e-commerce in a collaborative way. Such models will need to be replicated throughout the new economy.

Taking time

In the new economy, speed is critical to success. Technology moves fast, and because first-mover advantage is so powerful, internet companies have to move even faster. There are said to be three or four internet years to one calendar year. Yet slowness can also be a virtue. The e-business community does sometimes need to think in longer time horizons, which span not just the next investment decision, but also encompass the social and environmental changes that those investment decisions bring about. We need to learn to cope with the different cycles of time that operate in this debate: cycles of investment and innovation on the internet, which are measured in weeks and months; cycles of investment in the physical infrastructure of energy systems, roads and towns, which are measured in decades; and cycles of change in the natural environment, in the biosphere on which all economic activity ultimately depends, many of which are measured in centuries or millennia.

The way we view time is key to creating a sustainable digital economy. It doesn't mean abandoning the hectic pace of e-life. It means switching lanes occasionally. Things look different from the slow lane. You can pause, reflect, consider your wider responsibilities. Unless we occasionally stop and pause for breath, it's hard to think about the long-term issues that really matter. We need a bolt of inspiration to ease us into the slow lane every now and then. The Long Now Foundation (www.longnow.org) is one such attempt. Initiated by some of the biggest names in Silicon Valley, including Kevin Kelly (co-founder of *Wired* magazine) and the musician Brian Eno, the foundation aims to build a clock that will keep time for 10,000 years. It will tick once a year, bong once a century and, once every millennium, the equivalent of a cuckoo will come out. Such attention-grabbing reminders of the long-term implications of our actions are essential.

Taking up the sustainability challenge requires creativity, innovation and alliance building. It requires a different way of thinking; but this is what the dot-coms are so good at. There's everything to gain from channelling the dynamism of the new entrepreneurs into a force not just for economic good, but for social and environmental good too.

Notes and references

1   Federal Express press release, 10 July 2000. This example is discussed at greater length in Scott Matthews, H, et al 'Harry Potter and the Hole in the Ozone Layer', *IEEE Spectrum*, November 2000
2   Marbles/Echo Research (2000) *Dotcomment: How the Press See the Dot-com Boom*, London
3   Gates, B (1995) *The Road Ahead*, Viking, New York
4   *The Economist* (2000) 'What the Internet Cannot Do' 19 August
5   Leadbeater, C (1999) *Living on Thin Air*, Viking, London
6   Joy, B (2000) 'Why the Future Doesn't Need Us', *Wired*, April
7   Tim Jackson speaking at First Tuesday, 5 December 2000
8   Proddow, L (2000) *Heroes.com: The Names and Faces Behind the Dot Com Era*, Hodder & Stoughton, London
9   Borsook, P (2000) *Cyberselfish*, Perseus Books, New York
10 Castells, M (2000) 'Information Technology and Global Capitalism' in Hutton, W and Giddens, A (eds) *On the Edge*, Jonathan Cape, London
11 Pensions Investment Research Consultants (2000) *Environmental Reporting 2000*, PIRC, London
12 www.digitalpartners.org; www.siliconvalleygives.org
13 *Guardian*, 28 March 2000
14 Oakley, K (2000) *The New Victorians*, unpublished article

15 www.hp.com/e-inclusion
16 See eg Coyle, D (1997) *The Weightless World*, Capstone, Oxford; Leadbeater, C (2000) *Mind Over Matter: Greening the New Economy*, Green Alliance, London; Pine, J and Gilmore, J (1999) *The Experience Economy*, Harvard Business School, Boston
17 Romm, J (1999) *The Internet Economy and Global Warming, A Scenario of the Impact of E-commerce on Energy and Environment*, Center for Energy and Climate Solutions, Washington
18 *The Economist*, op cit
19 Leadbeater, op cit
20 Rifkin, J *The Age of Access* Tarcher/Putnam, New York
21 ACCPE (2000) *Choosing Green: Towards More Sustainable Goods and Services*, DETR, London, October
22 Interview in *Wired*, April 2000
23 Levine, R et al (2000) *The Cluetrain Manifesto*, Financial Times, London
24 ibid, p17
25 Cowe, R and Williams, S (2000) *Who Are the Ethical Consumers?*, The Co-operative Bank, Manchester
26 Interview in *Harvard Business Review*, September–October 2000
27 Thompson, B (2000) *E-Mutualism or the Tragedy of the Dot-commons*, The Co-operative Party, London
28 Sennett, R (2000) 'Street and Office: Two Sources of Identity' in Hutton and Giddens, op cit
29 SustainAbility (1999) *The Internet Reporting Report*, SustainAbility, London
30 Babcock, C (2000) 'Ethical Sourcing in a Wired Economy' in Thamotheram, R *Visions of Ethical Sourcing*, Financial Times/Prentice-Hall, London
31 *Red Herring*, August 2000
32 Levine et al, op cit

Response

by John Browning

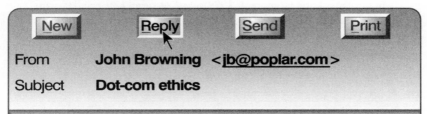

Something big has changed in the relationship of business to society. While James Wilsdon acknowledges this, he fails to carry his analysis to its logical conclusions, or to offer any real understanding of the new dilemmas and opportunities for business and policy makers. If someone like Wilsdon has come so adrift, maybe the revolution that is the new economy really is bigger than most of us now think. Wilsdon ends up with policy recommendations that threaten to not so much take advantage of the new opportunities being created, as crush them.

Part of the problem is that Wilsdon does too little to question the traditional assumptions of the left – that business is bad and government and unions are good – even when they are contradicted by his own evidence. Wilsdon starts with the assumption that 'e-businesses have failed to grapple with sustainability'. Yet his survey of e-businesspeople shows that two-thirds believe social and environmental issues to be important to their companies; the same two-thirds also believe that the advent of e-commerce will better enable companies to respond to environmental and social concerns. While executives could probably do more to act on their convictions, this hardly feels like failure. Indeed, if the survey of consumers cited by Wilsdon later in the article is correct, only 30 per cent of consumers take ethics into account when buying products. Executives may be leading the social and environmental agenda rather than resisting it.

The same unexamined assumptions cloud many of Wilsdon's recommendations. The fact that only 1 per cent of e-businesspeople consider unions to be important stakeholders in their business does not mean that they are a long way from good employment practices. Perhaps unions have simply become irrelevant. And while it may be a good idea for dot-coms, dot-orgs and dot-govs to 'share ideas and work together', Wilsdon begs all of the interesting questions about how or why. It would certainly be nice if government could, as he suggests, 'seek out good practice and use its influence to encourage it elsewhere' and 'intervene creatively, to foster innovation, not stifle it'. But government doesn't do these things, as Wilsdon tacitly acknowledges. And it's hard to see how it can bear the burden of expectations that his agenda puts upon it.

So how could government use the capabilities of communications technology to become more responsive? And what alternatives are there to regulation to promote social and environmental responsibility? These are key questions that Wilsdon never entirely answers, in large part because he doesn't seem to accept his own analysis of the new possibilities created by the changing nature of business.

At the heart of the novelty of the new economy lies a change in the nature of competitive advantage, and thus in the nature of companies themselves. When machines formed the core of companies, management didn't have to worry much about attracting higher-quality workers, or about improving how their people worked together. Workers could only produce where there were machines, so competition for talent was relatively limited. Government, in turn, focused largely on protecting people from the power of the machines – both by helping them to organize into unions, and by regulations that forced the capitalist owners of the machinery to think beyond maximizing return on their investment.

When people form the core of companies, however, attracting people and constantly improving the ways in which they work together is management's daily imperative. Notions of trust, community, shared values and shared goals move to the centre of the management agenda. Competition for talent intensifies and the balance of power shifts from manager to employee. (Imagine Microsoft, for example, trying to mimic the 19th-century millowners' tactic of locking workers out.) Along the way, what might once have been a relatively clear distinction between worker, consumer and citizen has becomes irretrievably blurred – and with those distinctions also disappear the relatively clear roles that once separated companies, voluntary groups and governments.

As distinctions fade, newly empowered consumers can nimbly step into areas where governments once clumsily trod. Thanks to the ability of communications technology to bring them information about all aspects of everything, people can now vote on many issues with their chequebooks every bit as effectively as they do at the ballot box. If people really oppose, say, genetically modified food, they don't have to buy it. If they really care about the wages paid to foreign workers, they will pay a bit more for goods made by companies that pay better. They can refuse to lend their talents to companies that pollute, or that violate their own code of social ethics.

Perhaps ironically, pushing the power and responsibility for ethics into the marketplace could well prove more democratic than leaving it in the hands of government – for markets, when functioning efficiently, provide a constant plebiscite on the public's concerns, while governments can only enforce diktat shaped by lobbyists and politicians. But while Wilsdon enthusiastically describes the possibilities of stakeholder activism, he never seems to take them seriously. Having listed a variety of new, sustainable business models, he asks 'What can be done to stimulate the wider uptake of ... sustainable models of e-business?' The answer: 'more of the same' – that is, regulation, government control and manipulation of markets.

Surely this misses the point. If there has been a revolution in business, then it makes little sense for everybody else to go on behaving as they did before. Instead of requiring people to do the right thing, perhaps it's time for government to look harder at how they can empower people to decide what is right for themselves. Instead of directing their energies at government policy, perhaps it's time for NGOs to turn more of their attention to educating and lobbying the public directly. Instead of worrying about how they can improve business, perhaps it's time for government and NGOs to turn their focus to how they can learn from it.

Of course there are limits to the forces now pushing companies to behave more ethically. But there are also real opportunities – at least for activists and politicians willing to admit that they hold neither a monopoly of righteousness nor even a monopoly on the forum for deciding what is right. Now is the time to grasp these opportunities. To fall back on 'more of the same' risks smothering the best of the new under the worst of the old, simply for lack of imagination and initiative. And that would be a shame. ∎

4 Surfing alone? E-commerce and social capital

Ben Jupp and Tom Bentley

Introduction

Do you generally trust others? Do you get involved in your local school or neighbourhood association? Are you interested in politics? Your answers to these questions indicate something about the UK's sustainability.

Sustainability requires much more than looking after our physical environment. Social and economic contexts are equally important. The UK needs people with skills and good health, low levels of crime, investment in infrastructure and technology. More than anything else, people need to be able to work together. While none of us can be sure of the challenges we will face in the future, we can be certain that meeting them will require cooperation. In general terms, three social conditions enhance our ability to work together.

Diverse social networks
The friendships and informal networks which criss-cross society are the sinews of cooperation. Through them we exchange ideas, support and information.

High levels of trust
To work together, people need confidence in each other. The more people are prepared to trust each other, especially those they do not

know very well, the less they have to spend time and resources covering their own backs.

Good civic institutions

Working together also relies on a whole raft of civic organizations, such as local residents' groups, political parties, pressure groups, unions, charities, schools and churches. These enable people to get involved in solving problems, provide a forum for debate and help democratic governance.

Collectively, these three conditions – networks, trust and civic institutions – are often called social capital.[1] They are resources that help us to cooperate.

Social capital is critical for societies to prosper economically. Countries with strong social capital also tend to have relatively effective governments and successful societies.[2] In the US, a recent study that compared social capital across different states found that those with high social capital tend to have lower crime, better educational results and healthier populations. The same can be true at the local level. Many of the most run-down neighbourhoods in the UK are characterized by fear, social isolation and weak community institutions.

Overall, the quality of social capital in the UK is mixed. To answer the questions above: 48 per cent of people trust others most or all of the time; about 10 per cent are involved in a local school or other local community activities; and about 2 per cent are members of a political party.

What of the future? This chapter investigates the possible impact of e-commerce. It asks whether the growth in e-commerce is likely to enhance or erode social capital, and what, if anything, government and others can do to encourage applications of internet technologies that help to create social and civic value.

Many are gloomy about the impact of e-commerce on informal social networks. We are generally upbeat. All sorts of social networks are already being supported by new technologies. Some of the chat rooms and virtual communities that e-commerce has directly fostered over the last three years are now declining; but e-commerce is supporting the infrastructure that will allow social networks to expand. These networks will gain from cheaper internet access through digital TV, internet service providers that are funded through advertising revenues, and software that is developed primarily for the e-commerce market.

We are also upbeat about social trust in an age of e-commerce. In contrast to the industrial revolution, which physically displaced people into cities, e-commerce is not yet forcing people into an alien virtual world. At the moment, electronic communication almost always supplements and strengthens traditional forms of relationship, communication and exchange. More information is available about individuals and companies, creating the potential for stronger, more open relationships, provided that transparency does not undermine trust by invading people's privacy.

In contrast to this overall positive picture, however, we argue that existing civic organizations and institutions are not faring well on the e-commerce-dominated Internet. Some civic groups are using e-commerce to improve their effectiveness. They are exploiting the networks it has spawned and are using the tools it has created, such as online trading systems and database technologies. Most are not. The vast majority of traditional civic institutions are failing to reshape their organizations around electronic exchange. At the same time, the new breed of e-civic groups, such as online local networks, are struggling to attract large numbers of users, or are being squeezed out by the cost of competing with cash-rich dot-coms.

Yet the slow progress of civic institutions in using e-commerce could change. They could learn from the successes and failures of businesses. In the last section of this chapter, we explore how they can learn to use the tools of e-commerce more effectively. We suggest that the building blocks of successful strategies include the following principles:

- *Think local.* Civic institutions need to harness the power of e-commerce tools and tailor them to local conditions. One of the opportunities presented by the internet is for civic and social organizations to join international networks; but the first waves of e-commerce have shown that success often begins with the local. Strategies might include using postcodes to give people information about their local environment, opening up local institutions such as primary schools to greater use and scrutiny, or undertaking street level referendums on local issues.
- *Think enterprise.* Civic institutions can make money in the new economy by trading local knowledge. New forms of reporting and web audits could allow people to see how such social enterprise balances commercial and civic objectives.
- *Think mutuality.* E-commerce is helping to establish new forms of exchange between individuals, from Napster to eBay. These forms of exchange could support a revival of mutual forms of organizations, particularly based around sharing knowledge.
- *Think distribution networks.* The main impact of e-commerce has been felt in the supply chains within and between business. The supply chains of the civic sector – grants, donations, and volun-

teering – remain largely untouched. We need trailblazing grant givers to start operating entirely through the web, automated monitoring and evaluation systems for groups who receive grants, and sites that allow people to inform charities of what they have to give away.

We also suggest that e-businesses can be encouraged to take on a more civic role, as partners in the creation of new content and web architecture.

The impact of e-commerce

Virtual communities are dead: long live community

Commerce and social networks have a long history of mutual dependency. Friendships ease commerce, from gentlemen's clubs to Tupperware parties. Commerce provides the infrastructure for friendship, from teenagers hanging out in shopping malls to the roads, railways and airports that have grown to service business, but which also help us to visit friends and relations. Many argue that the internet and its applications will generate entirely new forms of social network. People will no longer be restricted by physical limits, such as the boundaries of the local neighbourhood.

Enter e-commerce. What types of network is it supporting? A year ago the answer would have been simple. Chat rooms on the internet – or 'virtual communities' as many styled themselves – seemed the ultimate symbiosis between commerce and community. Here's how the business model was supposed to work. Companies encouraged people to form online communities by providing the infrastructure: a site with message boards, chat rooms, email lists and photo albums. In these communities, people would talk about their hobbies, their worries, their desire for sex – anything, really. The most important thing was that they hung around. By doing so, they would be viewing the adverts featured on the site. It was a bit like a company giving away a neighbourhood of houses, just so that the people who moved in could see the adverts in the surrounding streets.

The portal Yahoo! has invested heavily in this model. It encourages people to set up their own online club, and in May 1999 it paid US$5 billion for GeoCities, a homepage-building service. 'Our goal is to attract [visitors] and create an environment where they want to stick around' says Jeff Mallet, Yahoo!'s chief executive.[3] Sites for young people such as DoBeDo also help users build their own graphical 'avatars' (3D bodies), with which users can chat to each other and visit online stores.

Two problems have arisen with this model. First, many virtual communities have been fairly unattractive places in which to hang around. Full of half-sentences from complete strangers, some are worse than the worst singles bar. Even software such as Third Voice, which allows users to annotate web sites so that other users can see, gets pretty tedious. Who cares what a teenager from Iowa thinks about the website you are looking at?

More importantly, advertising revenue has been lower than forecast. Based on interviews with 50 community site executives, Forrester Research concludes that the concept of an online community is less effective than other forms of marketing in converting lurkers into buyers. They also found that people are particularly wary of adverts in chat rooms. In other words, the vital 'click through' to an e-commerce site just isn't happening. In response, companies are beginning to move away from the aim of stimulating general socializing, towards online communities that are much more tightly integrated with the content and commerce elements of the site.[4] For example, the clothing firm Lands End has introduced a tool that allows two people to chat in real time while shopping online.[5]

The idea that e-commerce will spontaneously create myriad new virtual social networks is probably a red herring; but there are mutually supportive links between online commerce and community. E-commerce is creating the types of electronic network and tools which people can also use to support broader social interaction. In this sense, social networks are free-riding on commercial networks in time-honoured fashion. In the same way that roads and railways, which were built primarily to transport goods, are also used for social purposes, the infrastructure of the internet creates opportunities for new forms of social connection.

Digital TV (DTV) is perhaps the best example. The cost of internet access through DTV is relatively low, largely because DTV companies have signed huge deals with retailers who will sell goods through the same channels. Much web architecture and software has also been developed to meet the needs of e-commerce (for example broadband technology), or because developers thought that they could make money from advertising (for example Hotmail).

The result is an explosion in social relationships that depend in some way on cheap electronic communication. The social network that has gained most from this is the extended family. Recent research in Trinidad found that the internet stimulated far greater contact between cousins who would traditionally lose touch as they moved to different geographical areas; and tracing family trees is one of the most popular research activities of the 21st century.[6] According to the National Genealogical Society, more than 80 million Americans are involved in tracing their roots, many of them using the web.

More generally, the internet is being used to reinforce a whole range of existing relationships. One study of America Online (AOL) users found that 9 out of 10 take up the service to communicate better with friends and family, and 8 out of 10 have suggested to friends that they should also get online.[7]

Other networks that may be strengthened are those that revolve around local neighbourhoods. A recent study of a Canadian neighbourhood, in which some people were given free internet services and others were not, supports this assertion.[8] The researchers found that those who were connected recognized 27 neighbours by name and talked to 7 on a regular basis. This compared with the non-connected residents who, on average, knew only 9 by name and regularly spoke to 4. Such evidence runs counter to the common concern that the internet could be the ultimate isolating technology, reducing our participation in communities even more than television did before it.[9] Self-help networks of people sharing advice and information are also being stimulated by the internet. These can link people facing similar challenges or life experiences, as the following extract illustrates.

'Newsgroups were an absolute lifesaver for me in the early days of motherhood. One of the first I found was misc.kids.breastfeeding which kept me sane and provided masses of advice, wisdom and support at a time when I really needed it. I really wanted to breastfeed my child, but had no family support apart from my husband... Crucially, it also gave me the opportunity to give support to others when I became an old hand myself. This was a real boost to me – that's the whole point of peer support.'[10]

Often, such sites bring together people who have been relatively isolated; those with disabilities, those with particular religious or political beliefs, those with specific illnesses. They do, however, build on what is already there. The number of self-help groups, from Alcoholics Anonymous to reading groups, was already growing before the internet. As with families and neighbourhoods, electronic communication often supplements existing networks, rather than creating something completely new.

Future challenges

The general influence of e-commerce-supported technologies on social networks appears to have been relatively benign. New virtual communities are rarely created from scratch; instead, two processes are underway. One is a strengthening of existing patterns of interaction. The second is a more spontaneous set of innovations, enabling people to exchange knowledge and coordinate activity around issues of mutual interest.

This does not mean, however, that all social networks are being strengthened. There are barriers to access for some people, particularly in lower income groups. Some traditional meeting places are likely to suffer. Studies suggest that high streets in major towns and cities will flourish, but in smaller towns and rural areas, retail facilities are likely to decline. This means that those who use them for socializing may well lose out.

Networks that are reinforced by new electronic forms of communication also raise an interesting challenge for social inclusivity. Societies with very closed networks tend not to be the most cooperative; people become wary of others. Such societies are held back economically and socially because they become unable to work together. Southern Italy is a good example.

The social networks being stimulated by the internet can tend towards exclusivity. Faced with millions of potential members, forums have to be selective. As one publisher of an electronic newsletter argues, 'I hate to sound undemocratic, but if you're going to have valuable discussion you have to limit it to people with valuable knowledge'.[11] Consequently, over the last couple of years, communities of interest on the net have become harder to join. Some require new members to be nominated by other members, just like the London clubs of old.

A degree of exclusivity is inevitable among self-selecting social groups; people have always mixed with others similar to themselves. However, it does reinforce the need for a more inclusive public realm of interaction and cooperation to develop alongside informal networks. Civic institutions are needed that can support these more open networks.

Trust me, I'm a dot-com

In February 2000, George Carey, the Archbishop of Canterbury, expressed a popular concern about the net. 'Access to information and the ability to tap resources not otherwise available can be a potent tool of empowerment. But it can also be exclusive and isolating', he noted. 'You may argue that email is a way of making important connections.

That's true, but it can also be a distorting and unsatisfactory one in which self-deception and evasion are prominent.'[12]

Others put this argument more scientifically. Professor John Locke of Sheffield University suggests that the internet is leading to 'de-voicing'. He cites a 1997 survey of 1000 British workers, in which nearly half said that the internet had replaced some form of face to face communication. As a result, he argues that trust will decrease because less information is capable of being exchanged in electronic form.[13] People are no longer able to make judgements on the basis of body language or speech intonation. This perception of online communications as untrustworthy is reinforced by news stories. Worries abound about online credit card fraud, and a handful of men have been convicted of raping women whom they met on the net, deceiving them into meeting up through their online personas.

So will e-commerce undermine social trust, even if it provides the tools to stimulate social networks? A lot of fears sprout from a general misconception that e-commerce is helping to create a virtual world – a space in which people never really see or meet each other and are there-fore unable to share enough information or common experiences on which to base their trust. In fact, as we noted earlier, the e-world is going in the opposite direction. Even if the initial contact with an individual or organization is electronic, it usually quickly turns into a face to face relationship as well. Internet banks have recently started opening branches. The CompuServe police discussion forum now has an annual barbecue. The AOL camping and caravanning group organize joint holidays and the Scottish community on AOL's Local Life channel have regular social get-togethers. The survey of a Canadian neighbourhood referred to previously found that 'relationships are rarely maintained through computer-mediated communication alone, but are sustained through a combination of online and offline interactions.'[14]

Far from de-voicing, electronic communication is often supplement-ing relationships. In particular, it is allowing people to find out more about the organizations and individuals they are dealing with. One click on Google throws up information on an expanding proportion of the population. Novell has developed software that allows people to send a bundle of useful information about themselves to commercial and social contacts. Likewise, people can use the new networks to find out about companies they want to buy goods and services from. Such additional information appears to be stimulating trust among those who access it. For example, Harvard political scientist Pippa Norris has found that those people who use new media to find out about politics and current affairs tend to become more trusting of the political system.

In the long term, e-commerce also has the potential to increase people's trust in organizations because fostering trust on the net is such a high priority for e-businesses. Companies are putting an incredible amount of work into increasing the security and reliability of the technology they use. For example, First-e, the internet bank, recently set up a six-person consumer council to act as a watchdog for the bank's customers.

Future challenges

Early trends suggest that social trust may increase as a result of the information available on the web. Tools for fostering trust are being developed by e-commerce companies. Individual relationships are generally being supplemented, rather than replaced, by electronic communications.

There is, however, an underlying challenge of maintaining privacy in this more transparent and connected world. Privacy issues on the internet have failed to generate much public excitement. People are concerned that their credit card details are going to get into the wrong hands, but few have paid much attention to the routine information that they provide about themselves when they are online.

Yet as financial pressures on dot-coms rise, so do the pressures to make money by using customer information. Kevin O'Connor, the 39-year-old chief executive of DoubleClick, has made his fortune from piecing together clues about people. His software tracks the sites people visit and banner advertising is then tailored to reflect their likely interests. But DoubleClick wanted to do more. It bought the largest database of household information in the US, for a cool US$1.7 billion. Its aim was to link that database to information collected on the internet, in order to create complete profiles of people's interests and patterns of consumption.

While companies argue that such information collation simply helps them target advertising better, it is unlikely that it will increase trust in companies. DoubleClick was eventually barred from merging its different databases, reflecting government and consumer wariness about companies holding such large amounts of personal information. The challenge is to ensure that data protection legislation keeps up with such developments. If it does not, trust levels are likely to fall.

E-commerce meets e-civics?

Trust and informal networks are crucial for social cooperation. They help individuals work together and share information and resources. Networks also form the basis for political and civic action. It was out of the informal networks in coffee houses that many of the political movements of the 18th century grew, and it was out of the workplace communities of the 19th century that unions and new political parties emerged.

Yet history shows that spontaneous, informal innovation of this kind must be reinforced and underpinned by institutional frameworks, in order for their longer-term potential to be realized and made available to large numbers of people. As we have already noted, informal networks may be relatively narrow. Society also needs public institutions that bring together many sections of the population. Solving common problems is also easier when there are formal structures for debate and action.

It is no coincidence that social progress has often followed the development of better civic institutions. It was improvements to the institutions of government in the 19th century – such as extending the vote, increasing accountability, and developing a neutral civil service – which laid the foundations for many of the social improvements of the 20th century. It was the development of mutual societies and voluntary hospitals and schools in the early 20th century that laid the foundations for the health and education services of today.

Staying offline

Many people hope that electronic networks will prompt a new wave of civic institution building, revitalizing democracy, community groups and public sector organizations. However, the evidence so far suggests that these hopes are not being fulfilled. The vast majority of charities, community groups, parent–teacher associations, political parties and so on have not yet started to use e-technologies to change the ways in which they work as organizations. Even among larger voluntary organizations, progress is fairly slow. Research in 1999 among NGOs with annual incomes of more than UK£250,000 found that 84 per cent used some form of computer networking. Of these, 67 per cent used email and just over half had a website; these figures are reasonable. Yet only 3.6 per cent said that new networks had led to changes in communication processes and only 4.4 per cent to changes in working practices.[15]

Some have improved their strategies since then. Greenpeace, for example, encourages people to become 'cyber-activists'. The Free Tibet Campaign has attracted five million people to its website. The majority of pressure groups, however, still confine their strategy to a basic website and the use of email. They have not used technology in innovative ways to create improvements in the efficiency of their activities or to boost their membership.

Dot-civics

If established civic organizations are not changing the way they work to incorporate tools developed for e-commerce, what about the new breed of internet-based civic groups? Like the dot-coms, some of the first civic organizations to use the web were start-ups – entirely new organizations established to exist solely on the web. Groups such as the Minnesota e-democracy project (www.e-democracy.com), or CharlotteWeb, the community portal and forum in North Carolina, set out to be the Amazon.coms and eBays of the civic world. They aimed to embrace the new technologies, using databases, discussion groups, and automated ordering systems to find new ways of addressing civic issues; but they hit a problem. The sector has no equivalent to the deep-pocketed venture capitalists who ploughed money into dot-coms as running costs increased, with the result that many sites have run out of money. Take CharlotteWeb: established in 1995, it received an initial grant of nearly half a million dollars, closely followed by several other large donations. It won awards. It spread to a large area. Now the site is largely abandoned, a rarely-updated adjunct to the local newspaper's online edition.

Many other local and civic sites have the same problem. Grassroots.com, established to provide online tools for political activists, has just converted itself into a consultancy and lobbying organization. Politics.com and OneDemocracy.com have both closed.

The difficulties for dot-civics are similar to those faced by many dot-coms. Firstly, they compete in a crowded market in which only the best sites develop a critical mass of interest. Many of the not-for-profit political sites in the US attracted far less attention during last year's presidential election than CNN, CBS and other mainstream news organizations. They just couldn't match the level of instant coverage and analysis that people wanted. The costs of marketing are also escalating, as search engines start to request payments for high ratings.

Secondly, developing and maintaining multi-functional sites can be extremely expensive. One survey found that it now costs around UK£1 million to set up a commerce-enabled web site, more than twice the cost of a year ago. A typical commercial web site costs £590,000 a year to run.[16] The money pouring into e-commerce has helped to inflate these costs. The millions flowing into dot-coms have priced civics out of the market, as software engineers, project managers and state of the art software become ever more expensive. One of the largest civic organizations in the UK told us that its internet strategy was being held back because it simply could not find enough technical staff; dot-civics have no share options to wave in front of potential employees. Whether these problems will be resolved now the dot-com bubble is deflated is yet to be seen.

Yet some dot-civics are thriving. VolunteerMatch (www.volunteer-match.org) uses online technology to link people and volunteering opportunities in the US. Timebank has set up a similar scheme in the UK (timebank.org.uk) supported by, among others, the Home Office and the BBC. Timebank's site provides users with information about a wide range of volunteering opportunities matched to the user's postcode or special interests. Oneworld (www.oneworld.net) hosts a network of 724 organizations that promote human rights and sustainable development. It includes information sites, fair trade retailers, and community groups, and also has an agreement to use content from *The Guardian* newspaper online.

Some of the more successful sites are actually commercial ventures, with access to the same sort of venture capital as mainstream dot-coms. At the GreaterGood.com shopping portal (www.greatergood.com), visitors can shop at over 100 leading online merchants – including Amazon.com, Nordstrom, Lands End, Dell and Office Max – and up to 15 per cent of each purchase automatically goes to an organization that they select, at no extra cost to them. In 2000, they anticipated generating over US$5 million for organizations such as Special Olympics, Save the Children and the Muscular Dystrophy Association.

Yet despite such successes, the general picture is that civic engagement has, at best, been only marginally stimulated by the new tools associated with e-commerce. If anything, e-commerce has priced some civic organizations off the internet. The challenge is to find better ways for civic organizations to exploit the tools and networks that e-commerce has created. Imagination and resources are needed to apply these tools to stimulate participation in all sorts of civic decisions, from how the local school is run to the priorities of national political parties. For those interested in the UK's sustainability, this institutional focus must be a priority.

Ideas for stimulating civic institutions

A number of suggestions for stimulating civic institutions through e-commerce flow from our analysis. Some of these can be supported by government. Most also require action by individuals and organizations.

Four ways forward

Think local

One of the conclusions of our analysis is that electronic relationships are closely linked to face to face relationships. The idea of a virtual world that floats in cyberspace is a myth. Instead, people bring their real relationships, their local identities and their tangible needs to all forms of electronic exchange. For civic organizations, the lesson is to combine online and off-line activities and strategies. Most people are not interested in joining purely virtual communities. They want to ground these connections in their day to day lives.

This grounding needs to incorporate a local element. Although most people spend a lot of time away from their local areas, and neighbourhoods are rarely homogeneous social groups, people are far more likely to get involved in local forms of activity than any other. This is the scale at which society influences house prices, fear of crime, their children's educational prospects and their enjoyment of public space. Community participation is still often strongest at the local level. A Home Office study from the early 1990s valued the contribution of local community organizations at UK£11–12 billion each year. Their contributions include:

- security for 5 million homes covered by 120,000 neighbourhood watch schemes;
- community-run playgroups and pre-school childcare for 1 million parents;
- transport from 5000 community transport schemes; and
- support for schools from 350,000 school governors.

Some of the most successful civic sites have drawn on local interest. The Environmental Defence Fund (www.scorecard.org) has established a website that gives people information about pollution in their neighbourhood. This is an example of how powerful database tools can provide new civic services for local people. Users simply type in their postcode and are given a local pollution analysis. The site also provides information and tools for responding to that information, such as advice on how to complain to local politicians. In its first year, the site was used by two million people.

Thinking local does not necessarily mean that sites such as CharlotteWeb should be revived. They were often too heavily focused on providing forums, with not enough emphasis on practical delivery of improvements to people's lives – the catalyst for voluntary participation. However, a local strategy should use e-commerce tools to extend the scope of local institutions and activities. Opportunities include:

- *Local feedback systems and referendums.* Many people will only get involved in very local issues – things that happen in their street or local school. A MORI survey for Birmingham City Council found that one-third of the population would like more control over their immediate public environment, such as roads and pavements. Often, issues flair up quickly, generating collective involvement, before subsiding equally rapidly. Online systems could be used to facilitate the quick resolution of such issues. For example, people could be asked to vote on whether a street maintenance firm should be sacked. On a longer-term basis, electronic communication and data analysis tools could help local organizations such as schools, parks and health centres to establish their own targets for improvement – a shift from the centrally-imposed target regimes that currently shape most public organizations.
- *Interactive websites.* Relationships between frontline staff and users are the foundation for community involvement in public services. Park keepers who know park users are far more useful than formal questionnaires. They can solicit feedback, encourage people to get involved, or just make them feel welcome. Online technologies could help to forge such relationships. Frontline staff could use the web to supplement their face to face relationships, by developing sites which provide and receive local information.

Think enterprise

The UK has a long tradition of community enterprise – voluntary groups developing innovative schemes to meet local needs, often based on a mixture of not-for-profit and for-profit activities. These range from the voluntary hospitals and schools of the 19th century to development trusts today. E-commerce creates opportunities for new forms of community enterprise. If companies like GreaterGood.com can make money, then so can the civic sector. An interesting example is the mutual learning and trading system for social organizations set up by the Community Action Network (www.can-online.org.uk). Groups may also be able to develop new ways of selling local knowledge; for example, networks of local residents might be able to provide useful information online to retailers who are considering establishing services in their communities.

E-commerce systems could help community enterprises increase the transparency of their work in order to attract grants. The UK's public services are in dire need of innovative, enterprising ideas, but using public money to fund non-public bodies raises serious issues of accountability. Government cannot just give money away without being sure that it is well spent.

Too often, the need for accountability leads to labyrinthine monitoring and audit arrangements that stifle the very innovation that the dispersing public funds aim to create. Electronic systems have the potential to change this. They could create new, open systems for decision making and financial transactions. Accounts and minutes of management meetings can be made publicly available. As openness increases, more money can be distributed throughout the sector.

Think mutuality

E-commerce is helping establish new forms of exchange between individuals. Sites such as Napster (www.napster.com) and Gnutella (http://gnutella.wego.com) are pioneering new models of peer-to-peer commerce. Linux, the operating system that rivals Microsoft Windows, is another example of the power of mutual exchange. It was developed by a network of individual programmers around the world, who continuously refined and updated the basic software, most of them working for nothing.

The challenge is to help these mutual-style networks embrace the wider issues that affect their members. That was the pattern of unions and friendly societies in the 19th century – they moved from being internally-focused systems of exchange and organization (shop stewards running the day to day organization of the workforce) into movements addressing the more fundamental issues of ownership, poverty, voting rights and working conditions.

In the same way, it is possible to imagine web-enabled mutuals starting to address some of the issues of the ownership of knowledge and information in the 21st century. These issues are growing in significance as information and knowledge become more valuable. Napster, for example, has already faced legal challenges from music companies because it challenges traditional forms of copyright ownership. Such mutual systems could be an important counterbalance to the increasing concentration of patents and other valuable information in the hands of large corporations. This does not mean that network communities should be given free reign over all forms of information, just as unions were wrong to demand the nationalization of all industrial resources; but they have a place, and should be given legal support to ensure that new forms of mutualism are not unfairly suppressed.

Think distribution networks

Civic organizations need to recognize that they can use e-commerce technologies to fundamentally improve the way in which they operate. The internet does not just enable effective communications. The main impact of e-commerce has been in restructuring supply chains, from global hubs for car components to the direct ordering of personalized Dell computers. In contrast, the supply chains of the civic sector – grants, donations and volunteering – have remained largely untouched. They could be radically improved. Organizations such as Timebank show what can be achieved, but far more is possible.

- Grant applications, assessment and monitoring could shift online almost completely. Today, most grant givers cannot even accept applications via email.
- We may need an eGive to match eBay; a national system for reallocating unwanted furniture, books and clothing to people and communities either in the UK or in the developing world who would find them useful.

Encouraging the dot-coms to move into civics

There is also a need to encourage IT firms and e-businesses to get more involved with civic activities. Some already make large contributions; for example Hewlett-Packard plans to target US$1 billion in products and services to the developing world through its 'e-inclusion' initiative. However, few companies are actually integrating social and civic responsibility into their core businesses, as Forum for the Future's recent survey highlights (see Chapter 3).

This integration of social responsibility could be the most important contribution that e-commerce makes to civil society. Often, it will involve partnerships between dot-coms and public or voluntary groups. One example from the field of education is Think.com, a set of secure networks supported by the Oracle Corporation to enable school students to exchange ideas and produce their own online content. The package provides a software tool to support communication and content development, and control network access. Think.com already has several hundred thousand users in the UK. It is no doubt driven partly by Oracle's recognition that educational markets will be increasingly important to its business success, but it has created a set of social and educational networks that span the boundaries between the public, private and social sectors. Stimulating these partnerships, and then linking them effectively with core public service provision, such as healthcare and education, is a key challenge for government.

Partnerships could also be developed around the creation of new content on issues of public interest, whether educational curricula, information about gardening and horticulture, or evidence about how to improve public safety. Such development would depend on the creation of open networks with shared ownership of content, rather than the model of separate development and content ownership offered by the BBC.

Conclusion: building institutions, looking wider

This chapter has focused on the impact that e-technologies can have on social networks, and the organizational challenge of using them to create civic and social value. We have argued that a wholesale process of institutional development and reorganization is key to realizing their full potential.

However, while focusing on change at an institutional level, we also need to flag up a few macro factors that are influenced by technological change, and which will impact on the quality of social relationships. The success of small firms rests not only on the quality of their business plans but also on the macro-economic conditions under which they operate. In the same way, civic institutions are influenced by factors such as population, mobility, working hours, family structure, ethnic and cultural diversity, and levels of income inequality.

Over the last decade, different commentators have pinpointed a number of factors to explain an apparent decline in social capital. Robert Putnam focuses on the negative effects of television, suburbanization and working hours.[17] Amitai Etzioni argues that communities have been undermined by too many individual rights. William Julius Wilson claims that poor urban areas have suffered from the flight of educated workers. Richard Sennett blames economic restructuring and flexible work patterns. All of these theories are important if we are to locate questions about social capital and new technology within a wider political context.

E-commerce is creating a space to think about these wider social forces. When economies undergo wholesale restructuring, the result is a combination of social disruption and renewal. In a period of dynamism and turbulence, we are able to reconsider the type of economy and society in which we want to live. That involves both innovation at the micro level – the focus of this chapter – and revisiting broader, older debates about how inclusive our society should be. Welcome to politics in the information age.

Notes and references

1   These elements often reinforce each other. For example, Paul Dekker of the Dutch Statistical Service has found that higher levels of volunteering tend to go with greater participation in civic debate.

2   See, for example, Norris, P (ed) (1999) *Critical Citizens: Global Support for Democratic Governance*, Oxford

3   'Yahoo offers community building', cnet news.com, August 18 1998.

4   Marther, J (1999) *Creating Community Online*, Durlacher Research Ltd, London (www.durlacher.com)

5   Marther, op cit

6   There is even a Jupp family research centre on the web.

7   Marther, op cit

8   Hampton, KN and Wellman, B (2000) 'Examining Community in the Digital Neighbourhood: Early Results from Canada's Wired Suburb' in Ishida, T and Isbister, K (eds) *Digital Cities: Technologies, Experiments and Future Perspectives*, Springer-Verlag, Heidelburg

9   *The Guardian* 'Only the Lonely' 2 February 2000

10 Cited in Burrows, R et al (2000) *Virtual Community Care? Social Policy and the Emergence of Computer Mediated Social Support*, ESRC Virtual Society? Programme. The questionnaire can be found at http://www.york.ac.uk/res/answers.htm:

11 Chao, J (1995) 'Internet Pioneers Abandon World They Have Created', *Wall Street Journal*, 7 June 1995, cited in Van Alstyne, M and Brynjolfsson, E *Electronic Communities: Global Village or Cyberbalkans?* MIT Press, Massachusetts

12 *The Guardian* 'Internet Isolates, Says Carey', 24 February 2000

13 *The Guardian* 'Can a Sense of Community Flourish in Cyberspace?' 11 March 2000

14 Hampton, K N and Wellman, B, op cit, p207

15 Burt, E and Taylor, J (1999) *Information and Communication Technologies: Re-shaping the Voluntary Sector in the Information Age?* Centre for the Study of Telematics and Governance, Glasgow Caledonian University

16 Flercher Research, cited in *Internet Statistical Backgrounder*, Citizens Online

17 Putnam estimates that changing patterns of work have created time and money pressures that account for 10 per cent of the decline in social capital. Suburbanization accounts for another 10 per cent decline, because people live further away from each other and their work, and spend more time commuting. Television accounts for a quarter of the decline, because it provides a more isolated form of entertainment. The majority of the rest of the decline he attributes to a rather vague change in the cultures of different generations. For example, those who lived through the Second World War appear to have established patterns of political and social engagement that their children have never learned.

Response

by Madeleine Bunting

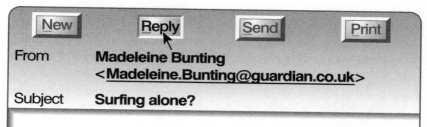

From   **Madeleine Bunting
        <Madeleine.Bunting@guardian.co.uk>**

Subject   **Surfing alone?**

The internet's rapid expansion has been accompanied by an astonishingly ambitious ideology; the claim that it will transform the way you live and work. Much of the early excitement, cultivated by massive advertising campaigns, was designed to panic people into getting online. It is now subsiding and, in an internet hangover, our understanding of what will and what won't be revolutionized is sobering up.

In the midst of this, the impact of the net on social capital is one of the most complex questions. One thing is for sure: that this is not a revolution, not the dawn of an era of virtual community and cyber-relationships, as Ben Jupp and Tom Bentley's measured analysis illustrates. We are beginning to place the net more properly as an increment on earlier technological development. Probably not as revolutionary in its consequences for social capital as the telegraph or the railway, but on a par with television. It will become just one in a range of communication technologies: we will pick up the telephone, turn on the TV, email or text message depending on the kind of communication we want. The net will supplement rather than replace.

By way of example, take Jubilee 2000, the debt relief campaign, which offers an excellent illustration of how the net can be used by a civic organization. The net was crucial; the tiny London-based team emailed about 500 activists around the world, generating a global movement from a network of email links. Information could be shared, breaking down one of the most insidious aspects of the debt issue – namely, that activists in developing countries often have little information about the negotiations of major creditors in the Paris Club or at the International Monetary Fund, which have a huge impact on their own countries' economies. Jubilee 2000's success is similar to that of other global activist groups such as those seen in Prague in September 2000 and Seattle in November 1999, both of which relied on the net to plan their demonstrations. The great assets of the net for social capital are its twin capacities to gather and distribute information and to keep people connected.

But these examples also show the limitations of the net. No amount of emailing replaces the demonstrations, the public meetings, the letter-writing campaigns and the local neighbourhood groups. There is an energy in the personal experience of physically *being* with people which can't be generated on the net. In all the discussion of 'effective communication' we lose sight of the crucial importance of the process of communication. It is a dangerous omission because it is in the process – the experience of other people's commitment – that radical, transformative politics is possible. It is the process that can transform the participants themselves, developing their confidence, bringing to fruition unexpected talents to articulate and assert themselves.

Many grassroots activist organizations are well aware of this. The East London Community Organization (TELCO) puts its energies into 'actions', such as confronting the chief executive of a bank that has pulled all its branches out of an economically-depressed neighbourhood. The actual event is almost as important as the end result, as TELCO members gain experience and confidence in negotiating with decision-makers. It is this human element – hard to quantify, spontaneous, unexpected and transforming – which is absent from net civic culture, and will always limit its role to a supplementary one.

This is particularly true of neighbourhood social capital, much of which is built around children – playgroups and schools. The role the net can play in triggering this kind of traditional geographical community is very limited (although it may play a supportive role as a useful resource for gathering information). The net can never deliver the chance meetings, social interactions and networks that develop at the school gate or over the garden wall, and are inspired by the powerful emotional instinct for the welfare of children.

Children break down boundaries; toddlers don't understand the concept of strangers. Here, we come up against another limitation of the net. As soon as you have a child, your attitude to your local environment is transformed; suddenly you care passionately about the quality of playgrounds, the safety and cleanliness of streets. Much of this social capital revolves around women with childcaring responsibilities. With a child to care for, a woman's social life shifts from being orientated around the office to being orientated around the children. None of this meshes easily with the net, as anyone who has struggled to log on with a baby on their knee well knows.

Finally, I want to raise the huge question of whether the net contributes to wisdom – the quality of our relationships with others and with ourselves. Ours is a culture fascinated by communication technologies. We are gripped by a fantasy of communication omnipotence and instantaneity; I can communicate with anyone, anywhere, anytime in the world. But with that has come a fragmentation of attention span. When a smorgasbord of information and entertainment lies at the touch of a finger, how long can we concentrate on any one train of thought? Can we allow ourselves the time to reflect, or resolve an emotional conflict? If office workers check their email on average every five minutes, what does that do to their powers of concentration? Both the speed of the net, and the wealth of information it offers, militates against certain thought processes. We become good at multi-tasking and skim-reading, but less good at the kind of reflection and contemplation that is essential for true originality and emotional wisdom. Dazzled by the technology of communication, we are in danger of losing sight of the fact that technology is secondary to the content: 'how' is less important than 'what'. The biggest danger of the net is its urgency; can we ringfence the internal space and silence essential for having something original and wise to communicate? ■

5 Sink or Surf? Social inclusion in the digital age

Alex MacGillivray and David Boyle

Introduction

Can't surf, won't surf? Not for long. The government has set itself the goal of ensuring that everyone in the UK who wants it will have easy, affordable access to the internet by 2005.[1] If you're not wired up via a home computer, DTV, mobile phone or personal digital assistant (PDA), then you should at least be able to surf at work– if you have a job – or in a handy UK Online centre. A stubborn or unfortunate minority will not 'want' access; we estimate that these will total about 10 per cent of the population in 2010, mainly well-to-do and elderly people, those with extreme disability, and the most hard-pressed of the socially excluded. However, if Tony Blair has his way, everyone else will be able to surf. The dreaded 'digital divide' will have been largely bridged.

This chapter looks beyond the issue of technical access, vital though that is. We start from the encouraging assumption that the government can meet its – highly ambitious – target and achieve near-universal access to online opportunities. Our focus is on whether e-commerce can be the missing piece of the jigsaw in the fight against ingrained patterns of poverty, deprivation and social exclusion. Comfortable Middle England is already beginning to reap the benefits of e-commerce. Fingers crossed, many believe that low-income communities will follow suit – if we can get them surfing (see Box 5.1).

Yet other critics argue that there is a dark side to the e-revolution; that the new economy could create new exclusions, no matter how many people are wired up. In this chapter, we argue that the structural

Box 5.1 Favourites: Angell Town

Angell Town is a so-called 'sink estate' in Brixton, South London. It is also an example of how communities are using the internet and e-commerce to challenge social exclusion. A computer re-engineering project, started by Community Logistics, is providing training for local young people and the IT equipment necessary to wire up every flat on the estate. A Lifelong Learning Centre is planned next door, along with a time bank devised by the New Economics Foundation (NEF), which will enable people to share skills and resources. The community hopes to have its own web portal soon, which will host websites for every business on the estate and every resident who wants one. Both the local school and the local doctor will be contactable via email; if your child hasn't turned up at class by 9am, you will get an email warning you. This is socially inclusive e-commerce in action.

tensions between local and global economies will be more than a match for local vim and vigour. Left unchecked, the commercial pressures of e-commerce could exacerbate exclusion and drain poor communities of precious cash flow and resources.

At the same time there is an emerging policy agenda full of opportunities to create the new human networks and new currency systems that will be needed to make e-commerce really work for poor people. The solution will lie in harnessing the power of e-commerce to invent:

- brilliant new ways of keeping money circulating among hitherto non-existent networks of producers and consumers; and
- surprising new forms of electronic currency – some based on time – that are more effective in linking local needs with local resources.

If seized, these opportunities will help sink estates and deprived rural communities alike to surf successfully on the e-commerce wave. How we tackle e-inclusion will provide valuable lessons for other countries that are hot on our heels. Encouragingly, the government's recent urban and rural white papers explore some of the necessary innovations; but more progressive initiatives are needed, particularly in the area of what we call 't-commerce' – using time as a new internet currency. The opportunities we outline are aimed at entrepreneurs and venture capitalists from all sectors. They point towards large and untapped e-markets, which need to be catered for if all sectors of society are to become full participants in the digital economy.

Beyond the digital divide

Access for all?

Only 5 per cent of the world's population has access to the internet; half the world's population has never even made a phone call.[2] Compared to this, the UK's digital divide doesn't look so daunting. But management consultants Booz-Allen & Hamilton still predict that only 60–70 per cent of the UK population will be online by 2003 without a more concerted effort to achieve universal access.[3] The government's response to this challenge is the UK Online initiative, which aims to ensure that everyone who wants it has access by 2005, at home, at work or in a nearby internet centre.

One in three homes in the UK is already connected to the internet, with almost one million homes going online in the three months to August 2000. Around half the adult population has already accessed the internet one way or another, and the advent of DTV and internet-compatible mobile phones, coupled to falling computer prices, will boost these numbers dramatically over the next few years. Yet despite this rapid growth, near-universal access is still an ambitious target. Government statistics show that women, ethnic minorities, the elderly, disabled people, and unskilled workers are less likely to use the internet – not always for reasons which are fully understood.[4] There will also be those who don't want to surf, particularly among the elderly. Add in severely disabled people and some categories of prison inmates who won't be allowed access, and you end up with up to 5 per cent of the UK population – three million people – remaining off-line.

And what about the socially excluded? Figure 5.1 shows how extrapolating current trends could bring practically all low-income households online in five years (the dashed line). However, there is an equally plausible scenario – the dotted line with its flatter s-curve – in which up to one-fifth of people on low-incomes fail to get online by 2010.[5] This would add up to another three million people who theoretically could get access to the internet, but who for a variety of reasons – poor education, grinding poverty, overwork, cultural prejudice, drug addiction, alienation – will not.

Although a majority of the UK population – perhaps 90 per cent or more – will have technical access within the next few years, the eventual size of these disparate groups who 'can't surf, won't surf' will become a major cause for concern.[6]

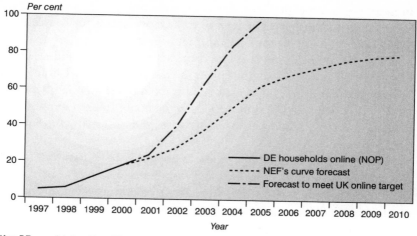

Figure 5.1   **Internet access in the poorest third of UK households**

Could surf, don't surf

In discussions around the digital divide, socially-excluded people are sometimes portrayed as passive and powerless recipients of new technology and government services; but e-commerce is not about giving information and patronage to the needy. It is the two-way inter-active exchange of goods and services using:

- novel electronic networks of producers and consumers; and
- electronic currencies of agreed value as the medium of exchange.

There are four obvious barriers to internet-inclusion: the cost of access (hardware and charges); lack of skills or confidence; fear of fraud and harmful content; and simply not seeing the relevance.[7] The first three are a major focus of government policy, particularly through the Office of the e-Envoy and the UK Online initiative. There are also numerous voluntary sector organisations which aim to improve access, such as Citizens Online, HumanITy and Cyber-Cycle,[8] and business-led initia-tives from companies like AOL, BT, Ericsson, and Hewlett-Packard. In general, there are grounds for feeling fairly optimistic about the progress being made in the provision of hardware and skills, and in levels of trust.

Yet there are some important exceptions. Long-term disabilities and health problems affect up to 8.7 million people in the UK.[9] For them, e-commerce could be very empowering, enabling them to work and shop in new ways, and explore virtual reality experiences. However, despite the many valuable efforts underway to improve access for people with disabilities, it is important that internet access is not seen as a substitute for the provision of 'real', physical access to places and services. Other people who cannot get far on the web are those without good literacy and numeracy skills, estimated to be more than one-fifth of all adults of working age.[10] Ethnic groups who are not fluent in English are also at a disadvantage because software and internet content are predominantly in English.

Getting all of these groups online is not going to be easy, but is just the start of the e-inclusion process. E-commerce also has a key role to play, but its impacts are still uncertain. It could impact positively or negatively on the bottom line of poor communities. It could build self-esteem and new networks, but could also isolate poor consumers with second-rate goods and services at higher prices. It could increase local cash flow, but may become another nail in the coffin of the local shop. Which is it to be?

Being taken into account: including consumers

Online, there are money-saving deals galore: higher interest rates, bulk-buy discounts and offers like PowerGen's 'Surf and Save', which gives a discount on electricity bills for internet users. All this is good news for consumers, unless you are one of the 6–9 per cent of people who have no bank account – mainly women, ethnic minorities, young people and the over-65s.[11]

The government's still-sketchy plans for a universal bank accessed through the Post Office network, and new basic bank accounts like NatWest's Step account, could provide the answer;[12] but to enable people to participate in e-commerce, these accounts will need to provide flexible debit cards, or some other system for letting websites extract money. Young people are particularly excluded because they do not have plastic. US websites like flooz.com provide young people with buying power on the internet, but with an unappealing reliance on parental supervision.

Up to a quarter of all households are excluded from credit of any kind.[13] A recent survey of Southwark residents showed that only four in ten had credit cards and less than a quarter had credit facilities for day to day purchases. It is suspected that many excluded people are blacklisted or 'red lined', unable to get credit simply because of their unfavourable postcodes.[14] Yet e-commerce offers the potential to give all consumers high-quality, tailor-made services. According to management guru C K Prahalad, the low-income market, which many financial institutions and retailers shun, could become an increasingly attractive proposition to e-tailers. He tells multinationals to think laterally about innovative ways of cashing in on the purchasing power of consumers in the developing world – an argument that applies even more forcefully to excluded groups in the UK.[15]

However, e-commerce can just as easily be used to exclude or provide desultory levels of customer service to small spenders. Many e-tailers find that half their income comes from just a quarter of their customers, and the latest techniques of online 'customer relationship management' identify the most valuable customers from their buying history, so that e-tailers can make sure they receive warm, responsive service.[16] A basic, automated service may be all that remains for less valued customers. The risk, say IT access experts Kevin Carey and Felicity Ussher, is that 'companies with reputable products no longer wish to sell to the poor, confining them to a street market "loan shark" economy'.[17]

Staying afloat: including business

Small businesses, so crucial for employment in deprived neighbour-hoods, have finally woken up to the internet; according to recent government figures, two-thirds of SMEs and 55 per cent of micro-businesses are now online.[18] Yet only a small proportion of these are actually trading online, despite numerous examples demonstrating how e-commerce can extend geographical reach and attract new customers.[19] For many, money and time are simply too tight to get online operations up and running. Ten local shops a day have closed over the last decade, and failure rates for new micro-businesses are alarming.[20] Big brand sites, with their 'walled gardens', can also make it hard for small business to gain access to e-markets.

Some neighbourhoods, particularly in rural areas, are already becom-ing retail deserts, and there is a risk that e-commerce will damage the profitability of the few remaining local shops, banks and services. According to the e-Envoy's office, 'no methodologically sound studies of the change in purchasing habits on the internet have been found',[21] but Forrester Research reports that just 9 per cent of US online spending in 1999 went to SMEs.[22]

Some local businesses – like fast food and hairdressers – look safe from e-commerce competition; but local book, video and music shops and convenience stores are under direct threat. In East London, the Community Action Network, a network for social entrepreneurs, has recently linked its website to Amazon.co.uk. Sales generate much-needed funds for bursaries, but may have the perverse effect of undermining local booksellers.[23] The situation for local business in Europe is not as severe as it is in the US, where online sales are free of local sales tax. There, Amazon.com has begun to develop supportive links with local bookstores, seeing them as an important shop window that can complement the online browsing experience.

Local shops are most vulnerable, but many other SMEs in deprived areas will struggle to survive the fierce competition of global B2B e-commerce. Purchasing departments in large firms can now award contracts to the lowest bidder worldwide through a reverse auction completed in a matter of hours. On the internet, capital is more mobile than ever before, and there is little or no attempt to assess the impact of purchasing decisions on local jobs and communities.

Watertight or leaky? Including local economies

Socially-excluded groups face big opportunities and major challenges on entering the e-economy. On the negative side, poor neighbourhoods that already leak local cash flow could be hit even harder by e-commerce. Local money flows have been identified as a key issue in the government's new strategy for neighbourhood renewal, yet the desired 'multiplier effect' – wherein local cash generates local jobs and more local spending – will be badly dented if small businesses collapse as a result of distant web-based competition, and if more consumer spending is diverted away from local shops.[24] More positively, inner-city estates and rural communities are a potent source of innovation and creativity, and could be a driving force in the development of new, more inclusive models of e-business. They have a tradition of making the most of non-financial resources, they urgently need more affordable products and services, and they will benefit most from vibrant online micro-businesses.[25]

Is it even possible to predict, let alone affect, these contradictory impacts of e-commerce on our local economies? NEF is just starting the UK's first comprehensive research programme on local money flows. Called Plugging the Leaks, it will attempt to measure these trends and impacts.[26] In the next two sections, we draw on lessons learnt elsewhere in the local economy to identify how e-commerce could be used to support small enterprise and keep local resources flowing.

New human networks

If e-commerce takes off in excluded communities, it will be about new networks between producers and consumers, and new currencies to enable trade among the cash-poor members of these new networks. Together, they could provide the key to socially inclusive e-commerce.

Building community networks

Community information networks are the online equivalent of cards in the corner-shop window; they enable local people to find or supply information about health, jobs, services, training and leisure. They are typically accessed in cybercafes, libraries, council offices, supermarkets or at home. One of the most successful, Newcastle's NewNet, now receives 12,000 visitors a month and acts as a virtual shopfront for community organizations across the city.

Wider networks, like the north-east's Regional Electronic Economy Programme (REEP), aim to link all relevant local networks together. And ukvillages.co.uk provides a template for all 28,000 villages and urban neighbourhoods in the UK to provide their own content, although the actual content is still patchy. At their best, these networks can deliver crucial information to individuals, allowing them to be active citizens, look for jobs, and update skills. Yet much more can still be done to make them searchable, interactive and fun, if they are to build enabling networks of individuals and communities.

Building local infrastructure for e-commerce

A simple logistical problem has provided the inspiration for some radical thinking about e-commerce infrastructure; bulky items bought online cannot be delivered successfully during working hours. Recent DTI and Cabinet Office reports have highlighted the potential for post offices and local shops to act as centres in which customers can collect their e-purchases and deal with returns.[27] In addition to its vast network of sub-post offices, the great strength of the Post Office is that it is highly trusted by consumers, particularly pensioners and the unemployed. Many corner shops also act as social centres, holding spare house keys for forgetful regulars and keeping an eye out for people who fail to pick up their newspaper.

The government is right to identify the role that post offices could have in e-commerce fulfilment. However, with investment and imagination, they could also become:

Box 5.2 Favourites: Craigmillar (www.ccis.org.uk)

The Craigmillar Community Information Service (CCIS) dates back to 1996 and is now the biggest free bulletin board in the UK. Based in Craigmillar, just east of Edinburgh, it provides: free IT training and email to local groups and businesses via CraigNet, a software archive; a means to share hardware; and a searchable database of local services and organizations. So far CCIS has successfully got 130 local groups online.

- universal banks coupled with time banks for LETS and credit unions for savings;
- online communication centres, including one-stop shops for central and local government services;
- demonstration and rental centres for the latest hardware and software;
- consolidators for online purchasing clubs to reduce delivery costs and obtain bargains in online auctions; and
- micro-manufacturing centres with CD writers, high-speed colour printers and other pieces of kit too expensive for most individuals to own.

Transforming themselves into local e-commerce centres could provide a sustainable livelihood for post offices and local shops that goes beyond benefits, scratch cards, fags and mags. To cope with such a varied workload, provide a friendly service, and train those who are all fingers and thumbs on the internet, will be a major challenge for staff. However, post offices and local shops have shown themselves to be enterprising and adaptable in the past, and the digital economy creates new opportunities for them to spearhead a renaissance of distinctive local high streets.

Building local skills networks

IT skills are a crucial requirement for participating in e-commerce. Thanks to government support, there is now widespread and affordable provision, but lack of time and motivation mean that many training resources in the community are not being taken up by the socially excluded people who really need them. The internet offers new ways to bring resources together with unmet needs. One such project is Learn-and-Earn, pioneered by LINCT (Learning and Information Networking for Community via Technology), based in Long Island, New York. The idea is

> ## Box 5.3 Favourites: Toby Peter and local retailing (toby@easynet.co.uk)
>
> Judging by the massive growth in farmers' markets in recent years, local food is more popular than ever. However, these markets have captured just UK£70 million out of the UK's £70 billion total grocery spend, and meanwhile over 500 post offices and thousands of local shops have closed. To get local food back into local shops, entrepreneur Toby Peter is developing a net-based directory that will match up small independent retailers with dozens of local food producers and suppliers. Small batch ordering, as most shopkeepers will testify, is a tedious process taking up to ten hours a week. The internet will allow retailers to manage their entire stock list electronically so that orders can be met automatically, making life easier and more profitable for local retailers, while providing a steady market for local producers.

that people, especially the young and old, can earn time credits while being trained on computers, which they can then cash in to buy a computer at the end of the course.[28] The lesson here is that being trained is a commitment that should be rewarded. Around 15 million computers are disposed of every year in the US, so it makes sense both socially and environmentally to refurbish them and make them available for these kinds of courses. Similar approaches are now being piloted in the UK.[29]

Building networks to keep money flowing

Real economic benefits can flow from the community information and advice networks that are being created – especially those that support the ability of SMEs to use the internet. However, the full potential of e-commerce for local economies is unlikely to be achieved unless they develop more direct ways of ensuring that local resources circulate locally. SMEs can be more flexible and faster than their larger counterparts, and there is potential for them to increase their economic clout by banding together in new e-clusters for purchasing and marketing.

Many of the best models for using the web to win new customers for local markets come from the developing world; for example PEOPLink, which links 130,000 artisans in 14 developing countries, allowing them to display and sell their products online. A similar idea is used by the UK company Tropical Whole Foods, which links together a range of fairtrade fruit cooperatives around the developing world. Other exciting examples include a farming coop in Chincheros in Peru; it multiplied its income by five by creating an online partnership with a US export company. There is also a project in Papua New Guinea that allows village elders to sell their highly accurate advance forecasts of coming storms.[30]

A few similar initiatives are now starting to emerge in the UK; for example the Gorbals Initiative, which was so surprised at getting 27,000 hits (40 per cent of which were from abroad) on its website in the months before its launch, that it now plans to help local businesses export their goods.[31] The idea of using e-commerce techniques to strengthen local business is also taking off elsewhere in Europe, notably through the EU's three-year Infoville project.[32]

The idea that local communities can trade their way out of disadvantage certainly shouldn't be dismissed. Pioneering examples of small firms that have benefited from e-commerce include the butcher Jack Scaife (jackscaife.co.uk), who now sells black puddings around the world. Trade associations and local retail forums could do more to replicate such examples, although this would require not just IT training for small businesses but e-marketing training too.

The internet can also be used by small hardware stores, pharmacies and bookshops to fight back against larger firms and retail chains. There are now several websites in the US which help local shops to stand up against the big brands. One of the most successful is Doitbest.com, a website cooperatively-owned by 4400 independent local hardware stores. The site stocks 70,000 items, and local stores pay just US$200 to join plus $15 a month. A percentage of each sale also goes to support the development of the site.

Other networks, such as Carbusters.com or Letsbuyit.com, allow ordinary people to generate online savings by buying in bulk. These networks don't distinguish between people or neighbourhoods, and could be used more creatively by community groups and voluntary organizations to bring cheaper prices to those who need them most. In future we are likely to see more online local clearing houses that promote local produce and build local e-commerce, as well as providing other kinds of support.

New currency systems

Money is round and rolls away. Most forms of e-commerce make it roll away even faster from local economies, as dot-coms siphon away yet more local cash. As we have seen, e-commerce can empower networks of excluded people, but enabling them to trade, often with very limited amounts of cash, will require innovative online currency systems.

> ## Box 5.4 Favourites: Hadrian Farm Meats (www.hadrianfarmmeats.co.uk)
>
> Hadrian Farm Meats was set up in response to a clear demand for high-quality meats, and a realization that farms could band together to supply these direct to customers through the internet. The company is based in a shop in Haltwhistle and sells traceable local beef, lamb and pork from the North Pennines. It currently employs two people and expects to double in size over the next year.

Building ways to pay online

The universal bank account method may seem the most obvious way of giving excluded people access to e-commerce, but it is not the only one. The development of DTV, m-commerce, smart cards and electronic money is set to create new, pre-paid methods of payment. Some of these could be online versions of existing voucher systems; others could be more ambitious. Electronic cash is yet to take off in the UK, but elsewhere consumers are getting used to new ways of making payments or drawing cash electronically without using credit cards. Europay and Barclaycard are working on a payment protocol so that people with smart cards can interface with their computers. DTV set-top boxes (STBs) have smart card slots and some – notably the boxes distributed by Sky – have two. There are currently around 3.5 million STBs with smart card slots in Europe, and by 2003 there could be 29m.[33] As a result, it may be easier to provide smart cards for excluded people than it is to get the banks to broaden the number of credit cards in circulation, given the resulting danger of debt.

Building the trust to trade

Even when people have the networks and there are mechanisms to pay for trading, trust remains a major obstacle to the large-scale uptake of e-commerce. This may be about to change with the emergence of guaranteed electronic markets (GEMs). GEMs are the brainchild of Wingham Rowan, host of the TV series *cybercafé*.[34] He envisages a vast network of local exchanges, bringing many informal skills and assets into the money economy, with the guarantee of insurance cover from buyers and sellers and access to a government-backed arbitration service (see www.gems.org.uk).

Box 5.5 Favourites: SmartCity (www.prodtech.com)

SmartCity is an electronic money system developed by ICL, which has been successful in countries in which cash security is a major headache. For example, the Siberian town of Purpe, which services a major gas field for the Purnefte Gaz corporation, has faced difficulties over wage deliveries being hijacked by the local mafia. Through SmartCity, wages can be transferred directly into employees' accounts and spent in local shops, all of which accept e-cash. The SmartCity card developed for the local PurBank pays interest, and has three sections: an interest-bearing rouble account, a non-interest-bearing dollar account, and a rouble credit card that charges interest.

A nationwide system of this kind would need major investment from government, not just in organizing the trading system, but also in setting rules for arbitration. It is no small project – Rowan likens it to the task of providing universal drainage or building the Channel Tunnel[35] – but there are ambitious local versions of the idea starting to emerge. Ericsson has been instrumental in trailing the concept in the small town of Vara in Sweden. AceNET in south-east Ohio includes 100 speciality food shops and farms selling their wares online. Digital City Amsterdam – which even includes a digital sex shop – attracts about 4000 hits a day.[36] Perhaps the most ambitious development is in Evanston, Illinois, where a coalition of the city council, university, school districts and chamber of commerce has created the e-Tropolis project.

For local e-commerce to work effectively, a reasonable proportion of the population must use it. Even if reticence can be overcome by ideas like GEMs, the cost will deter some towns from following Evanston's example. The legal responsibility for faulty goods sold over local internets also needs to be clarified. However, there are exciting opportunities for local authorities and cable operators to cooperate on such projects. Linking them to smart card payment systems would allow local authorities to recoup costs by selling access to other services – such as sports centres or transport – on the same cards. Local authorities could also make a real difference to the success of local networks by using them wherever possible for their own purchasing.

> ## Box 5.6 Favourites: e-Tropolis (www.technopolisevanston.org)
>
> The e-Tropolis project went live in 2000. It aims to go beyond existing community information networks by linking everyone in the city to a broadband network. The result has been an ambitious public–private partnership to wire up the city, and the creation of a virtual town square through which small local firms can sell their products in a trusted environment. The cost of linking up is quite high (US$49.95 a month), but 5 per cent of the revenue is ploughed back into IT training and provision for old, young and those on low incomes. The idea is that local people can book a tennis court, order a pizza, pay a parking ticket or read school reports – all online.

Building systems that keep goods and services flowing

The problem for poor communities is that, although they may be relatively wealthy in terms of time, skills and other resources, they do not have the cash to set up mainstream enterprises. E-commerce lends itself to converting almost anything of value into electronic forms that can be exchanged over the web. This principle could be extended to enable socially-excluded neighbourhoods to barter goods or time on the web, in order to match local needs and resources. There are a range of electronic currencies that could be adapted in this way.

Trade dollars and other commercial barter currencies
Between 10 and 20 per cent of world trade is now thought to be barter. Many barter schemes issue electronic money as a way of facilitating transactions, and this takes on many of the attributes of hard currency. It can be spent before surplus bartered stock has been sold on and transferred using smart card technology. Bartering over the internet has already begun in the US with the emergence of Ubarter.com, the product of a 1998 merger between Canadian and US barter interests.

Organizational barter currencies
The EU has embarked on a major study of the potential for small-scale barter in Europe, and has funded four barter systems for voluntary organizations and SMEs in central Scotland, County Mayo, Madrid and Amsterdam. In Scotland, a currency called SOCS (Scottish Organizational Currency System) is issued to small businesses to

> ## Box 5.7 Favourites: Ubarter.com
> ## (www.ubarter.com)
>
> Ubarter.com is developing into one of the pre-eminent e-commerce barter sites, with 40,000 businesses worldwide now using Ubarter dollars. Transaction volume stands at around US$30 million a year. Each transaction is charged at a fee of 5 per cent, but the advantage for small businesses is that members can receive credit in Ubarter dollars of up to $5000. This success has been noticed, and Ubarter now faces competition from three new sites in California alone – ebarter.com, Barter Trust and Doublebill.

provide them with interest-free mutual credit. Many such schemes are inspired by the Swiss currency system Wir, now 65 years old and Europe's most successful bartering operation.[37]

Social currencies

Local exchange trading schemes remain relatively small-scale; few have been able to attract more than 200 members. The total UK turnover of LETS when it was last estimated in 1995 was £2.1m in sterling equivalent – or about £70 per member per year.[38] One of the reasons for such low levels of trading is that there is an imbalance between supply and demand, with more luxury services available than the basic services which members actually need. Electronic currencies are designed to bring unused resources together with unmet demand. Given that resources in disadvantaged neighbourhoods – people's skills and know-how – go largely unrecognized and unmeasured by conventional measures of economic success, local barter currencies linked to e-commerce could provide an important means of giving people local buying power when they are short of cash. The strength of the systems would be in keeping local resources circulating locally, and reconnecting them with local needs.

T-commerce: internet trading using time as a currency

Excluded groups find it hardest to participate in e-commerce – but also have most to gain. Research shows that the main obstacle to using the internet is often time.[39] While some excluded people – notably single parents – suffer extreme time-poverty, time is one of the hidden assets of many poor communities. E-commerce could make use of this time to deliver 'hi-touch' as well as hi-tech services. New opportunities are emerging for time-based internet trading, or 't-commerce', which would reward people for work in the local community, creating new relationships of care and trust. Distributed through a time bank, the proceeds of t-commerce could be spent on a range of goods and services, from meals and medical equipment to rent and computers.

Although time banking was originally used to boost healthcare programmes, it is now being brought to bear on other social problems like truancy and youth crime. In the US, where there are now over 200 schemes, participants can use their hard-earned time dollars to:

- buy services from other people on the system;
- act as a form of insurance for when they are too old to earn any themselves;
- give to elderly relatives;
- donate back to the system for people who are too ill to earn them themselves; and
- buy a range of other goods and services, like food, insurance discounts or student loans.

A dozen schemes are either running or projected in the UK. Several of these are IT-based, but none has fully capitalized on the potential of e-commerce yet. There are a number of projects which point towards the long-term potential for t-commerce.

- Commonweal in Minneapolis uses a debit card known as the Community HeroCard, which holds both dollars and time credits. This can be used in the mainstream economy to purchase goods and services with a mixture of hard cash and time. The Mall of America – the biggest shopping mall in the US – was an early backer, charging in time instead of dollars in the restaurants and the theme park to encourage people to come during quiet periods.[40]
- TimeBank, a UK project with backing from the Home Office and the BBC, has a website (www.timebank.org.uk) linking people with local volunteering opportunities. This is not strictly e-commerce, but linked to a time bank at the local level it would enable people to earn time credits for taking part. During its first six months of operation in 2000, the TimeBank campaign attracted donations of over one million hours.
- iverb is a website (www.iverb.org) that provides a reserve of goods and equipment that time banks elsewhere can buy. Individual time banks donate products in return for time credits. Other time banks can log requests online, and iverb will match them with what they

have, or approach corporate donors if they can't. They also organize the paperwork so that donors can offset their donation against tax.
- London Time Bank, led by the NEF, will be a network of time banks across London linked by an umbrella internet bank, which will perform a similar function to iverb, and will also allow people to access their time accounts online.[41]

T-commerce has great potential to give resources that are sorely needed by the human networks in socially-excluded neighbourhoods (and many wealthy ones too). Schemes will increasingly be transferred to the internet so that t-traders can rapidly exchange goods and services, check balances, and search for other volunteer brokers. Local authorities and multiple retailers will also be interested in the opportunity to link time banks with smart cards and other emerging technologies, as a way of providing the benefits of the internet to those who will never own a home PC.

There is a tax issue to resolve. Time banking has been zero-rated for tax on both sides of the Atlantic, but it would affect benefits if time credits were spent on goods like refurbished computers. This has to be changed so that IT equipment suppliers – whether new or secondhand – can accept payments in time from socially-excluded people. There is also a big task for central and local government, businesses and voluntary organizations to collaborate in building up a local infrastructure of time banks. But t-commerce could be a very powerful way to promote inclusion in the digital age.

Conclusions

It is customary for researchers to conclude with a plea for more in-depth research about the impacts e-commerce is likely to have on disadvantaged neighbourhoods, and there is no doubt that it will be important to develop a more sophisticated understanding of these impacts if we are to accentuate the positive and obviate the negative. However, we already understand enough to outline a package of opportunities that exist to address the human and social weaknesses in mainstream e-commerce.

Opportunities for government
The following are some of the ways in which the government could contribute to inclusivity. It could:

- provide financial support to enable local information networks to transform themselves into GEMs, which provide a secure and trusted environment for local people and small businesses to trade goods, skills and other resources online;
- invest in e-marketing training for SMEs, and develop infrastructure that links small e-commerce sites to regional development and tourism sites. This process could be coordinated by the Small Business Service;
- outline a bold and clear vision for the Post Office network in the new economy as a centre for e-commerce delivery, micro-manufacturing, time banking and credit unions.

Opportunities for business and venture capital

The following are some of the ways in which business could contribute to inclusivity. It could:

- work with local authorities and community organizations to develop new ways for people without credit or debit cards to purchase goods and services online, for example with local smart cards.
- Major e-commerce sites and portals such as AOL, Yahoo! and MSN should make a commitment to provide local commercial content.

Opportunities for voluntary organizations

The following are some of the ways in which voluntary organizations could contribute to inclusivity. They could:

- establish a new-economy equivalent of the Peace Corps – a major volunteering network that can train local people in IT skills and set up web sites for communities and small businesses in low-income areas;
- extend computer refurbishment schemes and link them to a new generation of recycling centres to adapt IT equipment for excluded groups and disabled people.

Taken together, these measures would go some way towards enabling poor communities to reap the full benefits of e-commerce, to surf rather than sink on the waves of the new economy.

Notes and references

1   Office of the E-Envoy (2000) *UK Online Annual Report*, www.e-envoy.gov.uk, September

2   Schenker, J (1999) 'The Communications Revolution: Languages of Technology', *Time*, 11 October

3   Booz-Allen & Hamilton (2000) *Achieving Universal Access*, London

4   Data vary: figures from National Statistics (2000) *First Release on Internet Access*, London, September, are higher than NOP's regular Internet User Profile Studies.

5   Graph derived from NOP Internet User Profile Study, August 2000; data on actual access by D and E groups of partly skilled and unskilled workers, plus two s-curve extrapolations generated by NEF showing slow initial uptake, acceleration in the middle phase, and then a tailing off. In the pessimistic forecast, 20 per cent would not be online by 2010, meaning around three million people out of a population of 15 million low-income (DE) people in the UK over the age of 15.

6   This figure ties in with another estimate that puts DTV penetration at 87 per cent by 2008 (Henderson Crosthwaite Institutional Brokers, cited in ESRC Centre for Research on Innovation and Competition (1999) *Exploring the Effects of E-commerce*, ESRC, London)

7   Cabinet Office (1999) *Closing the Digital Divide: Report of Policy Action Team 15*, Cabinet Office, London

8   Department of Trade and Industry (1999) *Unwanted Computer Equipment: A Guide to Re-use*, London

9   Christie, I and Mensah-Coker, G (1999) *An Inclusive Future? Disability, Social Change and Opportunities for Greater Inclusion by 2010*, Demos, London

10 DETR (1999) *Quality of Life Counts*, HMSO, London, p74. See also www.standards.dfee.gov.uk

11 Mayo, E et al (1998) *Small is Bankable: Community Reinvestment in the UK*, New Economics Foundation/Joseph Rowntree Foundation, York

12 French, D (2000) *The Case for Community Banking*, New Economics Foundation Pocketbook, London

13 Kempson, E and Whyley, C (1999) *Kept Out or Opted Out? Understanding and Combating Financial Exclusion*, Joseph Rowntree Foundation, York

14 Unpublished New Economics Foundation survey for London Borough of Southwark, 2000

15 Prahalad, C K (2000) 'Let's Focus on the Digital Dividend' in *Is E-commerce Destined to Divide Us?* www.europeanbusinessforum.com

16 Williams, M and Boyle, D (1999) *The Customer Contact Continuum: A Model for Customer Relationship Management*, The Listening Company, London

17 Carey, K and Ussher, F (2000) *Can Europe Make IT Happen? Full Participation in the Information Age*, Centre for European Reform, London

18 www.ukonline.StatMap

19 Only 450,000 SMEs out of several million, according to DTI Press Notice P/2000/614, 11 September 2000

20 Mayo et al, op cit

21 www.ukonline.StatMap

22 www.forrester.com

23 www.can-online.org.uk

24 Social Exclusion Unit (2000) *National Strategy for Neighbourhood Renewal*, Cabinet Office, London

25 See www.innercity25.org, NEF's joint initiative with the Treasury to produce an index of the fastest-growing enterprises in inner-city areas.

26 Contact bernie.ward@neweconomics.org for details.

27 Retail E-commerce Task Force (2000) *Clicks and Mortar: The New Store Fronts*, Foresight/DTI, London; Performance and Innovation Unit (2000) *Counter Revolution: Modernising the Post Office Network*, Cabinet Office, London

28 www.linct.org

29 See for example Boyle, D (1999) *Virtual Currencies*, Financial Times Management Reports, London

30 www.peoplink.org

31 www.gorbalslive.org.uk

32 www.digitalsites.infoville.net

33 *Smart Card News*, February 1999

34 Rowan, W (1997) *Guaranteed Electronic Markets*, Demos, London; Performance and Innovation Unit (1999) *e-commerce@its.best.uk*, Cabinet Office, London

35 Rowan, W (1999) *Net Benefit: The Ultimate Potential of Online Trade*, Macmillan, London

36 www.home.digitalcity.com

37 Douthwaite, R (1996) *Short Circuit*, Green Books, Hartland

38 Hudson, H et al (1999) *Making LETS Work in Low Income Areas*, Forum for the Future, Cheltenham

39 DfEE (2000) *ICT Access and Use: Interim Summary Report*, London

40 Boyle, D (1999) *Funny Money: In Search of Alternative Cash*, HarperCollins, London

41 Boyle, D (2000) *Why London Needs its own Currency*, New Economics Foundation Pocketbook, London

Response

by Kevin Carey

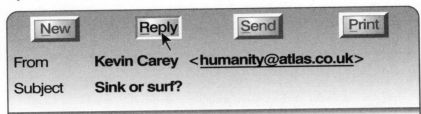

From   **Kevin Carey**   **<humanity@atlas.co.uk>**

Subject   **Sink or surf?**

The socially excluded, as defined for benefits payments and public expenditure, are a subset of the IT excluded; and the IT excluded, in the literal sense of being unable to access hardware, operating systems, software and telecommunications, are a subset of those who cannot operate effectively in cyberspace. The failure to understand this is the key marketing failure of e-commerce. Half of the potential market for e-commerce has not been properly analysed to identify the barriers to market expansion. If those managers responsible are on performance-related pay, their salaries should be halved.

The root of the problem is not economic, and will be even less so with the digital revitalization of telephones and televisions. The key to internet exclusion is the gap between people and information. This, of course, can be tackled in two ways: improve the functional efficiency of people; or improve the design and the ease of customization of information systems.

The UK government is repeatedly and dogmatically failing to reduce exclusion by adapting formal education to meet the challenges and opportunities of broadband multimedia. It still sticks to the rule that the more complex the system, the fewer people can use it unless they are given all the appropriate skills. This ignores two factors: as systems become more complex, it is useless to expect everyone to be able to do everything; and the more complex the system, the more people can contribute something. Thus, although reading and writing will continue to be vital, there are many tasks that internet users can perform that do not depend upon them. The metaphor for our time is the movie, not the novel.

At the other side of the gap there is design and customization. Just because a government report is available online does not mean that it is accessible. There will always be a limit to literacy, but to be only partially literate does not mean that you only have part of a vote. The science of information simplification is still primitive but is vital in all areas of presentation.

It is easy to see why a government rightly obsessed with improving basic educational standards has mistakenly focused on too narrow a definition of literacy, and why its civil servants are more anxious about the quantity of information posted on the internet rather than the form. But such a lack of basic understanding on the part of business is puzzling. The fundamentals of information and systems design are hardly daunting; the user needs to get hold of the information, understand it, navigate inside a system, respond to requests, and post unsolicited contributions. At the same time, the information must be adaptable for people with learning, physical, hearing or sight problems. These cases are not just the few emphasized by charity fund raisers. There are millions of people with minor, chronic disabilities, such as arthritis, which make contemporary cyberspace difficult if not impossible to navigate.

A difficulty lies at the heart of this discussion, which Alex MacGillivray and David Boyle hardly address. Excluded people of all kinds would prefer to be included in a society that makes financial and social allowances for each individual on the basis of equal concern and respect. They would prefer not to be specially categorized or to have special programmes that describe them as a 'problem'. A fully knowing market is a better way of dealing with this problem than altruism or regulation, but unless e-commerce takes seriously the prospect of making money from the 'missing half' of its market, we will have to fall back on older, supposedly discredited, ways. ∎

6 Towards the sustainable e-region

Ian Christie and Mark Hepworth

Introduction

Place matters: geography and the information economy

In many visions of the new economy, geography is seen as something to be transcended by technology. The electronic revolution brings about the 'death of distance' and ICTs free us to work anywhere, tele-commuting and connecting effortlessly with people and websites around the planet.[1] Perhaps it will turn out that way; but for the moment, this vision of the irrelevance of geography is quite wrong. Place matters, and it has a significant bearing on the social and environmental sustainability of the emerging information economy. Two stories from the year 2000 illustrate this point.

In September 2000, the internet recruitment business Boldly-go.com published research into the location of dot-com companies in the UK. Almost 80 per cent of these businesses are based in the south-east of England, with London accounting for almost 60 per cent. The two big clusters of ICT businesses in Scotland and Cambridge (Silicon Glen and Silicon Fen) account for just 4 per cent and 3 per cent respectively of UK dot-coms. As one entrepreneur explained, 'If venture capitalists can't drive to it, they don't invest in it. Start-ups go where investors are. That's why there is this concentration in London.'[2]

Secondly, an iconic image of futurist literature about the information economy is that of the wired rural community, with high-tech workers operating from rustic tele-cottages. Such a vision recently inspired the creation of an award-winning development of 39 'wired' houses in Crickhowell, Powys, in mid-Wales; but although it was intended to become a model 21st-century sustainable community, the development was forced to call in the receivers in October 2000, after one-third of the properties remained unsold.

Two important points and one crucial caveat arise from reflection on these stories. First, e-commerce is based in, and gravitates towards, the existing areas of greatest economic dynamism. It follows the contours of economic development. Second, there is no mass movement towards tele-commuting and rural location for e-business. The work of the information economy goes on in cities. Far from tele-commuting on a large scale, the workers of the information economy seem to be living in suburbs and rural areas and driving or catching the train to go to offices, just as old economy employees do.

All this points to an important issue for policy on the e-economy. It has no intrinsic dynamic that makes it socially equitable or environmentally friendly in terms of its impact on living patterns. The e-economy maps on to the existing geography of economic and social division, and the geography of car-intensive commuting. If it is to become more socially inclusive, and if its potential for contributing to more environmentally sustainable lifestyles is to be harnessed, policy will need to be devised to shape its evolution in a more positive direction.

The caveat is that e-commerce could be a powerful vehicle for sustainable development, opening up opportunities for marginalized areas and communities and helping to change the unsustainable geography of work and home. The UK is potentially developing some of the institutions and policies at regional and local level that could make this come about. The challenge is to make the connections between e-commerce, sustainability and regional governance.

The policy background: the new geography of governance

New Labour has committed itself to a radical programme of modernization of the UK's policies and institutions, to make them fit to meet what it sees as the major challenges of the new century. Heavily influenced by visions of the 'weightless economy' of services and information, it has embraced the idea that a new economy, powered by ICTs and e-commerce, is the paradigm for 21st century industrialism.

It has signalled its belief in a radical reinvention of governance in the UK, with devolution to Scotland, Wales and Northern Ireland; the beginnings of major reform in local government; and the establishment of a new regional framework for economic development. The Scottish Parliament and the Welsh Assembly have brought political leadership and accountability to economic development in their nations, building upon the regeneration programmes of Scottish Enterprise and the Welsh Development Agency. In April 1999, eight business-led regional development agencies (RDAs) began work across England, and the London Development Agency started work in 2000, following the election of the new mayor and the members of the Greater London Assembly.

The English RDA regions, plus the nations of Scotland, Northern Ireland and Wales – what we will call here, for convenience, 'the regions' – have already started to implement strategies for economic competitiveness, social cohesion and environmental sustainability. The RDAs and their counterparts, along with government, take the view that these long-term aims can only be achieved if the regions are successful in creating knowledge-driven information economies.

However, as we try to show in this chapter, there is a long way to go in integrating the vision of sustainable development and the vision of a dynamic ICT-led economy. The issues we consider are as follows.

- The unharnessed potential of the new economy to underpin many aspects of sustainable development.
- The strong regional, local and income variations in internet access.
- The lack, so far, of a virtuous relationship between e-commerce and tele-working.
- The difficulties in linking strategies for environmental sustainability and social inclusion with those to promote economic development and growth.

The new economy and regional development

The promise and problems of e-commerce and sustainable development

The literature and media hype surrounding the development of information technology have fuelled hopes that there is a deep affinity between the ICT revolution and more environmentally and socially sustainable development. There is much to be said for this – but also many caveats to be entered against it.

First, there is the claim that the e-economy is evolving towards dematerialization. The fact is that while there are many ways in which the new economy can contribute to reductions in energy and material use, there are also many ways in which it can fuel demand for products and environmentally-damaging consumption. This dual potential is displayed in relation to the other claims that have been made for the new economy.

A second argument is that the e-economy will create more environmentally-friendly patterns of mobility, by enabling tele-working and virtual commuting on a massive scale through technologies such as video conferencing, email, interactive TV and, in time, advanced forms of tele-presence. Again, in theory this is possible; but in practice, the e-economy seems overwhelmingly likely – in the absence of countervailing policies – to do what all previous advances in telecommunications have done; feed the demand for real travel and physical contact as well as virtual contact.

Third, there is the view that cyberspace is a space without a place, and that e-enterprise can be based anywhere as long as it is connected to the internet. This opens up the possibility of currently disadvantaged areas becoming more prosperous through engagement in the virtual economy, overcoming geographical, economic and social marginality; but it also means that there could be a reinforcement of the advantage of already prosperous areas. In spatial terms, the new economy displays features that have been apparent in previous waves of structural change and technological diffusion in the industrial economy. Some of them are outlined below.

The synergy between wheels and wires

Telecommunications and transport systems have always interacted in their contribution to the industrial economy. Telecommunication systems increase the level of transactions and negotiations, and stimulate mobility of people and goods. Advances in mobility increase the number of encounters and possible transactions, and in turn stimulate more use of telecommunications. Wheels and wires, in short, have a symbiotic existence in industrial economies.[3] There is no reason to expect that the new economy will be any different. It is not an autonomous entity – much of it depends on the old economy of manufacturing and distribution to provide and deliver the goods that are ordered over the internet.

The tendency towards clustering

The economist Michael Porter, among others, has drawn attention to the tendency of companies to form geographical clusters within the same or related sectors.[4] Clustering offers the advantages of proximity to finance, transportation, suppliers and customers; access to skilled workers and peers; and membership of networks of professional practice through which ideas and information may be swapped. As we will see later, the UK knowledge economy, of which e-commerce forms a part, shows all the classic signs of clustering, and this is being promoted energetically by national and regional policy makers.

These trends pose complex problems for sustainable development. First, the synergy between wheels and wires is overwhelmingly one between ICT and road use, for both commuting and freight. Any government introducing radical policies to curb road use in the name of sustainability is likely to be inhibited by fears of damaging competitiveness in the new economy, as well as in the old one. Enhancing the economic sustainability of the e-economy is potentially in conflict with measures to reduce the environmental damage inflicted by mounting volumes of road traffic.

Second, the tendency towards clustering can counter hopes of sustainable development. The concentration of the knowledge economy in clusters in already highly prosperous and congested areas means that these areas will become steadily less sustainable in environmental terms – a state of affairs prefigured in California's Silicon Valley, which is economically dynamic, yet badly polluted and lacking in quality of life as a result of over-development. Successful clustering also means that the less affluent in a desired area suffer from rising property prices and lack of affordable housing, while competition rises for social goods like access to good schools. The effect of an economically viable cluster might thus be socially unsustainable; recent reports on the Cambridge and Thames Valley clusters in the UK emphasize the problems of congestion and lack of housing provision for public-sector workers.[5] Also, clustering is a zero-sum game – not every area can have a Silicon Valley or Fen or Glen. Clustering works against sustainability on a wider spatial scale.

Nothing in these developments is surprising. Nor do any of these outcomes rule out the possibility that in the longer term the new economy could rewrite the rules of economic development. Yet this is highly unlikely unless the potential effect of the e-economy as a catalyst for more sustainable development is reinforced by active policy to shape national and regional change. Without that, the e-economy is likely to continue to reflect, rather than transform, the social, environmental and economic maps of the UK.

New governance, new strategies, old problems

The government's approach to sustainable regional economic development is based on creating new governance structures and processes, as well as promoting joined-up strategies that tackle economic competitiveness, social inclusion and environmental sustainability. This holistic view of regional development is reflected in the objectives pursued by development bodies in England, Scotland and Wales. However, in practice the goals that have most prominence tend to be economic, as shown in Box 6.1.

To judge by the evidence of published strategies, the linkages between ICT, e-commerce and sustainable development are few and far between. While all the RDAs and their counterparts are enthusiasts for harnessing the power of the e-economy, there is scarcely a reference to the ways in which e-commerce and ICT more generally can reinforce or hamper moves towards a more environmentally sustainable economy. Even in the otherwise admirable and comprehensive north-west England sustainable development action plan, the linkages between e-commerce and sustainability are not explored.

The environmental impacts of e-commerce have received far less attention than the social impacts, reflecting the more developed debate on the digital divide between information haves and have-nots in the UK. Very few of the strategic policy documents on regional development make the link between promoting e-commerce and its potential to support environmental sustainability through dematerialization and tele-substitution for travel.

The regions have become more attentive in their publications to the role of cleaner production in manufacturing, and to the scope for promoting renewable energy and other environmental technologies. There are few signs, though, of strategic thinking about how e-commerce and sustainable spatial development can go together. In particular, during our interviews and workshops with key stakeholders in the regions, numerous interviewees expressed concern that the rebound effect of ICT developments might not be adequately dealt with by national and regional policies. For example, little notice is taken of the environmental impacts of policies to promote knowledge clusters in areas that are largely dependent on road access.

Interviewees also noted a practical problem in joining up the social, environmental and economic agendas to achieve sustainable e-commerce at regional and local levels. They argued that RDAs and other agencies often lack good information about where the enterprises and other key players in the information economy are operating. While the

---

Box 6.1 Strategic objectives of development bodies in England, Scotland and Wales

The aims of the Scottish Enterprise Network Strategy are as follows.

- A Scotland powered by innovative and far-sighted organizations.
- A Scotland with positive attitudes to learning and enterprise.
- A Scotland with an inclusive approach to economic development.
- A Scotland that is a competitive place in the world economy.

Source: Scottish Enterprise (1999) *Scottish Enterprise Network Strategy*, Edinburgh

The vision for Wales as set out in *Pathway to Prosperity* is as follows.

- Our vision is based on developing a high-quality, innovative economy attracting inward investment but with a strong emphasis on helping indigenous Welsh enterprises to grow and compete. Achievement of this goal is inextricably linked to the need for a well-educated, highly skilled and well-motivated workforce, and to a first class business infrastructure. Wales needs quality enterprises, whatever their source or size, and we need them distributed throughout Wales.

Source: Welsh Office (1998) *Pathway to Prosperity: A New Economic Agenda for Wales*, Cardiff

The objectives of the English RDAs and the London Development Agency are as follows.

- Economic development and social and physical regeneration.
- Business support, investment and competitiveness.
- Enhancing skills.
- Promoting employment.
- Sustainable development.

Source: See, for example, South East England Development Agency (1999) *Building a World Class Region*, Guildford; One North East (1999) *Unlocking our Potential*, Newcastle.

RDAs and their counterparts are active in developing databases to inform their research and strategic planning, most have yet to build up a clear picture of the key elements of local and regional sustainability in relation to e-commerce. These elements would include:

- Where and how the new information economy is developing, and what policies (if any) are being developed by dot-coms and other information economy players to promote social inclusion and environmental sustainability.

- Where community initiatives are closing the digital divide locally, and where there are particular concentrations of digital disadvantage.
- Where good practice in environmental strategies, technologies and business operations is developing, regionally and locally.

Without such mapping of the regions, it is very hard to forge partnerships between the information economy, local communities and environmental initiatives. One respondent noted that in his region he could identify scores of projects to promote e-commerce and foster links between business and the public and community sectors, but hardly any of these made any reference to sustainable development and environmental policy; nor would he know how to start in making connections between the e-commerce world in his region and the regional players in environmental technology and green business.

ICT and e-commerce in regional economic strategies

Economic competitiveness

In drawing up their economic strategies, the regions have paid greatest attention to benchmarking themselves against other EU regions. This approach has fostered a degree of competitiveness between regions, which many of our respondents regarded as negative and harmful to the cause of sustainable development.

Only two out of the eleven UK regions – London and the south east – reach the European average for economic prosperity, measured by GDP per capita. The key economic challenge facing the new regions, according to guidance from Whitehall and their own strategies, is to grow faster than the rest of Europe over the next 25 years. For the majority of the regions, this means achieving record-level growth rates, starting from positions that lag well behind the EU average.

At the same time, the government requires the regions to improve social inclusion and environmental sustainability. Thus, it seems likely that even in the more advanced regional economies, there will be great pressures to integrate economic, social and environmental objectives. Most respondents suggested that short-term economic priorities will win out much of the time.

Competitiveness is increasingly determined by immaterial or intangible investments in knowledge and information. These weightless investments mostly take the form of services, such as marketing and advertising, research and development, and engineering, management and administration. The contours of the knowledge economy and its impacts on growth, productivity and employment are difficult to identify, let alone quantify. Market boundaries are blurred by the convergence in telecommunications, computing and broadcasting. Most businesses do not or cannot assign a book value to their knowledge assets, and are only just beginning to take an interest in knowledge management. The problems of measuring the new economy are also underlined by the fact that the e-commerce revolution is taking shape across sectors rather than within one, new, dot-com sector.

Social cohesion and the digital divide

The DTI Future Unit's report on the knowledge-driven economy argues that universal internet access should become a cornerstone of the government's information society policies:

'Just as with the telephone network, there are strong social and economic justifications for promoting universal access to these services. Beyond simply the world of work, they will become fundamental components of education and health care, entertainment and social contact ten years hence.'[6]

By 2008, it is likely that most of the UK's population will be able to gain some kind of access via PC, DTV, mobile phone or other devices which will be affordable to nearly every household. The key question regarding the social element of internet take-up is basically about the quality of access and the affordability of regular and extensive use. In many areas, we will witness a skewed pattern of use and access, with poorer households lagging far behind the more affluent majority owing to a variety of factors, some of which are listed below.

- The entry costs of equipment for people on very low incomes.
- The running costs of IT use and line charges for internet access for people on low incomes.
- The inadequacy of IT interfaces for people with impairments of sight, hearing and dexterity.
- The rapid obsolescence of equipment as new technologies are improved and new standards emerge.
- Lack of skills and confidence in using the internet among many people on low incomes.
- Lack of access to the internet via work as a result of unemployment.
- Lack of interest and a perception that the internet is not relevant to one's lifestyle.

Affordable access to telecommunications is a necessary but far from sufficient condition for enhancing social cohesion. Providing greater volumes of information over ICT networks will not lead to greater social cohesion if consumers, employees, investors and citizens lack the knowledge and the financial, political and cultural resources needed to create real economic value out of the information they receive. Access alone is no panacea if the policies do not also address the quality of access, and the ways in which people can make the most of it.

RDA policies that seek to increase social cohesion through ICT need to be aimed at the root causes of information inequalities and the social and economic divisions that lie behind them. Public technology policies aimed at improving ICT skills need to be linked with mainstream policies to improve employment, education and training. Making ICTs an integral dimension of RDA social strategies aimed at tackling social exclusion is a process that can draw on a range of government initiatives. These include the UK Online programme for making government services accessible by internet, the commitment to universal internet access by 2005, the 'IT for All' initiative that will strengthen the role of public libraries as internet gateways, the National Grid for Learning centred on schools, and the University of Industry scheme for delivering online training to workplaces.

Environmental sustainability

ICTs can contribute to environmental sustainability in a number of ways, but making the link is not easy. While the regions are developing increasingly weightless economies in terms of monetary value and intangible services, it is plain to see that even the knowledge-driven economy moves on 'wheels and wires' – the argument made by Mark Hepworth and Ken Ducatel in their book *Transport in the Information Age*.[7] Most information and knowledge is ultimately embodied in physical goods or people's brains – tangible weighty things that still have to be moved around the UK on commuter trains and cars, large trucks and small vans, ships and planes.

All of the regions are focusing in their competitiveness strategies on ways to develop a sustainable transport system and better road and rail links. As one of the major threats to environmental sustainability, the growth in road-dependent transport is a key target for regional sustainable development policies. In this regard, there are a number of applications of telecommunications:

- electronic road pricing to reduce congestion pressure on town centres;

- guidance to improve route selection;
- real-time traffic management to optimize the use of existing roads;
- passenger information systems to make public transport more attractive;
- inter-modal information services; and
- smart card ticketing systems.

The government's ten-year plan for transport, unveiled in 2000, and its programme for urban and rural regeneration, will create opportunities for local and regional partners to develop new strategies and technologies aimed at improving the environmental sustainability of towns and cities. However, our interviews revealed considerable scepticism about the extent of commitment in RDAs and elsewhere to tackling road traffic and car dependence rather than building new road capacity. To achieve greater momentum, the regions should develop stronger Local Agenda 21 initiatives, working closely with the planning authorities, regional chambers and regional government offices.

The geography of the knowledge-driven information economy

Although the UK's nations and regions are at different starting points, they are looking towards the same finishing line; a knowledge-driven information economy that is competitive and sustainable. How far apart the regions are, and how wide a gap there is between current patterns of development and more sustainable ones, is illustrated below.

Mapping the e-economy

It is possible to benchmark the different regions of the UK in relation to the knowledge-driven economy, but we need to acknowledge that there is a major difficulty in measuring the new economy of immaterial services. The knowledge economy has many faces, given its focus on creativity, innovation, learning, technology and entrepreneurship. These are features of all industries and cover the private and public sector to different degrees. The existing sectoral classifications can only give an approximate picture of what is going on, and there is a great need for better regional and local data on the emerging e-economy and its social and environmental dimensions.

Figure 6.1 below shows the degree to which local economies special-ize in information society sectors, and the degree to which knowledge workers are geographically concentrated by residence. Information society sectors are defined broadly to include ICT-goods production, ICT-related services, and the content and multimedia industries.

The map shows that the main geographical features of the informa-tion economy in Great Britain are:

- Metropolitan dominance; larger cities dominate the information economy at the regional and national levels – London most obviously, then regional capitals, such as Bristol in the south west, Birmingham in the west Midlands, Edinburgh in Scotland and Leeds in Yorkshire and Humberside.
- North–south divide. There is a deep north–south split across the UK; the knowledge economy fans out from London northwards to Cambridge and Birmingham and westwards and southwards in the M3–M4 arc.
- Local divides. There is considerable local variation in the depth of the knowledge economy within each region – it is glaringly shallow in vast swathes of the UK, both north and south and within London itself.

The geographical distribution of knowledge workers is more even across the country. This is due to several factors:

- Large numbers of knowledge workers live outside metropolitan employment centres and commute to work, mostly by road, from suburbs and smaller urban centres;
- High technology manufacturing is more evenly distributed across the regions, with strong local pockets, though its share of regional employment is very small;
- The public sector is a major employer of knowledge workers, with population-led services being more dispersed, within local govern-ment, health authorities and so on; and
- Micro-firms are top-heavy in managerial functions. They are widely dispersed, often home-based, and account for a growing share of new jobs.

Figure 6.1 highlights the degree to which London and the south east regions dominate the information economy within Great Britain. More generally though, what the map shows is that the information economy is characterized by metropolitan dominance – that is to say, bigger cities

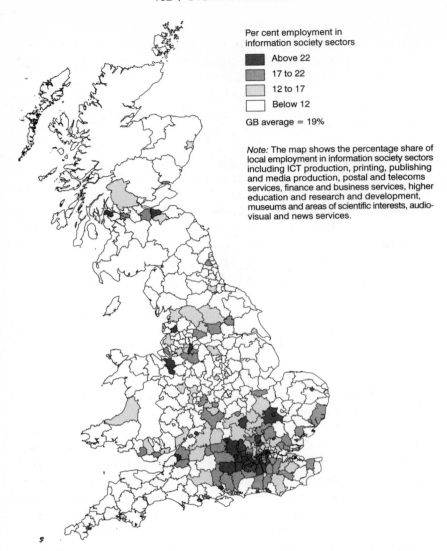

Per cent employment in
information society sectors

Above 22

17 to 22

12 to 17

Below 12

GB average = 19%

Note: The map shows the percentage share of
local employment in information society sectors
including ICT production, printing, publishing
and media production, postal and telecoms
services, finance and business services, higher
education and research and development,
museums and areas of scientific interests, audio-
visual and news services.

**Figure 6.1   London dominates the knowledge-driven
information economy**

are emerging as powerful economic centres in their own right, linking
their regions to the global economy. Yet the pattern is more complex
than this suggests. Not only is there a clear division between regions,
and between big cities and their regions, but there is a further division
within the cities. For example, within London, as Figure 6.2 shows,
different boroughs are in quite different positions. This pattern is
repeated across the UK in cities and wider metropolitan areas.

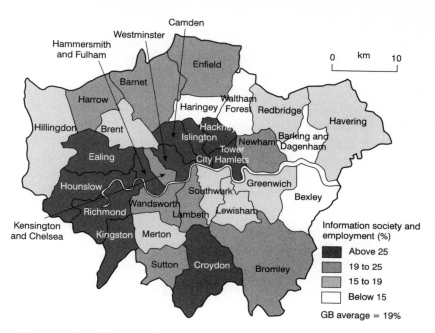

Figure 6.2 **The different positions of Camden and Lewisham in London's information economy**

The relative competitiveness of Camden and Lewisham cannot be seen in Figure 6.1. On the surface, they both appear to be located at the very core of the UK's knowledge economy. However, as Figure 6.2 shows, London's dominance of UK economic growth – and the better paid jobs that go with this – is not reflected across the whole of the capital. Local competitiveness varies significantly within Europe's most powerful global city. Whilst Camden is one of the strongest local information economies in the country – being part of the global city core – Lewisham is located on the weaker south-eastern side of London.

Through our Local Internet Futures programme,[8] we have examined social exclusion in four different case study areas. Ward-level maps were generated to indicate patterns of deprivation in each area – the inference being that a digital divide correlates closely with low incomes, weak educational attainment and other aspects of social deprivation. For example, on the basis of the government's index of deprivation, Bradford is a 'divided district'. Bradford City Council's recent vision statement includes a long-term ambition to combat deprivation by building a knowledge-driven economy. However, the Camden experience suggests that realizing this economic vision will not necessarily end Bradford's social exclusion problems. Camden is located in the glittering core of the information economy, but significantly its deprivation problems are among the worst in the country. We have dubbed this 'the Camden paradox'; in the knowledge economy, extremes of economic competitiveness and social exclusion co-exist alongside one another.

The digital divide is accompanied by a division between cities as centres of ICT work and rural or suburban areas as residential places for knowledge workers. It is a feature of the UK's major cities that great swathes of the knowledge workforce abandon urban areas at night and weekends, and return home to the suburbs and countryside. This reinforces the pressures for housing development in green belts, which have caused so much concern among policy makers and the public and led to calls for an 'urban renaissance'.[9]

Few of these findings are surprising: growth in new sectors will always tend to be concentrated where money, clients and skills are to be found. The e-economy maps on to the contours of the old economy. The tendency for clustering of e-commerce and the information economy in and around cities is the result of many factors:

- Cities provide access to a critical mass of finance, brokers, partners, contacts, customers, suppliers, distribution networks, business services, ideas, amenities and workers;
- Clusters of enterprises within a sector or centred on a supply chain relationship form in cities for similar reasons – access to people, money, ideas, leisure services, high quality housing and transport;
- Dot-com enterprises that need access to finance, and find that service sectors are already concentrated in cities, will tend to cluster there;
- Tele-commuting on a large scale has yet to take off because of the reluctance of employers and workers to embrace the organizational changes it requires;
- Long-standing preferences for living in suburbs and the countryside and commuting to towns have yet to be challenged by the new economy. They are in any case reinforced by the failure of urban regeneration strategies to persuade more people that living in cities can be good for their quality of life;
- The roll-out of ICTs naturally begins in areas of greatest demand where infrastructure can be easily installed; this gives cumulative advantage to urban areas, while remote rural areas remain less economically attractive for cabling and other ICT investment; and
- The information economy depends on well-educated and motivated workers, and has relatively little need for people at lower skill levels, so the socially excluded find few job openings in the absence of much improved education and training opportunities.

The regional and local challenge

The structure of the information economy in Britain is clearly evident in Figure 6.1 above. The challenge of economic modernization is immense in regions such as the north east, the north west and the Midlands, in which traditional manufacturing and rural development are still important to growth and employment. In regions where the information economy is strong overall – such as the south west, the east of England and the south east – there are clear east–west sub-regional divides that mirror the north–south divide in the UK as a whole. These sub-regional divides are evident within London, with the east of the capital lagging behind the west. The centralized structure of the information economy in Scotland and Wales is also widely recognized.

History and market forces have combined to create the contemporary geography of the UK information economy; but what does the future hold, and what do the regions face? Three factors need to be considered as potential barriers to more sustainable development.

1   The national map of average male earnings is strikingly similar to the map shown in Figure 6.1. This gives lagging regions a powerful incentive to try to emulate development patterns in the south east, which are clearly at odds with environmental and social sustainability.
2   The national map for the roll-out of broadband ICT infrastructure is also similar to Figure 6.1; London, the big cities and the clusters of development in the south east and along the Thames corridor will have priority in the absence of policies to stimulate provision in more marginal areas.
3   Figure 6.1 also shows a clear correlation with the map of car ownership, and the clusters map on to the worst zones of road congestion and pressure for housing development. The information economy has evolved along with, and has promoted, intensive road use.

Clearly, the regions need to develop highly skilled workforces if they are to compete in a global economy that depends on creativity, innovation and entrepreneurship. In the absence of a dynamic, market-based information economy, we are likely to witness a brain drain from the lagging regions in the Midlands and the north to London and the south, adding to pressures on transport and housing.

This pattern is already present in the market for IT skills. London and the south east have a huge monopoly on the country's best IT talent, with university graduates migrating southwards to the heartlands of the information economy. As Figure 6.3 shows, 9 out of the 11 regions have

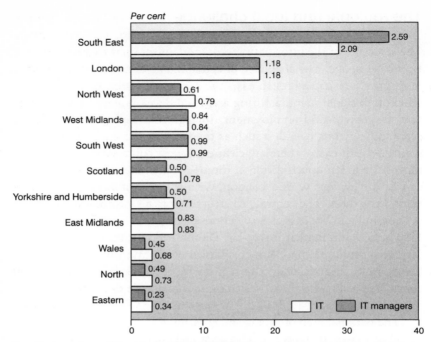

Note: Regional share of IT employment in Great Britain (%); the figures are location quotients that measure the degree to which IT employment is under (<1) or over represented (>1) in the region

Figure 6.3   Regional concentration in the British IT workforce, 1997

massive ICT skills deficits. How will they attract inward investors, for whom ICT skills are now more important than telecommunications infrastructure? How will they develop new technology-based businesses and high-tech clusters as the government's white paper on competitiveness envisages? These are key issues that the RDAs will need to address in partnership with the Small Business Service and the learning and skills councils.

These regional and local imbalances cast doubt on the capacity of e-commerce and ICT to become a motor for rapid economic development outside London and the south east. People and opportunities are gravitating to the south east, shifting talent and resources from the disadvantaged areas. The regional advantage of the south east is so great, and the urban bias of the new economy so substantial, that it is hard to see how e-commerce can be a decisive factor in regenerating other areas in the absence of wider policies for regional redistribution and promotion of demand.

Extending access to ICT is not a panacea in the disadvantaged areas; ensuring that everyone in the worst-off parts of, say, Merseyside has access to the internet will not necessarily do anything to improve their social inclusion and economic prospects. For that to happen, internet access needs to be accompanied by access to money, jobs, education, healthcare, training and markets. To attract more clustering by new enterprise, such areas need to offer the same high quality access to services (finance, transport, well-educated recruits and so on) that attracts clusters in the south east and in big cities. In short, ICTs and e-commerce cannot do the job of economic regeneration on their own. Even if they could, deprived regions would still be far behind the core areas of the information economy in the south of England, where the right ingredients for rapid e-commerce development are already in place.

The spatial tensions of the e-economy

It seems clear that the geography of the information economy, as it has developed so far, has reflected and contributed to existing social and economic divisions, and to the environmental problems caused by road transport. The key patterns are:

- clustering in and around major cities;
- significant divisions between and within regions;
- divisions within urban areas between wealthy and deprived neighbourhoods;
- the 'Camden paradox', which states that strong local information economies exist alongside deep social deprivation and exclusion from ICTs; and
- correlation between the information economy and the pressure points on transport and housing.

What is also clear is that further market-led development of the information economy in itself will not do much to tackle the problems posed. If we are to get more sustainable development, then policies to promote ICT need to run alongside, and be integrated with, policies to combat poverty, to regenerate cities, and to curb road use by making public transport and tele-working more attractive.

Our research suggests that RDAs and their counterparts so far lack the strategic tools to tackle these issues in a joined-up way. What all this implies is the need for the rapid development of a coherent culture of regional governance in which such tensions can be aired and resolved. New forums for consensus building, and the development of clear regional strategies that can be communicated effectively to the population at large, will be vital for this. ICTs will play a key role in making new linkages.

Towards more sustainable development: an e-region strategy

The conclusion we draw from our interviews and mapping work is that the UK needs a strategic approach to e-commerce, ICT and sustainability that starts at the national level and is followed through regionally and locally. This approach should use public–private partnerships to embed ICTs into all aspects of the new regional development strategies, economic, social and environmental.

At present, the information economy is reinforcing some unsustainable elements of the old economy. We see major inequalities of access to the internet by class and area; large gaps between and within the regions of the UK; and close correlations between areas of unsustainable demand for road use and housing and those areas of greatest prosperity. It seems clear that national, regional and local strategies for sustainable development do not yet have sufficient grip on actual activity on the ground. Many respondents fear that there is a serious failure to join up policies that could harness the potential of e-commerce and ICT to promote sustainability. RDAs in particular seem to be driven principally by a vision of increasing GDP growth and of creating clusters of knowledge-intensive business, with little practical attention to sustainable development thinking despite frequent references to it in strategy documents. In the light of this, we propose an e-region strategy for moving the regions into the information age as a new and important dimension of sustainable development.

A vision of the future: the sustainable e-region

We have proposed elsewhere[10] a vision of the e-region that could be applied to all nations and regions of the UK. The e-region would connect the information society with the three dimensions of sustainable development. It would make creative and innovative use of ICT to bring about long-term improvements in the competitiveness of its economy, the cohesion of its society and the quality of its environment. Most importantly, it would be backed by political and business leaders and widely understood across the region. Political, voluntary sector and business champions will be essential to making the vision a reality.

The e-region would need to be integrated into wider economic strategies so that the impacts of technology could be assessed in terms of organizational and regional performance. This was also found to be a critical success factor in the European Digital Cities programme, which found that information society initiatives tend not to be sufficiently integrated into wider development policies.[11]

Regional economic strategies should contain five types of basic competitiveness initiative: building a strong base of information society businesses; applying e-commerce to supply chains; developing a competitive base of ICT skills; creating an effective business support system for SMEs; and mobilizing the regional science and knowledge base to create clusters. These are all goals that RDAs and their counterparts are pursuing.

However, they need to be accompanied by, and integrated with, the pursuit of social and environmental goals. This requires a clear perspective on the spatial problems of an information economy which still depends on road-borne mobility and commuting patterns. As one respondent put it, we need strategies that enable people in rural areas to work more often where they live, and enable those in cities to live much nearer to where they work. RDAs need to work with government and local authorities to pursue policies that will regenerate rural areas to make them less marginal in the information economy and more capable of providing jobs and affordable housing. They also need to focus on urban renaissance strategies that make city living more affordable and attractive to those currently forced into long commuter journeys from the suburbs and countryside.[12]

There is a need for joined-up action at national, regional and local levels to ensure that the digital divide is truly overcome. As we have stressed, securing universal internet access will not be enough to achieve this. The key issue in disadvantaged areas is the lack of money, skills, confidence, access to networks of opportunity and learning, and local capacity for partnerships between business, public and community bodies. Overcoming these problems will require strategy and policy to combat poverty, rather than the provision of physical access to the internet via PCs, DTV or other media. The regions could apply the e-region concept to improve social cohesion in several ways.

- They should aim to develop socially cohesive information societies that guarantee universal and equal access to the labour market, welfare, community life and local governance;
- They should ensure that a training and education infrastructure is available, offering affordable training in core IT skills and in the use of the internet;

- They should promote the integration of ICT into regeneration projects wherever possible. These projects should be framed by local information society strategies, tuned to the particular needs and aspirations of the areas concerned, and integrated with policies for enterprise, training, education, health, libraries and community care;
- Where appropriate, they should produce rural information society strategies that address the ICT needs of specific sectors, such as tourism and agriculture, and of isolated towns and smaller settlements. These should focus on the use of ICT-based services like teleworking, tele-medicine and tele-shopping to promote sustainability; and
- They should implement electronic governance systems that improve public and individual access to policy-making forums, as well as providing the information needed to make an effective input.

Our review of existing competitiveness strategies shows that modernizing regional transport systems is a top priority in all regions. Even in the information age, the regions need world-class 'wheels' and 'wires' to compete successfully. However, policy makers also need to focus on reductions in the demand for road use and on ways to boost ICT-based alternatives to mobility. The e-regions concept could be applied to improve environmental sustainability and quality of life in the following ways:

- Communications 2020 action plans that exploit the joint potential of 'wheels and wires' could be developed to enhance sustainable mobility and accessibility. The impacts of this should be measured in terms of trip reduction and online labour markets;
- The production and use of transport telematics, such as electronic road pricing and passenger information systems, could be promoted, building on the region's science base and EU research and development funding;
- ICTs and other environmental initiatives could be integrated through community intranets, electronic conferencing, and environmental monitoring and information services that can be easily accessed; and
- The sustainability of existing clusters of enterprise should be assessed, especially in terms of road dependence, and international best practice in planning should be explored for 'industrial ecology' clusters of green business, where one business can process the waste of another, and organizations work together to reduce waste, energy consumption and road travel needs.

Implementation: partnerships and benchmarks

The UK government and the EU place great emphasis on the role of regional private–public partnerships in driving the information economy. However, these partnerships are not yet well developed, and where they are driven by EU funding they tend to be dominated by the public sector. Moreover, UK government funding for regeneration projects aimed at integrating ICT with social and environmental objectives in the regions is heavily criticized by our interviewees for its short-termism and focus on capital spending rather than revenue support. All too often, promising joined-up projects fail to realize their potential because funding is over-complicated and does not support long-term development.

To overcome these obstacles, the regions should develop best practice models of private–public partnership to ensure sustainable levels of investment. RDAs could boost partnership activity by promoting an e-region challenge competition, in which consortia of towns and cities would compete for innovation funding. The regions could also set up information society forums made up of private, public and voluntary sector partners who can move the e-region concept forwards in terms of policy and institutional frameworks.

Many different national and EU initiatives would contribute in some way to the development of e-regions. However, no agency has an overview of these initiatives or is able to measure how e-regions are developing against a meaningful set of benchmark indicators. To this end, the government should create an e-regions agency to promote awareness, partnerships, research and standards, so that issues are tackled more holistically and partnership opportunities are fully exploited.

Regions should also carry out a benchmark audit of ICT infrastructure in their areas and link this to better information about social and environmental projects, so that key players can be put in touch with one another. This process could perhaps be supported by regional equivalents of the First Tuesday network that has been successful in brokering contacts between e-entrepreneurs and financiers.

Conclusions

The e-region framework is intended to promote the integration of ICT-related initiatives that are in place, or being planned. Its success will also depend on a joined-up approach between national, regional and local levels of governance. We have proposed the e-region as a way of bringing together those different approaches to the information economy which are currently failing to join up. The geography of the information economy is skewed; it is reinforcing existing divisions, while simultaneously bringing new energy and wealth to the areas in which it clusters. The new RDA economic strategies also seem to be skewed towards an over-emphasis on GDP targets. We need policy frameworks that can harness the potential of e-commerce and ICT to produce a more socially and environmentally sustainable map of the UK for the 21st century. The e-region concept offers a tantalizing glimpse of what could be achieved.

Notes and references

1   Cairncross, F (1997) *The Death of Distance*, Orion Business Books, London
2   Goodley, S (2000) 'Putting You Streets Ahead', *Daily Telegraph*, 28 September
3   Hepworth, M and Ducatel, K (1992) *Transport in the Information Age: Wheels and Wires*, John Wiley, London
4   Porter, M (1998) 'Clusters and the New Economics of Competition', *Harvard Business Review*, Nov–Dec; Seely Brown, J and Duguid, P (2000) *The Social Life of Information*, Harvard Business School Press, Boston
5   Ablett, S et al (1998) *Cambridge 2020: Meeting the Challenge of Growth*, Analysis, Cambridge; Clark, A (2000) 'Rooting For the Now and Fen', *Guardian*, 15 June; Islam, F and Doward, J (2000) 'Space: The Fen frontier', *Observer*, 1 October; Hyland, A (2000) 'Corridor Lined with Gold', *Guardian*, 13 June
6   Future Unit (1998) *Converging Technologies: Consequences for the New Knowledge-Driven Economy*, DTI, London
7   Hepworth, M and Ducatel, K, op cit
8   LFG (2000) *Local Internet Futures: National Report*, Local Futures Group/Cable and Wireless, London
9   Urban Task Force (1999) *Towards an Urban Renaissance*, DETR, London
10 LFG (1999) *Telecommunications and Regional Development: National Report*, BT, London
11 IST (2000) *Towards a Sustainable Information Society*, European Commission, Brussels, June; Van den Berg, L and Van Winden, W (2000) *ICT as a Potential Catalyst for Sustainable Urban Development*, EURICUR, Rotterdam
12 Urban Task Force, op cit

Response
by Jim Norton

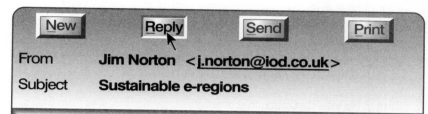

From   **Jim Norton** <**j.norton@iod.co.uk**>

Subject **Sustainable e-regions**

I welcome the paper by Ian Christie and Mark Hepworth as a vital contribution to the debate on extracting real benefits from the potential offered
by e-technologies and harnessing these to improve environmental
sustainability and social cohesion. I found much in the paper with which
I strongly agree.

No new economy

Christie and Hepworth lay to rest the ghost of a separate 'new' economy.
In my view, the widespread use of the term 'new economy' by politicians
and others is unhelpful. It tends to suggest that there is some form of
economic nirvana available to the few while the many are trapped in an
'old economy' ghetto. The reality is that the tools of e-business are applicable across *all* areas of economic activity, bringing both efficiency
savings (for example through supply-chain re-engineering and integration) and new product and service opportunities (for example, tailoring
otherwise generic products to individual needs). Much e-business
simply represents a new (and often complementary) channel for delivering existing products and services. Indeed the more far-sighted
entrepreneurs actively combine internet, telephone call centre and
physical channels to generate an overall approach much more responsive to customer needs. It is thus hardly surprising that the e-economy
is following the contours of the UK's economic and social geography.

No simple panacea for e-inclusion

While I applaud much of what government is seeking to achieve on inclusion through its UK Online programme – for example providing internet
access in every public library – there are further layers of this challenge
still to be addressed. For me, the challenge of digital inclusion is like a
Russian doll. Each time you solve an issue, and thus open the doll, there
is another issue inside. Once physical access to the internet is resolved,
the next challenge is access to payment systems for those who, through

personal choice or exclusion, exist outside conventional banking and hold no debit or credit cards. Once this is resolved, there is the challenge of functional illiteracy, building voice and picture-based systems to support the surprisingly large minority in the UK who cannot easily use existing systems.

Unleashing the creativity of SMEs

I tend to the view that much true creativity in business comes from SMEs. Can we use that inherent creativity to push out the boundaries of the UK's existing economic and social geography? Are there new types of business such as e-business intermediaries ('info-mediaries') that can be established outside the existing economic power centres? Can we unleash the potential of already existing SMEs in underperforming areas? My own experience, based on some 90 presentations to audiences of SMEs in all parts of the UK during 2000, suggests that this potential can be unleashed. We are now seeing awareness of the e-economy rising very sharply among SMEs.

DTI benchmarking figures suggest that even for the worst-performing element – micro enterprises of 0–9 employees – the numbers connected to the internet have risen from 15 per cent in 1999 to 55 per cent in 2000. To what extent is this awareness being carried forward into a true under-standing of the potential of e-business? I believe that if RDAs could help their existing and potential SMEs to address the core business issues of the e-economy – rather than just the technology – then dramatic progress might be made. Some time with a trained business facilitator, patiently holding the feet of the SME decision-makers to the fire while they work through the process of developing their own unique e-business strategy, would pay immense dividends.

A final thought

The RDAs have a crucial role. As Christie and Hepworth suggest, success will come from a holistic approach that embraces social cohesion and environmental sustainability as well as the pursuit of economic improvement. The private sector has long used tools such as the 'balanced scorecard', which highlight separately the financial, customer, process improvement, innovation and learning aspects of performance measurement and reporting. Might such tools be applied to the RDAs? ■

7 Virtual traffic: e-commerce, transport and distribution

Peter James and Peter Hopkinson

Introduction

E-business is already changing the movement of goods, components and materials, and could transform it over coming decades.[1] These changes raise many important questions for sustainable development, including the following.

- Will residential areas be overwhelmed by fleets of white vans delivering growing volumes of internet-ordered goods?
- Will internet shopping mean that consumers keep their cars parked and use their extra time at home or in their neighbourhood – or will they find replacement destinations or activities to drive to?
- Will there be a network of local drop-off and collection points for goods which can't be delivered to homes and, if so, will these be accessible by bicycle and foot as well as by car?
- When other continents are just a mouse-click away, will there be even more international transport of goods?
- In a world of virtual organizations and supply chains, where does environmental and social responsibility lie?
- Can e-business help to reduce the waste and underutilized capacity found in many existing supply chains?
- Will e-business-optimized supply chains be more vulnerable to disruption?

Some argue that the answers to these questions are very positive for sustainable development. They believe that e-business will increase the efficiency of goods distribution – and thereby reduce prices – as well as dampening demand for freight transport. They also claim that e-business can give disadvantaged suppliers and consumers easier access to markets and goods, and encourage a more community-based distribution structure.

This 'quieter roads and fuller baskets' scenario can be contrasted with one of 'e-road rage' in which home shopping increases delivery van movements while consumers use their increased vehicle availability to travel more. The result will be increased congestion, and more inconvenience from van movements in residential areas. Pessimists also believe that the increased – and often automated – ordering options created by e-business will result in more geographically-extended supply patterns, longer transport hauls, and increased difficulty in monitoring the environmental performance of suppliers. Later we'll return to these points and discuss the evidence for and against them. Firstly, however, we briefly discuss the characteristics of current logistics activities, and the key variables which influence their environmental and social impacts.

Sustainable logistics

Logistics is of great relevance to sustainable development. It influences people's access to goods and services and creates transport movements. These consume non-renewable energy and other resources, generate noise and vibration, and create emissions of carbon dioxide, nitrogen and sulphur oxides and other pollutants. There are also high levels of wastage in many supply chains as a result of goods in storage and transit.

In broad terms, the environmental and social impacts of logistics are influenced by a number of factors.

- The amount (weight) of goods lifted and transported.
- The distance they are transported.
- The mode (eg air, rail, road or water) and sub-mode (eg articulated lorry, LGV) used to transport them.
- The loading of the transport unit.
- The power source of the transport units, and their performance.
- The nature of the infrastructure (eg congested roads, site footprint and design).

Box 7.1 Criteria for sustainable distribution

The DETR has defined sustainable distribution in terms of a number of outcomes.[2] For the economy these are:

- growth – promote continued economic growth;
- jobs and prosperity – new and secure jobs, relevant skills;
- fair pricing – reflect the direct and wider costs of transport;
- competitiveness – ensure fair and open competition at home and abroad; and
- choice – ensure a plentiful and cheap supply of goods through an efficient system of goods distribution.

For society they are:

- safety – improve vehicle, driver and other road-user safety;
- health – protect the health of the road user and the public;
- disturbance – minimize the impact of noise and vibration on the public, and minimize community severance;
- access – promote wide access to markets, goods and services; and
- equity – ensure that efficient distribution services are available to all, using the user-pays principle.

For environment they are:

- climate change – contribute to greenhouse gas reduction targets;
- air quality – meet UK and EU air quality standards;
- noise – meet UK national and EU noise standards;
- land use and biodiversity – minimize impacts on the biodiversity of species, habitats and landscapes; and
- waste management – minimize waste and impact of waste produced.

- The number of times they are handled (which influences mode, loading and other factors).
- The storage of goods and requirements for storage (eg duration, location, temperature and climate control).
- Packaging requirements.

Before considering how these might change in response to e-business, it is important to describe the current baseline. By weight, most UK imports and exports travel by sea, but the gap between sea and air freight is much less in terms of value. UK air freight has grown by around 7–9 per cent a year during the 1990s, and industry forecasts anticipate a similar rate of growth in coming years.[3] This is worrying because, per tonne carried, air is the most environmentally damaging form of freight transport.

Within the UK, the most detailed data available are for rail freight and heavy goods vehicles (HGV, over 3.5 tonnes in weight).[4] One striking point from the HGV data is that food, drink and tobacco account for one-quarter of total tonne-kilometres, with shipments of minerals and construction materials not far behind. Hence, the impact of e-business on these sectors is particularly crucial.

The national road traffic forecasts

Moving freight by rail or water is less environmentally damaging than by road, and government policy is to increase the relative share of these modes. However, the most recent forecasts predict a 72 per cent increase in HGV traffic between 1996–2031 (approximately 1.6 per cent per year).[5] This is mainly due to an increase in the tonnage of freight being lifted (which is closely correlated with GDP growth), and increased handling of goods. The average length of haul is expected to remain constant because of rising fuel and transport costs.

There is less detailed data for freight carried by LGVs (under 3.5 tonnes), or by individuals in their own vehicles. LGVs are mainly diesel-engined and account for only 5 per cent of road freight by weight, but 9 per cent of total road traffic. Their use has been increasing rapidly, causing some disquiet about their impacts in urban and residential areas.[6] Government forecasts estimate that LGV traffic will continue to grow at a faster rate than HGV traffic over the next 30 years, but with a declining annual rate of increase.

Recent changes in logistics

Information technology has been a major cause of changes in the distribution infrastructure. Food and other areas of retailing have seen direct store deliveries by manufacturers largely replaced by deliveries to regional distribution centres (RDCs). Suppliers deliver directly to the RDCs, from where dedicated trucks ship consolidated loads to individual supermarkets.[7] These have greatly reduced vehicle movements to individual stores and, probably, total freight-kilometres. They have also increased vehicle utilization because consignments can be collected from several suppliers.

However, some of these gains have been offset by the move to out-of-town shopping locations, which means that consumers are often driving more in their own vehicles. Some urban shop locations also have tight time restrictions and limited access, which reduce loading factors and fleet flexibility.

Similar consolidation points have been introduced into B2B sectors – for example, auto components. However, these are sometimes accompanied by small warehouses near points of production in order to meet 'just in time' delivery requirements. This can result in more frequent movement of lightly loaded vehicles.[8]

At a European level, a number of importers and suppliers have also reorganized their distribution. They now have a small number of central warehouses serving several countries, with either direct shipping to customers or small warehouses in national markets. Such systems are generally heavy users of air freight.

Underpinning many of these changes is the rise of 'third party logistics', which involve external suppliers taking complete responsibility for the logistics function.

There are also moves towards shared use of distribution facilities to reduce costs in the petroleum and retail industries. However, there remains considerable resistance in other areas due to problems with a previous generation of shared use distribution in the 1960s and 1970s.

Despite these changes, considerable inefficiencies in European logistics remain. A German study found that the average delivery time for electrical, electronic and communication products was 29 days within Europe, compared to 11 days within the US and only two in Japan.[9] The discrepancy was less marked, but still important, for international shipments. These ranged from 45 days for exports from Europe, 23 days for the US and only 18 days for exports from Japan.

The main reason why international shipping is so much slower – and more expensive – is high transactional complexity and costs. The UN estimates that these account for no less than 7 per cent of the US$6,000 billion annual value of international trade.[10] One software company examined the administrative trail for an export consignment of goods and found that it involved 60 phone calls, 50 emails, 30 different types of documents, 21 printed sets of documents, 20 faxes and 30 sets of photocopies.[11] Air freight is more advanced than international rail or shipping in streamlining these procedures.

The measures announced as part of the government's recent sustainable distribution strategy are intended to dampen the forecast increases in road freight, and increase the volumes of rail freight. A number of these measures are aimed at greater application of information technology. For example, delivery scheduling is being encouraged to optimize vehicle capacity utilization, and minimize distances travelled.

To some extent, therefore, e-business may already be taken into account by government thinking; but will e-business create further changes which are not reflected in the DETR's forecasts and policies?

E-business and the supply chain

The founding application of e-business was electronic data interchange (EDI). This uses a dedicated communications link to send orders, confirm receipt and make payments. EDI generates considerable savings over manual alternatives for large volumes of transactions, but has been too expensive for many SMEs.[12] The development of e-business based on low-cost, flexible, web-based interfaces is now creating a qualitative change in much logistics and distribution activity. This transformation has three main dimensions:

- e-commerce;
- supply chain management and data exchange; and
- virtual organization.

E-commerce

When e-commerce is defined in a narrow fashion, as an activity concerned with the buying and selling of goods and services, it has four essential elements: ordering, invoicing, payment and order fulfilment. 'Closed channel' e-commerce links a single supplier or buyer with its customers – typically through an online catalogue or under a pre-negotiated contract. 'Open channel' e-commerce links a range of suppliers and customers through online market places.

B2B e-commerce has been slower to develop and less publicized than B2C e-commerce, but most forecasts suggest that it will eventually account for 80–90 per cent of the value of e-commerce transactions. Such predictions are notoriously unreliable, but in late 2000 many of the leading forecasters were suggesting that the volume of European e-commerce transactions will reach between US$1–2000 billion a year by 2004, with almost a quarter of this in the UK.[13]

B2C e-commerce
To date, the most rapidly-growing area of e-retailing has been lightweight products such as books, CDs, games and software, which consumers feel no need to touch before buying. As these are of low weight, they generally use existing distribution channels such as courier and postal services,

and have only marginal effects on overall logistics patterns. However, they may increase demand for warehousing, increase LGV movements in residential areas, and cause the closure of some shops.

Some start-ups such as in 60, Kozmo and Urban Fetch have also introduced quick (often one hour or less) home and office delivery services for similar goods and takeaway foods in large urban areas. Their main impacts are local, in the form of increased vehicle movements. Although these could be significant if the services take off, high operating costs have created considerable doubts about their viability – resulting, for example, in Urban Fetch abandoning its UK home delivery service.[14] The economic drive for tightly defined delivery areas may also raise access issues; in the US, Kozmo has been accused of refusing to deliver to some neighbourhoods with ethnic majorities.

Technology is also creating the option of delivering some products such as music, film, software and documents in electronic rather than physical form. Electronic document delivery is already reducing the growth of courier markets.[15] However, while this can produce significant savings in paper and packaging, the low weight of the products means that the logistics impact is relatively insignificant. Increased downloading will also require energy and may increase demand for hardware. Nonetheless, there may be environmental arguments for exempting such downloads from internet taxes, should these ever be introduced.

Home shopping for food and other consumer staples is of potentially greater significance. UK activity in this area has been dominated by existing retailers, with the market leaders picking orders from supermarket shelves. This is estimated to cost anywhere between UK£8–20 per customer, with the exact figure depending upon the cost of picking, the number and location of deliveries, and the utilization of the delivery fleet. With an average £5 delivery charge, most current services are losing money on all but the most valuable deliveries. Delivery to workplaces – which is Waitrose's strategy – is said to be 30–50 per cent cheaper than home delivery because it can be consolidated. However, there may be some employer resistance to the large-scale development of such schemes.

The domination of UK home shopping by established food retailers contrasts with the US, where new entrants such as Webvan have command. They have built dedicated picking centres that have high capital costs but low operating costs, achieved through cheaper locations and buildings – said to be 75 per cent less per square foot than those used by supermarkets.[16]

A recent Verdict study argues that current leaders such as Iceland, Sainsbury and Tesco will maintain their market leadership in home

Box 7.2 The automatic shopping cart

Webvan (www.webvan.com), which recently merged with its largest competitor, HomeGrocer, is the leading US e-retailer of groceries. Its business model is to avoid delivery charges and still achieve higher margins than supermarkets, through using lower rental sites and a high level of automation. It also focuses on routine purchases of branded goods, accepting that people will prefer personal shopping for non-standardized items such as fruit and vegetables.

Webvan's stores are typically 80–90,000 square feet – twice the size of an average supermarket – and located in warehouse parks. Each site employs up to 100 staff in stocking, picking and delivering goods. Customers order from a database of around 13,000 items, most of which have an image and information about the producer, size, price and (for food) nutritional information. The precise range offered varies by location. So too does pricing, which is determined by competition.

All orders received before 11pm are picked at night in a highly automated process – some of Webvan's warehouses have over 25 miles of conveyor belts. Deliveries are made during the afternoon and evening of the following day. Customers are given 90-minute windows and the company claims that 99.5 per cent of deliveries are on time. Webvan also says that it encourages 'customer rapport', especially with those who are elderly or housebound.

grocery shopping in the UK.[17] It also foresees a gradual move to picking centres as volumes rise, in order to reduce costs and avoid inconvenience to normal shoppers. Some of the centres may be co-located with supermarkets, but most are likely to be developed in low-cost warehousing locations. In some cases, dispersed picking centres may deliver in relatively large vehicles to local centres, from which smaller vans will deliver to homes.[18]

There is likely to be more competition for non-food staples such as clothing, many of which may be sourced on an international basis. This may create increased transport. For example, one international mail order company reduces its inventory by fulfilling orders from five warehouses – three in the US, one in Japan and one in the UK. Each warehouse serves its national market, but orders from other countries can be fulfilled by any of them. This can mean that an order from Germany is fulfilled from the US even if the product is available in the UK.[19]

The three key influences on all forms of home shopping will be: consumer access to ordering channels (PCs, DTV and third-generation mobile phones); delivery charges; and the level of returns.[20] Rapid growth is unlikely, especially for consumer staples, until delivery prices approach or reach zero. This is only likely to be achieved with a move to more automated picking, mechanisms to reduce returns, and/or aggressive market expansion by the supermarket chains.

Reducing returns will be especially important. One solution will be to give customers more accurate delivery times (although this can require expensive technology, and is at the mercy of road congestion problems). Another solution is to install drop-off boxes in customers' homes, although this means overcoming concerns about hygiene and security. Sainsbury is trialling the use of secure boxes for packaged goods, and the housebuilders Laing are installing fixed containers in their new developments. There will also be pressure for more evening and weekend deliveries; this is still in its early stages in the UK, but is rapidly growing in the US. Finally, there is likely to be development of local distribution centres where goods can be dropped if people are not at home.

B2B e-commerce

The main growth in this area is expected to come from electronic marketplaces that link buyers with sellers via the internet. There are now almost a thousand such sites, but these are likely to consolidate in the medium term. E-marketplaces vary in operation, but most provide:

- access to buyers and sellers;
- auction or tendering mechanisms for individual contracts;
- the means of conducting and completing transactions, often including provision of logistics services; and
- industry-specific information.

In addition to providing an open marketplace, many sites also provide restricted areas that allow sellers to deal with selected buyers. Some are also starting to provide project-management support by providing a central information-clearing house. In the case of packaging, for example, this would include job design specifications, graphics files, amendments, progress data, and approvals. The potential advantage is the reduction of waste and fewer problems stemming from bad communication and out-of-date information.

Forecasters suggest that B2B marketplaces will account for a high proportion of industry transactions within a few years, and become powerful forces within their sectors. In the auto industry, Goldman Sachs has estimated that e-marketplaces such as Covisint (a collaboration between leading manufacturers) could save US producers more than US$60 billion a year, or $3650 per vehicle.[21] At the other extreme, market research for GroupTrade, a provider of e-supplies to small businesses, calculated that it could save UK SMEs an aggregate UK£24 billion a year, the equivalent of 3 per cent of GDP.

Exchanges are also likely to have a significant impact on logistics and distribution itself. One reason for this is provision of instant logistics as a service to buyers. PaperExchange, for example, provides this through a partnership with the US logistics company C H Robertson. Another influence is the creation of online markets in freight capacity. There are now over 250 freight exchanges worldwide, of which approximately 60 are in Europe. One UK-based example is the FreightTrader portal developed by Mars and IBM, which provides an online market for temperature-controlled loads, and which will soon be extended to other areas of road haulage and shipping.[22]

One effect of both B2B and B2C e-commerce is increased demand for warehouse space. In the US, the market for rented warehousing is now growing by 10–15 per cent per annum, much of it driven by e-commerce vendors.[23] Some of the early pioneers, such as Amazon, have developed their own distribution facilities. This includes one of the UK's largest warehouses, a 500,000-square-foot facility which is approaching completion in Slough.

In the UK, e-commerce warehousing is mainly concentrated in the south east, where the surveyors FPP Savills have estimated that e-retailing accounted for two million square feet in 1999, or 10 per cent of the available space. A study by Lambert Smith Hampton has also found that there is now a shortage of suitable sites in several areas of the country.[24]

Packaging

An important environmental question connected with e-commerce is whether it will increase or reduce the volume and nature of packaging. One argument is that because there is no longer a requirement to influence consumer choice, packaging will become simpler and primarily focused on the protection of goods in transit. Online vendors such as Amazon are also pressuring suppliers to use more simple and less bulky packaging to reduce postage and storage costs. However, an alternative view is that this approach poses a considerable threat to brand identity, such that packaging could become more, rather than less, important as a means of communication between suppliers and their customers. The rough handling that occurs in many e-fulfilment channels – and customers' propensity to return anything that appears to be damaged –

may also mean that packaging increases in weight and volume. Indeed, one consultancy predicts that this trend will create demand for an additional 1.5 million tons of containerboard in the US by 2005.[25]

Supply chain management and data exchange

The lower costs and easier accessibility of internet-based data exchange can make critical data – such as levels of inventory and orders – available to all players.[26] The result, when combined with enabling technologies such as bar-coding and tracking of items in transit, is a 'glass pipeline' that allows a much greater collective knowledge of where goods are, and what will be required in future. This reduces the need for extra stock holdings.[27]

The inventory and cost benefits of this can be partially offset by other developments. There may be a need for more inventory management close to production plants to reduce any risk of disruption, and there may be increased handling costs from delivering smaller consignments on demand.[28] Nevertheless, there is still a considerable net reduction in inventory costs which, other things being equal, reduces interest, storage costs and waste. Tesco, for example, recently announced savings of £60m from closer ties with suppliers and consolidation of distribution centres.[29]

These outcomes are potentially beneficial for sustainable development. The reduced costs can make goods cheaper for customers, and also free up resources for investment in other areas. A reduction in waste levels – which can be as high as 40 per cent of inventory costs in areas such as perishable goods – is also environmentally beneficial. However, the move to just-in-time delivery that often accompanies more integrated supply chains can result in additional vehicle movements. Reduced logistics costs can also create a rebound effect of greater dispersal in supply chains, so that longer distances are travelled. Finally, the tighter connection between the different elements within the chain, and reduced levels of stock, greatly increase the vulnerability to disruption. This was demonstrated by the speed with which the UK petrol blockades of September 2000 disrupted not only fuel supplies but, perhaps more surprisingly, food supplies. This reflects the fact that only limited stocks are held at any one point in the highly-efficient UK food chain.

Whether positive or negative in their effects, glass pipelines are likely to develop further. To date, they have been driven by powerful buyers such as supermarket chains and large manufacturers, who are able to ensure that all their suppliers conform to common standards. However, many other supply chains have yet to achieve this, primarily because it is difficult and expensive to link many different IT systems together.[30] Eventually, this is likely to be achieved by the falling cost of software, but in the near future the difficulties may create serious access barriers for many SMEs.

Virtual organization

A broader reconfiguration of business relationships is occurring in many organizations, involving the outsourcing of many activities, and the formation of partnerships and joint ventures to handle others. Many of these relationships are handled partially or exclusively via the internet; so too is a growing proportion of customer service and marketing. Indeed, the archetypal virtual organization is one that has a brand and a website but no physical assets. Instead it relies on a network of sub-contractors and business partners to make and distribute the goods it sells. These may form what consultants Cap Gemini have called a 'collapsible supply chain' – one that is established to exploit a short-term opportunity, and then reconfigured or replaced when new opportunities arise.

One common aspect of virtual and non-virtual organizations engaged in e-business is a reliance on what has been termed 'fourth-party logistics'. Providers of this service take responsibility not only for the movement of goods, but also for activities such as inventory management and product return. For example, Joint Retail Logistics monitors and manages the performance of manufacturers, hauliers and other suppliers to Marks & Spencer at all stages from order to final delivery.

The development of e-commerce has also been accompanied by e-fulfilment, in which vendors take responsibility for all activities, from taking an order to customer delivery. An interesting UK example is the new Cenargo e-logistics centre at Eaglescliffe, near Darlington.[31] This is a 250,000-square-foot combined call centre and warehouse, and it will employ up to 700 people. The centre recently won its first contract, to handle 1.3 million orders a year for Virgin Vie cosmetics. One important criterion for the location was access to broadband communications.

Virtual organizations can also have a considerable indirect effect on logistics. By extending the number and geographic range of business relationships, they are a powerful driver of globalization. The low administration costs of these new organizational forms also means that they are less sensitive to many traditional cost drivers. This was demonstrated in the recent debate about inward investment to the UK, which reached record levels in 1999 despite the high level of sterling. One of the main reasons appears to be the relative indifference of e-business –

Box 7.3 E-commerce fulfilment – just do it

UPS is the world's largest provider of e-commerce fulfilment. The first step in this process was the provision of online tracking of shipments. According to the company, it costs only 10 US cents for customers to check progress via a website, compared to $1.78 if they call a customer service representative.[32] UPS now offers a complete e-logistics outsourcing service. Its collaboration with the sports goods company Nike provides an example of how this works. Nike's previous distribution model had involved shipment to a distribution warehouse, and then onward distribution to retail outlets via pallets. However, the development of direct selling through www.nike.com required a separate fulfilment channel, which is completely outsourced. UPS handles all orders – including those using the telephone number on the Nike website – and transmits them to a Nike warehouse. UPS software then arranges the picking, packing and shipping to final customers.

one of the fastest-growing areas of inward investment – to changes in national currency rates.

Virtual organization can also exacerbate vulnerability to disruption. In the case of petrol, the major oil companies have increasingly outsourced haulage to third-party providers, who in turn are heavily reliant on sub-contracting to owner-drivers, either directly or through further intermediaries. It was therefore very difficult to make decisions quickly when the crisis hit. The rising oil prices that fuelled popular discontent were also influenced by low levels of oil stocks, which make markets very sensitive to even small fluctuations in supply and demand. One cause of this is organizational changes in refining, as the oil companies have sold a substantial proportion of capacity to independent operators. These 'financial refiners' (so-called because they are solely focused on short-term financial returns) can only prosper by reducing costs. One of the easiest ways to do this is to reduce stocks by moving from 'just-in-time' to 'almost-not-enough' production, in which output responds very quickly to market changes.

One potential advantage of e-business outsourcing is that it makes it easier to share distribution facilities, thereby increasing capacity utilization. As well as joint use of warehouses and transport, this can involve more fundamental changes. Some forecasters predict that there could be a move towards downstream assembly, filling, and labelling. This means, for example, that orange juice could be shipped in bulk to a local warehouse which would then fill and label own-brand cartons for a number of supermarkets. Depending on the stage at which it occurs, shared use can also reduce the need for land and warehousing, and improve the utilization efficiency of goods vehicles.

E-business in three sectors

To illustrate the variety of ways in which e-business can impact upon logistics, Tables 7.1–7.3 provide a summary of initiatives in three supply chains.

1   Documents – chosen as a significant driver of air freight and LGV transport, and as an area with potential for substituting electronic for physical distribution.
2   Food – chosen as the biggest single freight category, and also the one in which the effects of e-business have been most discussed, especially for home shopping.
3   Petroleum – chosen as a representative bulk goods sector.

We have also provided a broad-brush assessment of whether the developments appear to be positive for sustainability (denoted with '+'), have no apparent effects (denoted with 'N') or may have negative effects (denoted with '–'). Those that have mixed impacts, or are contentious (for example, globalization), are indicated with '?'. The concentration of available data on environmental impacts means that these are analysed in greater depth than social impacts.

Two broad conclusions can be drawn from Tables 7.1–7.3:

1   Although most discussion of e-business and sustainability has focused on B2C areas such as home shopping, the greatest impacts of e-business on logistics are at upstream B2B stages.
2   Many e-business initiatives appear to be positive for sustainable development. The potential negatives often concern second-order effects which are difficult to forecast (for example, increased transport due to falling logistics costs) or contentious (for example, the development of more globalized patterns of production and consumption).

Table 7.1   E-business and the document supply chain

	Supply Chain Components	Sustainability Impacts (+ve/-ve)
Origination	Centralized, online image banks accessed by multiple document creators (eg national subsidiaries participating in a worldwide product launch)	Avoids physical transport of files, duplication of storage and wasted output from the use of old images (+)
	Internet-based file transfer	Avoids physical transport of files (+)
Production	Creation of documents from direct customer input to a website	Personalization reduces waste of unwanted material (+) but low cost may encourage more printing (–)
	Online auctions/tenders for print jobs	Utilizes spare capacity (+) but extends reach (?)
	Online project management of document production process (coordinating originators, printers, print buyers etc)	Reduces printing of erroneous output and inefficiency due to poor communication (+)
Distribution	Distribute and print – files transmitted for local printing and distribution	Avoids transport of printed material and supports localized print employment (+)
Consumption	Content read on screen	Can potentially avoid printing (+) but cheap internet distribution may lead to more copies being printed by relatively inefficient local printers (–)
	Content downloaded to e-books/newspapers etc	Avoids materials, printing and transport impacts of physical product (+) but may stimulate further globalization of media sector (?)
	Personalization of printed outputs, making people more likely to read them	Personalization can reduce waste of unwanted material (+) but low cost may encourage more printing (–)
Organization	Emergence of communication 'solution providers', providing a one-stop service for all stages of the product chain	No obvious environmental implications (N) but might encourage global distribution strategies (–)

Table 7.2   E-business and the food supply chain

	Supply Chain Components	Sustainability Impacts (+ve/-ve)
Origination	Online auctions for foodstuffs	Can reduce waste of unsold items and increase the income of local producers by cutting out intermediaries (+) but extends market reach (?)
Production	Production driven by real-time downstream scheduling/ purchasing decisions	Reductions in inventory waste (+) but may move to just-in-time delivery (?)
Distribution	Online supply-chain management systems	Stimulus to air freight (13% of imported UK air freight is fruit and vegetables) (–) but reductions in inventory waste (–)
	Shared use of warehouses and/or transport fleets	Avoids duplication of resources and increases capacity utilization (+)
	Warehouse-based filling and packaging	Can reduce inventory waste and potentially reduces supplier movements (+)
	Fleet optimization using vehicle tracking	Supports reverse logistics and can improve energy efficiency through route optimization (+)
	Online markets for unused distribution capacity	Increases capacity utilization (+)
Consumption	Internet ordering with direct delivery to home	Van delivery of multiple loads environmentally better than individual car trips (+) but may increase evening/weekend deliveries (–) and cars may be used for other purposes (–)
	Use of local drop-off centres	Reduces LGV traffic in residential areas (+) but benefits depend on proportion of pick-ups by car (?)
	'Info-mediaries' aggregate demand from consumers and solicit automated bids from suppliers	Specialized knowledge could be positive if sustainability is a high priority, but may not be (?). Will make supply-chain initiatives more difficult (–)
Organization	Possible competition between supermarket-based models of existing players and attempts of new entrants and grocery manufacturers to develop direct delivery systems	Potential for plethora of lightly-loaded distribution networks (?)

Table 7.3   E-business and the petroleum supply chain

	Supply Chain Components	Sustainability Impacts (+ve/-ve)
Origination	Online trading of crude oil and derivatives	Extends existing well-developed market so no obvious changes (N)
	Online markets for unused bulk tanker capacity	Increases capacity utilization (+)
Production	Online trading of refined oil products and derivatives	May increase capacity utilization through easier ability to sell output (+)
	Production driven by real-time downstream scheduling/ purchasing decisions	No obvious implications (N)
Distribution	Online markets for unused midstream/downstream distribution capacity	Increases capacity utilization (+)
	Info-mediaries aggregate business customers and solicit automated bids from suppliers	Specialized knowledge could be positive if sustainability is a high priority, but may not be (?) Could make supply chain initiatives more difficult (−)
	Real-time data exchange with both upstream and down-stream and resulting optimization of operations	Increases capacity utilization (+)
	Dedicated product movers provide a one-stop service to oil producers	Specialized knowledge could be positive if sustainability is a high priority, but may not be (?)
Consumption	Internet purchase and direct delivery of products, eg lubricants to consumers	Few trips undertaken solely for this and may fragment delivery loads (?)
	Development of multi-use sites combining retailing with other functions, eg local drop-off hub	May reduce returns (+) but favours car-based transport (−)
	'Gas bots' searching for cheapest local services of fuel, with global positioning satellite (GPS)-based road directions	Reduces cost (+), but may lengthen journeys (−) and reduce ability to introduce environmental factors into purchasing decisions (−)
	Online account information and settlement	No obvious implications (N)
Organization	Development of virtual oil companies, purchasing from separate producers, product movers, refiners and filling station chains	Increased efficiency (+) but may be more difficult to develop supply chain initiatives (−)

Implications of e-business for sustainable logistics

There has much general debate about the relationship between e-business and sustainable logistics. The following sections examine some of the most common propositions which have been made in the literature.

E-business and logistics: some common assumptions

By making supply chains more efficient, e-business can significantly reduce prices and thereby create considerable environmental and social benefits

The improved information flows created by e-business have already helped to make supply chains more efficient. In the US, for example, the average stock turn was 8 a year in 1995 but reached 13.2 in 2000.[33] The net effect was a record fall in the inventory-to-sales ratio. Cheaper and faster-moving inventory management often translates into significant reductions in waste levels, and increased utilization of capacity. The environmental benefits of these may increase as the volume of B2B transactions grows.

On the other hand, when e-business results in a fragmented supplier base it might reduce opportunities for efficiency gains from supply-chain integration. Efficiency gains could be offset by demand for high-speed delivery, which is costly and makes it difficult to achieve high vehicle utilization. Reductions in costs could also mask greater environmental and social externalities; increased use of transport is an obvious example. Another is the potentially adverse effect on producers, such as small farmers or local businesses, whose incomes are reduced or working conditions made worse.

A final issue is whether price reductions could stimulate higher consumption, which many would consider to be unsustainable. Tangential evidence that this might happen is provided by a recent McKinsey study, which notes that one UK retailer selling both online and from shops found that the combination of both media increased total purchases by 10 per cent. It also noted that the average value of customer purchases from leading e-retailers is up to 20 per cent more than their bricks-and-mortar competitors. However, it is uncertain whether this represents a shift in consumption, or a net increase. McKinsey itself attributes the findings to a greater percentage of premium products, the bundling of products and services, and easier cross-selling in e-retailing.[34]

One area in which e-retailing does seem to have increased the overall market is books. While this expansion is not solely due to price – online retailers may tap some latent demand by offering easier access than existing stores – it seems to have been an important element. Of course, books are different from other products, and many people will see an increased demand for knowledge as a very positive, and thoroughly sustainable, outcome. However, current experience is sending some early, if faint, warning messages about the impact of e-business on future levels of consumption.

E-business can provide easier access to markets for suppliers in remote or disadvantaged locations, and easier access to goods for disadvantaged consumers, and therefore helps to overcome regional and national inequalities

There are many examples of this. For example, www.fromages.com was created to sell artisan-produced French cheeses and now exports 95 per cent of its sales, usually within 24 hours of receiving an order. There are similar examples in developing economies; Indian farmers have used the internet to check prices in regional markets, which can be much higher than those offered by local merchants.[35] They are now bypassing local outlets and transporting their produce directly to regional markets. Although this means longer hauls, the prices they can obtain are sometimes 50 per cent higher.

The question is whether this will be anything more than a niche phenomenon – one which is sometimes replacing relatively eco-efficient bulk shipments with other, more transport-intensive, forms of consumption (as may be the case with www.fromages.com).

Electronic home shopping can reduce the demand for travel and associated environmental impacts

Complete replacement of car-based shopping trips by internet ordering and van-based delivery could certainly reduce distance travelled – by 70 to 80 per cent according to one simulation.[36] However, complete replacement is unlikely as consumers could use the spare time and vehicle availability to make other journeys. The limited survey evidence of consumer responses to home shopping has found that they reported less car use. It would be useful to validate this through larger-scale studies. One point to note is the finding from some US teleworking studies that initial reductions in car travel are partially offset over time by the stimulation of new driving.[37] This results from people moving further away from the workplace, or making short trips from home to shops during lunch breaks.

The retail sector also has a strong interest in diverting time and cost savings into further shopping. People shop not only to buy specific goods, but for a variety of other reasons such as social interaction, excitement, and the creation and maintenance of personal identity. Many forecasters predict that future stores will place more emphasis on these factors.[38]

A business model that consigns low-margin staples to internet ordering and delivery, and replaces them with higher margin goods on the shelves, would be very profitable for retail chains. Indeed, this is already emerging in embryonic form in the US, where the strategy of at least one home-shopping company has changed from seeking to replace supermarkets, to concentrating on staple items. It accepts that its customers will continue to visit supermarkets for fresh and speciality items. It is also possible that the internet might produce an 'unbundling' of multiple orders that, for convenience, were previously made from a single location. This could mean that a single car trip is replaced by a number of van deliveries, leading to an increase in delivery units.[39]

On the supply side, Sally Cairns has identified six key factors that are likely to influence the environmental impacts of home shopping.[40]

1   *Returns*, which create the need for additional journeys and delivery of replacements (and which constitute a potentially higher proportion in home shopping because of the absence of any physical contact with goods before purchase).

2   *Cost structures*. The impacts vary according to whether these reflect the full environmental costs of the transport used, and – more specifically – whether they encourage deliveries of small value and weight at non-congested times.

3   *Delivery locations*. Home storage units, local pick-up points and shared distribution channels could reduce returns and the movements of delivery vehicles.

4   *Vehicle use*. The impacts vary according to the mode used and, for road vehicles, the extent to which they use conventional or alternative fuels, have advanced engines and emission control systems, and are well-driven and maintained.

5   *Routing and scheduling optimization*. This may be based on sophisticated software systems and accurate GPS data to track vehicle locations.

6   *Load consolidation*. This involves the sharing of distribution facilities and delivery vehicles, increasing utilization and reducing vehicle movements and the amount of warehouse space required.

The importance of the two latter variables is demonstrated by a Swedish research project that examined all the deliveries made to 15 shops, restaurants, schools and day nurseries, and compared them to an ideal pattern involving trip optimization and shared use of delivery vehicles. They found that the latter could produce a 39 per cent reduction in distance travelled, a 42 per cent reduction in the number of vehicles used, and a 58 per cent reduction in number of journeys. The work is now being extended into the central shopping area of Uppsala with the involvement of Skandi System, a local haulage company.[41]

Two aggregate forecasts of the transport impact of electronic home shopping have recently been reported. In the UK, the economic consultancy NERA has estimated that home shopping will reduce car-based shopping travel by 5 per cent by 2005, and 10 per cent by 2010.[42] This outweighs a forecast increase in delivery traffic of 0.25 per cent by 2005 and 0.5 per cent by 2010. The study also estimates that the greater diffusion of IT within the freight sector (route planning, freight exchanges and so on) will lead to a 17 per cent and 19 per cent reduction respectively in goods vehicle mileage by 2005 and 2010.

A recent study in The Netherlands by the Dutch road haulage association TLN has estimated that 11.5 per cent of total retail sales – approximately 3.5 million tonnes of goods – will be purchased online and home delivered by 2005. In urban areas of The Netherlands, this will often replace cycle or foot trips, which are the two most frequent modes of transport for shopping. The net effect is forecast to be a 17 per cent increase in road vehicle movements over the next five years.[43]

The two studies indicate the sensitivity of the outcomes to the assumptions made. Until there is more empirical evidence on how customers respond to home shopping, and which delivery patterns suppliers use, it is impossible to validate or disprove either proposition.

E-business creates an opportunity for a more community-based distribution structure and a reversal of the move to out-of-town development that has occurred over recent decades

The high cost of distributing goods to homes – both because of low population densities in residential areas and high levels of returns – is the Achilles heel of B2C e-commerce. One solution would be a nationwide network of drop-off points, used when people are not at home or as the primary distribution point, with the incentive of lower charges. There are a number of options for the physical location of this network. Existing premises which may be used include superstores, shopping centres, convenience stores, filling stations, post offices, mail sorting

Box 7.4 The e-post office

The Post Office's e-fulfilment service aims to use its existing infrastructure to offer e-commerce vendors and customers a wide range of home delivery and local collection choices. These include the ability to specify alternative collection points (so if no one is at home the next location will be used), and the use of a local post office as a collection, payment, returns and ordering centre. This may require an extension of opening hours to allow people to collect before or after work, or at weekends. The Post Office is also looking at the prospect of using post offices and warehouse facilities to consolidate orders for local pick-up or home delivery.

centres, public transport nodes, community halls and schools.[44] It has also been suggested that purpose-designed facilities could be built in business parks, and at major employment sites, drive-in shopping centres and park-and-ride sites.

One striking feature of many of the collection discussions to date is that car access is a primary criterion. While this is obviously important, especially for bulky goods, no equivalent attention is paid to cycling or walking as alternative means of collection. There has been little discussion of community distribution models aimed at minimizing vehicle movements, particularly in residential areas. These would give people the option of collecting lighter consignments by cycling or walking to a neighbourhood drop centre. The economics of such schemes would depend on delivery cost savings when compared with home drop-offs. One possibility is that they could become local meeting places, providing an alternative means of fulfilling the social functions of shopping.

The increased ordering options that e-business provides to both business and consumers will result in more geographically-extended supply patterns, and therefore higher transport-intensity for goods

There is considerable evidence that this is happening at a global scale. The best objective indicator is the high rate of growth in air freight, which is being partially driven by e-business. The growing sophistication of specialized supply-chain management by importers and exporters, and the creation of online markets in most sectors, is likely to strengthen this trend.

E-trade would of course be less transport intensive if more goods were shipped by sea and rail rather than air and road. However, e-commerce usually demands highly flexible supply chains, whereas rail and sea transport are the least flexible modes, with high infrastructure costs and a reliance on regular volume. This inherent disadvantage is compounded by the limited application of e-business within the rail and maritime sectors. The latter is particularly slow in adopting the electronic documentation that could reduce costs and waste and, more importantly, increase speed, reliability and customer confidence.[45] The slow pace of e-business also impedes the development of intermodal transport, which is only likely to grow substantially with the development of centralized info-mediaries who can provide an integrated tracking service over all transport modes.

Online ordering will increase the number of suppliers and reduce average order size, making it harder to persuade supply-chain members to behave responsibly in environmental and social terms

Over the last decade, the general trend in supply chains has been to work with fewer suppliers. However, the development of B2B market-places makes it easier to source products from a larger number, and wider geographic range, of suppliers. This is especially true of the maintenance, operating items, and commodity components that form the bulk of B2B purchases by value. The limited evidence available suggests that this phenomenon is occurring. For example, one Digital Futures partner that moved to online procurement increased its supplier base almost tenfold as a result. The main reason for this appears to be the high transaction costs of the previous system when finding the optimal supplier for every individual item.

Competition authorities are beginning to be concerned about the potential impacts of B2B marketplaces, and it is likely that new forms of regulation will be developed for them. It is important that this regulation takes environmental and social considerations into account because, on present trends, B2B exchanges may make it more difficult to consider these in many purchasing decisions. This is particularly true of indirect goods and services that have limited visibility and no immediate connection with the environmental or social parameters of the final products. Price is likely to be the predominant factor in these purchases.

There is also more specific concern about the impact of B2B exchanges on logistics. Trade bodies fear that these may further increase the extent of sub-contracting and draw in more suppliers from outside the UK, who may have lower costs for fuel and other factors. One anxiety is the vetting of even more complex sub-contracting structures for safety considerations. Another is the issue of liability.

The organizational and personal ties between customers and suppliers may also be weakened by B2B exchanges, making it difficult for individual customers to exert informal pressure for improvement. The best means of overcoming these forces is likely to be some kind of pre-qualification procedure for environmental and social performance. An alternative or complementary option would be to require buyers to provide environmental and social information about the goods they are selling, perhaps based on standardized parameters. Both these activities could be undertaken by the online certification agencies that are starting to emerge. However, the cost-reduction focus of exchanges and their users, and the dangers of violating free trade regulations, may constrain market-led initiatives, meaning that some kind of policy intervention could be required to achieve 'green e-certification'.

Conclusions

The relationship between e-business and logistics is in its early stages, so it is difficult to make definitive judgements. However, Table 7.4 presents some provisional conclusions about the impacts of e-business in terms of the DETR's criteria for sustainable distribution.

One important distinction is between first- and second-order effects. First-order effects are those that result directly from the application of e-business, for example in supply-chain integration or home shopping. Second-order effects represent the response of business and consumers to these first-order effects; examples include the extension of supply chains because of cheaper logistics, or the use by consumers of car capacity that had been freed up by electronic home shopping. A broader second-order effect concerns the effect of easier access to cheaper goods on the overall levels of consumption and transport. It is also important to distinguish between one-off changes – such as reductions in waste from better management of supply chains – and continuing effects, such as the long-term influence of delivery and collection infrastructures after they are built.

There are many positive first-order effects that have been created by e-business. It seems likely to increase distribution efficiency, reduce waste, increase capacity utilization, and cut costs for consumers. It creates access to broader markets for many small producers, especially in remote regions; and there is scope to reduce environmental impacts by substituting electronic for physical distribution in some areas.

The negative effects on sustainability include greater use of air freight, extra LGVs in residential areas, and the increased demand for

Table 7.4 E-business and the DETR's criteria for sustainable distribution

Supply Chain Components	Sustainability Impacts (+ve/-ve)

Environment

Climate change	+ Reduced emissions from increased efficiency and growth of electronic distribution – Possible adverse effects from increased handling, length of haul, use of air freight, and use of electricity for internet technologies
Air quality	+ Reduced emissions from increased efficiency and electronic distribution – Possible adverse effects from increased handling, length of haul, use of air freight and use of electricity for internet technologies – Increased local impacts around airports and urban residential areas
Noise	– Increased by growth of air freight and possible adverse impacts from greater LGV traffic in residential areas, especially at evenings and weekends
Land use and biodiversity	– Increased demand for distribution space ? Possible changes in volume and pattern of car travel
Waste management	+ Greatly reduces inventory obsolescence and other waste within the supply chain, and makes it easier to find users for unwanted goods and materials + Facilitates reverse logistics and waste take-back – Some increases in waste due to unpredictable demand, shortening product life cycles and increasing the return of goods ? Possibility of reduced packaging

Economy

Growth	+ Significant positive impact due to greater distributive efficiency and expanded trade (on conventional criteria)
Jobs and prosperity	+ Growth creates more jobs in distribution and other sectors – Jobs may be insecure ? Pattern of employment may change
Fair pricing	+ Air-cargo economics greatly influenced by absence of duty on aviation fuel ? Also issues of whether road-vehicle users pay the full cost of their impacts + Better information for customers, bringing costs down
Competitiveness	+ Distribution costs potentially more transparent; more could be done to enhance the competitiveness of shipping
Choice	+ Online ordering, and the increased efficiency and reach of distribution, will reduce prices and extend the variety of goods

Supply Chain Components	Sustainability Impacts (+ve/-ve)
Society	
Safety	+ Positive effects of increased information, eg on vehicle choices – Effects of increased traffic in residential areas
Health	– Increased use of LGVs may have health impacts in some urban locations
Disturbance	? No likely reductions in HGV traffic and increases in air-cargo and LGV traffic, with more traffic in residential areas and at evenings and weekends
Access	+ Online ordering greatly expands opportunities – Limited by the digital divide and possible red-lining of urban home delivery routes
Equity	+ Efficiency increased, and wide availability – User-pays principle not in place for air cargo

warehousing. The extent of the latter two impacts will partly depend on the degree of shared use within buildings and delivery fleets. Another key uncertainty is what consumers will do with any vehicle capacity freed up by home shopping; if this is used for replacement journeys, it could produce a net increase in transport.

Second-order effects are even harder to predict. There will clearly be economic benefits from e-business-driven reductions in logistics costs. Disadvantaged countries, regions and social groups potentially could benefit from improved access to goods and services. The development of B2B marketplaces could also provide a new gateway for integrating sustainability into supply chains, but could equally result in even less emphasis on sustainability than at present. There might be an increased average length of haul in response to falling distribution costs and easier transactions; and the increased possibilities of global availability with cheap delivery could provide a major stimulus to unsustainable consumption.

Some of the effects of e-business are already anticipated in the government's sustainable distribution strategy, and the forecasts that underlie it. This is particularly true of the supply-chain integration and inventory reduction that e-business enables. Some of the unanticipated developments should also be positive – in particular, the fact that B2B marketplaces make it easier to sell unused logistics capacity.

Yet there are other developments that could seriously undermine current policy assumptions. There may be more frequent deliveries by less heavily-loaded vehicles, making it more difficult to achieve the government's aspiration of increased volume utilization. There could also be a substantial increase in LGV traffic, which would counter forecasts that the rate of increase will slow in coming years. There could also be an increase in the already-high growth rate of air freight. This would have a disproportionate impact on sustainability, both directly (through emissions, noise and energy use) and indirectly (through its influence on broader structures of supply and demand).

It is important to remember that the situation could change rapidly. For the next few years, any growth in home shopping will be based on the existing infrastructure of supermarkets (for order picking) and, to a lesser extent, distribution channels (parcels carriers and collection points). However, there is a critical level – probably between 5–10 per cent of total retail sales – beyond which there are likely to be significant changes. These will include the increased development of picking centres, the closure of some supermarkets, and the creation of new distribution channels, possibly including purpose-built drop-off and collection networks. New distribution systems are likely to rely on car-based collection, and could therefore undermine the government's longer-term objective of reducing car dependence. There is also a danger of a plethora of different distribution points creating confusion for customers and excessive vehicle movements.

Our general conclusion, then, is that both the scenarios identified at the beginning – 'quieter roads and fuller baskets' or 'e-road rage' – could come to pass. Hence it is too early, despite the obvious first-order benefits, to give e-business the green light as a creator of sustainable logistics; but equally, there is not sufficient evidence to argue that it should be impeded. The current signal is amber, with some warning signs that the second-order effects could be at variance with sustainable development. Now is the time to take precautionary action to ensure that e-business is compatible with the government's sustainable development objectives.

Recommendations

Business

What can business do to respond to this amber warning? It can be assumed that competitive forces will lead many companies to take advantage of the positive eco-efficiency benefits created by e-business; but dealing with the more complex environmental and social challenges can be problematic because of the organizational fragmentation that e-business creates. Nonetheless, possible action points for companies include the following.

Do more to measure and monitor the transport and wider sustainability implications of e-business decisions

It is clear that substantial moves towards e-business will have great environmental and social significance. They will result in many activities that were previously carried out in-house being outsourced, generating new patterns of environmental and social impact. However, substantial discussion of this topic seldom (if ever) occurs in corporate environmental or social reports. When it is considered, it suffers from a lack of consistency and standardization. It would therefore be desirable for companies to engage with appropriate expert and representative bodies (for example, the Global Reporting Initiative) to provide guidelines on how e-business issues should be treated. More information is also essential to obtain an accurate picture of each company's sustainability footprint.

Pay greater attention to the environmental and social performance of e-business and e-fulfilment suppliers

It is also likely that e-business will displace a growing proportion of the environmental and social impacts created over the life cycle of goods and services. It is therefore important that companies pay careful attention to the sustainability performance of their e-suppliers, such as e-fulfilment services or B2B exchanges. This is particularly important given that such services often operate in 'internet time', and are under great pressure from increasingly sceptical capital markets to provide short-term performance.

Government

In the case of government, action is needed in the following areas.

Improve the knowledge base

In order to provide early warning of adverse trends, it would be helpful for the DETR to collect more detailed data on the volume and characteristics of air freight and LGV traffic. Increased knowledge of the transport behaviour of car-owning home shoppers and the impact of e-marketplaces on vehicle utilization would also be desirable, as would better monitoring of the impact of e-business in the construction and minerals industries, which generate a large proportion of freight tonne-kilometres.

Tax fuel for air freight

The growth of air freight demonstrates that e-business is changing patterns of production and logistics. This is the most environmentally-damaging freight mode, so it is important that it is not subsidized in any way. Unfortunately, aviation fuel is currently exempt from taxation, which sends a misleading signal about its true costs. Introducing or increasing fuel taxes is not a popular political option, but it is vital that the government continues its policy of pressing for international agreement on this issue.

Examine trends in home-based distribution and experiment with new options

It would also be desirable for the DETR to undertake a detailed examination of the potential for local distribution channels and their transport implications. This should be a prelude to the preparation of a planning guidance document for local authorities. There is also scope for local experimentation with the introduction of multi-use collection points that are accessible to pedestrians and by bicycle, as well as by car.

Introduce tighter controls on freight vehicles in residential areas

It seems inevitable that there will be an increase in overall LGV traffic in residential and urban areas, especially at evenings and weekends. The parking, pollution and safety implications of this could become an issue for many people. One possible solution would be to introduce a system of residential certification for vehicles and drivers, so that only those in possession of a certificate would be allowed to drive in designated areas.

Examine the future demand for, and the likely location of, warehousing

E-commerce is also encouraging demand for warehousing. Already there is a shortage of large warehouses in parts of the UK, which may emerge as an impediment to economic development. This is also another issue to be taken into account in traffic planning.

Give greater policy support for shared use

The problem of warehousing also raises the question of whether policy should be more supportive of multi-use distribution facilities – for example, through preferential treatment of planning applications or tax concessions (such as partial exemption from business rates). These could reduce van movements and the land requirement for warehousing. Multi-use facilities may also make it easier for smaller producers to gain access to markets.

Increase the application of e-business to rail and shipping

Water and rail are, in general, the least environmentally-damaging transport modes. However, they are less developed – particularly in the case of marine shipping – than air and road freight. It is important that this imbalance should be addressed by examining opportunities to substitute electronic for physical documentation, and introducing inter-modal tracking systems for freight in transit.

Increase access to home shopping for the housebound

There is one group for whom home shopping is definitely likely to be more sustainable; those who are housebound because of age or disability. Some of these will already be shopping indirectly, through car journeys by relatives or home helps, and are unlikely to increase their personal or indirect journeys as a result of home shopping. Internet access could also improve their quality of life by enabling them to feel more in control of their lives and less isolated. Trials should be undertaken to demonstrate the feasibility and value of home shopping for the housebound. Should these be successful, consideration should be given to subsidizing home shopping, which may well be cheaper than employing home helps to do it and would free their time for other, more productive, tasks.

Regulate B2B exchanges with regard to environmental impacts

Finally, competition authorities are beginning to pay greater attention to the potential role of B2B marketplaces. On current forecasts, these will become an intermediary in many transactions, and will therefore have great influence on buyers and sellers. They could become either a new obstacle to incorporating environmental and social factors within supply chains, or a new mechanism for collating and transmitting sustainability information. To date, discussion of B2B exchanges has focused on their ability to reduce costs, and it is questionable whether market forces alone will make sustainability a more critical factor. Hence, some form of policy encouragement may be required. The embryonic nature of these exchanges makes it unlikely that action will be required for some years, but it would be worthwhile for the government to monitor the extent to which they take sustainability into account, perhaps in collaboration with the EU.

Notes and references

1   The term 'e-business' includes e-commerce, but also encompasses other
    kinds of electronic interaction such as exchange of data. 'Logistics' is the
    management of inventory stocks and movements within the supply chain
    – it incorporates not only distribution of produced goods and services but
    also upstream movements of raw materials and management of inventory
    during transit.
2   DETR (1999) *Sustainable Distribution: A Strategy*, London
3   Lobo, I and Zairi, M (1999) 'Competitive Benchmarking in the Air Cargo
    Industry, Part 1', *Benchmarking*, Vol 6, No 2, pp164–190
4   DETR (1997) *National Road Traffic Forecasts Working Paper P3 – Non Car
    Traffic Modelling And Forecasting*, London
5   ibid
6   Lex (2000) *The Lex Transfleet Report on Freight*, Lex and Freight Transport
    Association, London
7   Foresight Retail E-commerce Task Force (2000) *@Your Service*, DTI, London
8   Huppertz, P (1999) 'Market Changes Require New Supply Thinking',
    Transportation and Distribution, March, pp70–74
9   Zentrum für Logistik (2000) *Trends in Distribution*, paper presented to Pira
    Conference on Electronic Shopping, 26 May 2000; Pira, Leatherhead
10 Croft, J (2000) 'Overboard! Paperwork on Way Out', *Financial Times* supply
    chain management supplement, 25 October, p6
11 Tyler, G (2000) 'Taking Centre Stage', *Supply Management*, 31 August,
    pp24–28
12 Angeles, R (2000) 'Revisiting the Role of Internet EDI in the Current
    Electronic Commerce Scene', *Logistics Information Management*, Vol 13, No
    1, pp45–47
13 Grande, C (2000) 'Electronic Commerce Bulls Exude Confidence', *Financial
    Times*, 26 October, p13
14 Booz-Allen & Hamilton (2000) *Last Mile to Nowhere*, New York
15 Keynote (2000) *Express and Courier Market*, London
16 Helft, M (2000) 'Webvan Goes Shopping', *The Standard*, July 3, see
    http://www.thestandard.com
17 Verdict (2000) *Home Delivery and Fulfilment*, Verdict, London
18 Foresight Retail E-commerce Task Force, op cit
19 Richardson, H (2000) 'Virtually Connected', *Transportation and Distribution*,
    March, pp39–44
20 Verdict, op cit
21 Burt, T (2000) 'Industry Faces Up to Challenge of E-commerce', *Financial
    Times* auto supplement, 14 June, p1
22 Hastings, P (2000) 'Tender Care for Transport Companies', *Financial Times*,
    1 June
23 WERC (2000) *Warehouse Inventory Turnover*, Warehousing Education
    Research Centre, Miami University, Ohio

24 Lambert Smith Hampton (2000) *The Right Connections*, Lambert Smith Hampton, London
25 Malinen, H (2000), paper presented to 9th International Containerboard Conference, Miami, 13–15 September, Jaakko Poyry Management Consulting–North America
26 Werner, T (1999) 'EDI Meets The Internet', *Transportation and Distribution*, June 1999, pp36–44
27 Fransoo, J C and Wouters, M J F (2000) 'Measuring The Bull Whip Effect In The Supply Chain', *Supply Chain Management*, Vol 5, No 2, pp78–89
28 Huppertz, op cit
29 *Supply Management* (1999) 'Tesco Sweeps Up Purchasing Savings', 29 April, p9
30 National Research Council (2000) *Surviving Supply Chain Integration*, National Academy Press, Washington DC
31 Lambert Smith Hampton, op cit
32 Nairn, G (1999a) 'Vital Links for Customer Satisfaction', *Financial Times* electronic business supplement, October 20
33 WERC, op cit
34 Calkins, J, Farello, M, and Shi, C (2000) 'From Retailing to E-tailing', *The McKinsey Quarterly*, No 1, pp140–147
35 Lloyd, M (2000) 'Magic Box a Lifeline to India's Poor Farmers', *South China Morning Post*, May 24, p20
36 Cairns, S (1999) *Home Delivery of Electronic Shopping: The Environmental Consequences*, ESRC Transport Studies Unit, University College, London
37 Hopkinson, P, James, P and Selwyn, J (1999) *The Environmental and Social Impact Of Teleworking*, paper presented to the 6th European Conference on Telework and New Ways of Working; Aarhuus, Denmark
38 Pine, J and Gilmore, J (1999) *The Experience Economy*, Harvard Business School, Boston; Royal Institution of Chartered Surveyors, Vision 21, London
39 Marker, J T and Goulias, K (1999) *A Review And Framework For The Analysis Of Household Replenishment And Its Impact On Travel Behaviour And Goods Movement*, Pennsylvania Transportation Institute, University Park, Pennsylvania
40 Cairns, op cit
41 IST/Information Society Directorate (2000) *Case Studies of the Information Society and Sustainable Development*, European Commission, Brussels
42 National Economic Research Associates (NERA) (2000) *Motors and Modems Revisited*, National Economic Research Associates, London
43 Transport en Logistiek Nederland (TLN) (2000) 'Nieuwe wijn in oude zakken' ('New wine in old bottles') TLN Research Department, June (www.tln.nl)
44 DTZ (2000) *A Research Study into Potential Collection Points*, English Partnerships, London
45 Nairn, G et al (1999b) 'IT and the Maritime Freight Industry', *Financial Times* electronic business supplement, 20 October

Response

by Stephen Joseph and Tara Garnett

From   **Stephen Joseph and Tara Garnett**
                <info@transport2000.org.uk>

Subject   **Virtual traffic**

This chapter does an excellent job of demolishing the popular misapprehension that e-commerce will inevitably make everything better. On the contrary, the authors point out that one of the internet's key commercial strengths – its ability to get more goods moving further, more quickly and cheaply than ever before – may also be its Achilles heel, leading to yet more polluting, long-distance goods transportation, particularly by air. Also disturbing is their warning that even where e-commerce can help create environmental gains – less waste, for instance – these savings could simply translate into lower costs, increased production, greater resource use and the penetration of markets even further afield. Left to its own devices, it appears then that e-commerce will simply enable us to destroy the environment in new, improved and ever more ingenious ways.

This said, we are encouraged by the anti-fatalistic stance of the Digital Futures project. Faced with dire warnings of global environmental collapse, it's as well to remember that e-commerce is not a force beyond our control. As far as transport is concerned, we can and should act both to restrict its propensity to increase freight mileage, and to develop that capacity which it does have to benefit the environment.

As far as restrictions are concerned, many of the measures needed to manage e-related traffic are the same as those that Transport 2000 has always advocated. These include the promotion of rail freight, and the implementation of taxation systems that specifically penalize long-distance goods transportation. A tax on aviation is, as the chapter's authors point out, an urgent priority here. We also need to see taxation changes for surface transportation. For some time now, Transport 2000 and others have been advocating weight–distance charging, a 'pay as you go' system whereby the heaviest lorries travelling furthest pay the most – an eminently sensible tax that is looked upon quite favourably by many within the freight industry. To these financial measures we might add the need for a better regulated haulage market. At present we have too many hauliers driving after too few jobs, the consequences being artificially low haulage prices and yet more power to the major retailers who can play one half-broke haulage firm off against another.

As far as personal travel is concerned, action to reduce the likelihood of people spending the time freed from shopping journeys on other, equally car-dependent, pursuits can include congestion charging, car parking restrictions, car-free areas and housing developments, more investment in public transport, cycling and walking, and the transformation of our towns and cities into places where shops, services, leisure facilities and workplaces are within walking or cycling distance of people's homes.

Such damage limitation measures are essential. But we also need to adopt more positive ways of meeting the challenges that e-commerce presents. Although the internet has the ability to link businesses and customers across the globe, so hastening the process of globalization, it can also link local producers with local markets, leading to an overall reduction in freight mileage. By acting as a virtual noticeboard or auction space, the internet could map local and regional needs and resources, match 'wanteds' with 'offereds', and identify gaps where further investment and skills development are needed. It could help to create a fine mesh of networks and connections at the local and regional level, which would keep air freight and long-distance surface transportation to a minimum. Moreover, in rural areas, local producers could also serve as collection points for their local catchment area, providing rural communities with a sustainable alternative to the weekly trip to the out-of-town superstore.

Of course, these networks of local producers will need substantial support if they are to compete against the massively more powerful major retailers. Government must clearly take the lead here. The RDAs also have a useful part to play. Up until now their role has been, as far as we can see, to serve as the meek and adoring handmaidens of foreign inward investment. But perhaps it is time they started to live up to the 'regional' part of their names, by helping to develop and support local and regional economies and enterprises.

Transport 2000 is currently developing a project to explore the potential for greater reliance on local production and distribution to meet local needs. Once it is up and running, we hope to work closely with those associated with the Digital Futures project, as well as with a range of other NGOs.

Finally, perhaps we need to look beyond e-commerce and explore the role that information technology as a whole might play in reducing the environmental impact of the goods we manufacture, order and distribute. Some institutions have, over the last few years, worked hard to develop life-cycle assessment (LCA) models, which they can use to assess the sustainability – in terms of energy, resource and water use –

of a given product. Such LCA modelling is, however, far from mainstream. Technological advances should mean that ever-increasing numbers of products, including those on any supermarket shelf, can be subjected to this kind of sustainability testing. E-commerce can then perform an invaluable function in disseminating and marketing environmental and social 'best buys' to the general public. ■

8 Bricks versus clicks: planning for the digital economy

Andrew Gillespie, Simon Marvin and
Nick Green

Introduction

The hyperbole and speculation associated with the e-commerce revolution is no new phenomenon. Pioneering technologies from railways to automobiles, electricity to the telephone, have been greeted with an expectation that they will completely transform people's lives. Early readings of new technologies show a marked tendency to both exaggerate and simplify their impacts on society.[1] The central question of this chapter is actually rather simple: how does e-commerce shape the physical environment of cities? The answer is less straightforward, but what we aim to do is take a closer look at e-commerce and better understand its environmental paradoxes.

There is little empirical research on the significance of e-commerce for towns and cities, and no well-developed data set against which we can benchmark the environmental implications in the UK or elsewhere. Worse, there are certain pitfalls along the way that we need to be aware of. The most prominent of these is the focus on urban dissolution. This is not the first time that a new technology has been hailed as the end of the city, nor will it be the last. Put simply, electronic forms of communication and transaction are seen by some as a substitute for face to face contact and physical movement. It is claimed that people will be able to live anywhere and negotiate all their needs and services through electronic media. The problem with such a view is that all the evidence points to the growing (rather than declining) importance of cities in the digital age. Cities have the densest communications infrastructure, in terms of both roads and electronic networks. The consumers of e-commerce services are much more likely to be located in cities and have access to the internet at work and home. The bulk of innovation in the development of e-business takes place in cities.

So it is reasonable to argue that cities are actually at the centre of the e-commerce revolution. Our analysis starts with a brief tour of the theoretical terrain, looking at debates about the relationship between the physical and virtual environments. We examine how this relationship has been addressed in UK planning policy, and look particularly at the implications of e-commerce for retail centres. We then return to the four scenarios which are mapped out in Chapter 2, and explore how they might be applied to an urban context. We end by examining the implications for national, regional and urban planning policy.

Physical and virtual environments

There are competing ideas about the environmental impact of e-commerce, based on different understandings of the linkages between electronic and physical flows and spaces. Urban sustainability policy is mainly concerned with physical resources such as water, waste, energy, goods, services and people, and how they move through fixed infrastructure networks. The associated environmental emissions and externalities can be measured, monitored and potentially shaped to meet environmental targets. Usually, the environmental problems created by these flows of resources are conceived of in physical terms, such as the ecological footprint of a household, building or city.

The electronic environment associated with e-commerce and telematics is in sharp contrast to this way of thinking. Information flows quietly, invisibly and unobtrusively through websites, cables, fibre optic wires, or the air around us, with insignificant direct environmental impacts when compared with physical movements. The telecommunications networks themselves are also hidden, often beneath the city, and have largely intangible physical effects in comparison to the construction and use of road networks. E-commerce services recreate physical functions in cyberspace and so do not have the same physical presence as the services and functions they replicate or displace. These new spaces are almost ethereal, and their environmental impact cannot easily be measured or monitored in the same terms that would be applied to the tangible city.

Nonetheless, there are parallels between electronic and physical cities. Telecommunications networks are often laid alongside roads, railway tracks, energy and water networks. E-commerce uses physical metaphors such as the 'superhighway', while websites recreate the layout of stores and facilities such as the 'shopping basket'.

These electronic flows and spaces represent a major challenge to conventional urban policy. Superimposing a conventional physical view of the city on the electronic city is a fraught affair. In the physical city, the development and location of buildings and the management of transport networks are all tightly regulated. In the electronic city, an e-commerce provider needs no planning permission for a new retail or commercial development. This makes it extremely difficult to assess the indirect effects of telecommunications networks on urban environments.

There is a problem of context. Urban sustainability debates have focused on the physical environment, while making the assumption that the electronic environment is fundamentally benign, with few negative implications for the physical city. IT and telecoms companies have also promoted the view that the electronic environment can displace or substitute for damaging physical flows and spaces. The challenge for the future is to determine how urban environmental policy, which is firmly embedded in the concept of the physical city, can begin to cope with new conceptions of the city based on electronic spaces and flows.

The e-materialization of cities?

A central feature of the debate about the environmental implications of e-commerce is the concept of 'e-materialization', the substitution of electronic equivalents for physical products. Examples include replacing CDs with music downloaded from the internet as MP3 files, or the replacement of paper documents with electronic ones – the 'paperless office'. This focus on the ability of e-commerce to substitute electronics and software for material products, electronic delivery for movements of goods by road, and websites for buildings, posits a future based on the gradual decoupling of the links between resource use and economic growth. The prevalent viewpoint assumes that there is potentially (if not actually) a high degree of congruence between the development of e-commerce and a more sustainable society. The e-materialization thesis draws upon a number of strands of evidence to support the idea that e-commerce displaces the physical environment, and these are discussed below.

Dematerialization of the economy

The first strand concerns the broader changes in the structure of the economy, supported by e-commerce, that are leading to a decline in the resource intensity of economic growth. Obtaining adequate data and ensuring comparability between countries is difficult, but several recent studies provide evidence of declining material and energy intensity over time, despite increasing GDP.

The 1999 report produced by Joseph Romm of the Center for Energy and Climate Solutions is particularly supportive of the e-materialization thesis, and has been influential in shaping the debate about the environmental benefits of e-commerce in both the US and the UK.[2] The report examines how e-commerce may be fundamentally altering the traditional relationship between energy use and economic growth, and how this 'historic shift may benefit our economy and environment'. Its central argument is that:

> 'Two remarkable, though seemingly unrelated, changes have taken place in the US economy in the past two years. The first is well known – the remarkable growth of the internet. The second is not well known – that in 1997 and 1998 while the US economy grew by some 8 per cent, US energy consumption hardly grew at all, about 1 per cent. Had the historical relationship between US economic growth been the same in those two years as it had in the previous 10, we might have expected 6 per cent growth in energy consumption.'[3]

The report takes a very positive view of the connection between the growth of the internet and energy trends. Consequently, the US Energy Information Administration (EIA), a statistical and analytical agency in the Department of Energy, was asked to report on the potential impacts of computer use and the internet on electricity consumption. The EIA considered contradictory claims that the internet would result in substantial increases and falls in energy consumption, and specifically addressed Romm's assertion that between 1997 and 1998 the US economy exhibited substantial increases in economic growth with little growth in energy consumption. The EIA's response is that the drop in energy intensity 'is almost entirely due to the decrease in the use of natural gas in the buildings and industrial sector' because 1998 was warmer than 1996. As the EIA points out:

'One would expect the change in energy consumption and intensity to have occurred over a much wider range of fuels and sectors if energy efficiency and structural changes were responsible for the lower use of energy over this two year period, which was not the case.'[4]

The EIA report concludes that current understanding of the relationship between the internet and energy consumption is limited; 'at this point in time, it is too soon to come to any conclusions as to the precise path of electricity use resulting from internet and internet-based commerce.'

Substituting telecommunications for travel

The second strand of the e-materialization thesis concerns the question of whether travel substitution takes place. Evidently there is potential for telecommunications to displace trips in ways that have clear environmental benefits, particularly when teleworking or teleconferencing are substituting for a long commute. However, the evidence is more complex. Californian academic Patricia Mokhtarian has undertaken a great deal of research into the relationship between telecoms and travel. In a paper entitled 'The Information Highway: Just Because We're On it Doesn't Mean We Know Where We're Going', she reflects on the hype associated with the development of ICTs, and then examines in detail the commonly-held assumption that they reduce congestion and improve air quality.[5]

Like many policy makers and planners, Mokhtarian believes that telecommuting can have a positive impact on travel but 'the question is how much of an impact, and what the indirect and system wide impacts will be'. To illustrate the complexities involved, Mokhtarian provides an account of the refereeing of an academic paper that attempted a rigorous empirical evaluation of two telecommuting pilot projects.[6] The paper found that telecommuters travelled on average between 52–54 miles on regular weekdays, compared to 13 miles on telecommuting days, producing a 75 per cent saving due to the elimination of work-related trips.

'We thought we had placed this result quite firmly in context. But when the paper was submitted for publication, one of the reviewers commented that it seemed generally well done and well written, but the claim that telecommuting would reduce travel by 75 per cent was too extravagant to be credible... We suddenly had visions of this number being pulled out of context and carelessly quoted just as the reviewer

did: "telecommuting will reduce travel by 75 per cent". So we inserted even more caveats – in the text, in the tables, everywhere we possibly could.'

The three caveats in the paper directly question the potential environmental benefits of telecommuting. First, the 75 per cent only refers to weekday travel by employed telecommuters, and excludes weekend and non-work-related travel. Furthermore, the telecommuters in the pilot project were not typical of the workforce, as they tended to live twice as far away from work as the average person. Second, the 75 per cent refers to telecommuters, not the whole population. The study estimated that in 1991 only 6 per cent of the workforce was telecommuting over one day per week, and that this saved only half a per cent in total vehicle-miles travelled. This saving was much less than the potential margin of error in the quantitative assumptions made in the study. Finally, even if the percentage of the population telecommuting were to increase, research evidence tends to indicate that new drivers would respond by filling the new capacity made available to them.

The lesson Mokhtarian draws from this example is carefully phrased:

'Don't count too heavily on the trip reduction benefits of telecommunications technology. Yes, they will be there – at the margin. But they will be counteracted and perhaps completely swamped out by impacts in the opposite direction.'

So how does this all come together at the level of an individual city or region? With considerable complexity. True, overall material production might become more efficient, but strong incentives to promote ecological benefits will still be needed, simply because there will be increasing demand for more movement. Looking specifically at e-commerce, the question for cities is how to ensure that the environmental benefits associated with restructured business processes are enhanced, particularly through increased efficiency of resource use.

Cities in the digital economy

Planning policy and practice in the UK has consistently attempted to concentrate urban development, and to limit sprawl through mechanisms such as new towns, green belts and planning-policy guidance from central government. The 1980s saw this planning regime put into temporary abeyance, and the location of activities largely determined by market forces, tempered only by the strength or otherwise of NIMBY reactions against new development in particular places. The results were a population exodus from metropolitan areas, a massive shift towards investment in new out-of-town retail facilities, and a marked decentralization of service activities from large cities to smaller urban settlements – a process examined recently by the Town and Country Planning Association (TCPA) in their investigation of the changing geography of jobs.[7]

During the 1990s, however, the traditional objectives of UK planning were gradually reasserted, a process that has been accelerated since 1997 by the Labour government. These objectives, now cloaked in the new mantle of sustainable development, include facilitating an 'urban renaissance', strengthening the role of established town and city centres, and bringing about a closer balance between homes and jobs in order to limit the growth of commuting.[8]

Land-use planning is now trying to get to grips with the likely implications of the digital economy for urban areas. Here we examine the extent to which a digital economy is likely to contribute to more extended urban forms, and hence pose a challenge to a planning regime that is attempting to bring about more concentrated urban forms.

A new urban form?

Starting from the premise that in order to avoid transportation humans invented the city, some have argued that advances in communications technologies will dissolve the glue that holds cities together, in that more and more of the traditional roles and functions that first generated the need for urban concentration can be achieved at a distance via telecommunications links. However, cities seem destined to persist for the foreseeable future, due to their dense webs of face to face relationships, transactional opportunities, agglomeration economies; their abundant hard and soft infrastructures; and their social and cultural resources. Indeed, some are suggesting that electronic networks, far from undermining cities, are actually bolstering the role of major cities as centres of interpretation of the vast flows of information circulating instantaneously around the globe. As Tony Fitzpatrick, the director of Ove Arup, puts it:

'cities reflect the economic realities of the 21st century. Remote working from self-sufficient farmsteads via the internet cannot replace the powerhouses of personal interaction which drive teamwork and creativity.'[9]

Even if the city as an entity is not threatened by the emergence of a digital economy, the spatial form that cities take does seem to be changing in significant ways as a result of space-shrinking technologies. These new spatial forms seem to pose marked challenges for our current planning paradigm. For planners, the superseding of the familiar 'space of places' by a new 'space of flows' poses both conceptual and practical challenges. How are urban inter-relationships to be conceptualized when they are no longer based on size and proximity, and are highly variable over time? How can the traditional tools of planning, such as land-use controls, be adapted to cope with flows rather than the static nature of land use and location? According to Borja and Castells, writing in 1997:

> 'The new metropolitan city is best understood as a system or network, with variable geometry, articulated by nodes, strong central points, defined by their accessibility. Quality in the new urban-region reality will depend on the intensity of relations between these nodes, on the multifunctionality of the nodal centres, and their capacity to integrate the whole of their population and their territory through a suitable system ensuring mobility.'[10]

Similarly, Graham and Marvin contend that even if a 'post-urban shift' is not taking place, we do seem to be witnessing 'a transition from traditional, core-dominated, monocentric cities towards complex, extended, and polycentric city-regions made up of a multitude of superimposed clusters, grids, and internal and external connections'.[11]

Although there are elements of this new urban form that are compatible with a concern for enhancing sustainability, it is clearly inimical to the preservation of the existing fixed urban hierarchy, as it depends on high levels of mobility and interaction across the whole metropolitan system. This has profound implications for pro-sustainability spatial development policies. In the specific context of The Netherlands, these implications have recently been explored by Hajer and Zonneveld. Their analysis is of particular interest because Dutch spatial planning is regarded as having been successful in achieving the kind of concentrated urbanization that current UK planning philosophy – encapsulated in the Urban Task Force report *Towards an Urban Renaissance* – is trying to achieve. Hajer and Zonneveld argue that a combination of new technologies and transport innovations means that the importance of proximity has been seriously eroded:

> 'the network society immediately seems to undercut the axiomatic idea of "proximity" as an orientation for planning... It poses a direct

challenge to the key planning concept of the compact city that, after
all, uses spatial proximity as its organizing principle.[12]

The planning concepts currently being applied in the UK embody very similar principles, for example in attempting to reduce unnecessary travel by locating jobs and residences closely together, and by steering development into existing urban centres. It is almost as if the sustainability principles that underpin current planning policy in the UK, most notably the desire to preserve traditional urban forms through land-use control measures, are attempting to reverse the reduction in the friction of distance that technological advances have made possible.

New urban forms are coming into being, characterized by high levels of movement and mobility on the scale of extended metropolitan regions. Although the familiar urban hierarchy of small towns, larger towns and cities appears still to be in place, the functional relationships between the elements in this hierarchy have changed completely. Existing physical entities add up to something new, which is articulated by high levels of electronic and physical interaction, and which is only comprehensible on a region-wide scale. There are likely to be important conflicts in attempting to reconcile the network society with a planning paradigm that seeks to preserve traditional urban hierarchies and reduce travel.

The hyperlinked high street

While a digital economy is likely to recombine existing physical places to produce new urban forms, the possibility also exists that particular components of the existing built environment might be rendered redundant by processes of e-materialization. One obvious question posed by the recent growth of e-commerce is whether new forms of online retailing threaten existing retail outlets.

The answer to this question has great significance for planning, given that current policy in the UK is attempting to protect the existing retail hierarchy of high streets, town centres and major city centres, turning the tide against the massive decentralization of retailing that occurred during the period of laissez-faire planning in the 1980s. National planning policy concerning retail location was revised in 1996 to adopt a sequential approach to selecting sites, starting with sites in the town centre, then edge of centre – defined in terms of easy walking distance – and only then other sites that are well-served by other means of transport. Just as the tide begins to turn against the drift of retailing to out-of-town locations, is a new threat suddenly posed by the migration of shopping towards the internet?

Answering this question is far from straightforward, both because of uncertainty about how B2C e-commerce is going to evolve (even the most successful examples of B2C e-commerce, for example Amazon.com, remain highly unprofitable); and because even if e-commerce does grow rapidly, there will be no simple impact on existing facilities. As a recent report from the Retail and Consumer Services Foresight Panel notes:

'E-commerce is only one ingredient in the mix of social, demographic and economic forces that are reshaping the high street. While it is possible that e-commerce could be perceived as being responsible for current trends impacting on the high street, it need not be seen as a substitute for existing retail. It may be complementary or involve novel transactions and services. The make-up of the high street could continue to evolve from retail towards a service sector orientation.'[13]

Established retail centres have already undergone considerable change in the wake of the decentralization of retailing to out-of-town locations, while enhanced competition from telephone banking has also impacted on their service role. If we look at the way B2C e-commerce is evolving, we find a long list of town centre retail and service activities that will be subject to competition from e-commerce over the next decade, ranging from food and book retailing to banking, travel and estate agency.

For most city centres and larger town centres, the competition posed by e-commerce to existing retail and service facilities is unlikely to be severe. However, for smaller town centres and high streets, particularly those that have already been detrimentally affected by out-of-town retailing, we can anticipate a more pronounced challenge from e-commerce that they will need to respond to. High streets will need to adapt by emphasizing their service and leisure (rather than retail) functions if they are to survive and flourish. The prosperity of their catchment areas will be an important influence on their fortunes, though here the effects are complex. On the one hand, a prosperous catchment area adds viability to the shift of emphasis in the high street towards leisure and dining out; but on the other hand, prosperous catchment areas are likely to witness higher levels of e-commerce.

The outcomes, then, are difficult to predict with much certainty, but already weak high streets and secondary retail centres are likely to suffer disproportionately from the advent of e-commerce, in that many of their businesses are already operating at the margins of profitability. Of particular concern are the rural market towns that provide retail facilities and services to their hinterlands. The range and quality of internet-based alternatives to these facilities and services may lead to relatively high levels of e-substitution, which could undermine remaining physical outlets.

From a policy perspective, the growth of e-commerce challenges existing planning policies that aim to protect the established retail hierarchy. There is also a contradiction in policy that needs to be addressed: if e-commerce is successful in reducing the number of shopping journeys, and hence contributing to transport reduction policies, is it likely to do so at the expense of the very existing retail centres that planning policies are attempting to preserve?

Planning for a digital future

In a recent review of the relationship between planning and telecommunications at the European level, Dabinett and Booth conclude that 'the role of telecommunications as a driver for change is only marginally integrated in current planning policy and practice'.[14] Developments in the UK over the past three years with respect to regional planning allow us to gauge the extent to which this is true. Each of the regions of England has been involved in preparing new spatial development strategies, known as regional planning guidance (RPG), following extensive consultations amongst local authorities and other stakeholders.

The draft RPGs cover the period to 2016. Given the likely impact of ICTs over this period, it seems reasonable to expect that the following issues would be addressed in some detail:

- the role of ICTs within spatial restructuring;
- the importance of telecommunications infrastructure;
- the potential contribution of ICTs to economic development;
- the potential contribution of ICTs to rural development;
- the implications of e-commerce for retail provision; and
- the travel substitution potential of ICTs, within travel reduction strategies.

To assess this, we looked in detail at five of the draft RPG strategies: the south east,[15] south west,[16] north east,[17] Yorkshire and the Humber,[18] and east Midlands[19] regions. A summary of our findings is shown in Table 8.1.

All five of the draft RPGs display clear and consistent evidence of the new sustainability ethos of planning, with a common emphasis on policies to reduce car travel and to concentrate development in existing

Table 8.1   Incorporation of ICT impacts into draft regional planning guidance

	South east draft RPG	South west draft RPG	North east draft RPG	Yorkshire and Humberside draft RPG	East Midlands draft RPG
Role of ICTs within spatial restructuring	✗	✗	✗	✔	✔
Significance of telecoms infrastructure	✗	✔	✔	✔	✔
Forces shaping telecoms infrastructure	✗	✗	✗	✗	✗
Contribution of ICTs to economic development	✗	✗	✔	✔	✔
Contribution of ICTs to rural development	✗	✗	✔	✔	✔
Implications of e-commerce	✗	✗	✗	✗	✔
Travel substitution potential	✗	✗	✔	✔	✔

urban centres. With the exception of the south east RPG, they have all begun to address the social and environmental issues surrounding the digital economy, though extremely patchily and from a very limited starting point. The following observations can be made concerning the nature of their engagement with these issues.

- There is limited recognition (with the exception of the east Midlands and Yorkshire and Humberside) of the role of ICTs in contributing to the decentralization of activities, or in influencing the context within which spatial development is taking place.
- There is some recognition of the importance of telecommunications infrastructure for economic development, but limited understanding of the market drivers that are producing spatially-differentiated levels of telecommunications provision. The influence of planning in the development of these infrastructures is seen as limited.
- The potential contribution of ICTs to rural diversification and development, and improved access to services in rural areas, is recognized across the regions, although the mechanisms for realizing this potential remain largely undeveloped.

- Although there is a strong emphasis on measures to reduce the demand for travel, there is little reference to the role of teleworking or the travel substitution potential of ICTs more generally.
- With the exception of the east Midlands, there is remarkably little understanding of the extent to which future patterns of retail provision might be affected by the growth of e-commerce.

What is perhaps most apparent is that while awareness of these issues is rising, policy responses remain undeveloped. Planners, it seems, have neither the specialist expertise nor the mechanisms with which to influence the spatial development of a digital society. And yet, as William Mitchell has argued, perhaps the most crucial task for the planning community at this early stage in the development of the new economy

> 'is not putting in place the digital plumbing of broadband communications links... but rather one of imagining and creating digitally mediated environments for the kinds of lives we will want to lead and the sorts of communities that we will want to have.'[20]

Planners urgently need to seize the opportunity to shape these digitally-mediated lives and communities in ways that will contribute towards more sustainable futures.

Digital cities: four scenarios

The evidence suggests that unless the tendency of ICTs to generate movement is curbed, e-commerce will not necessarily contribute to wider sustainability objectives at an urban or regional level. However, this does not have to be the case. Through the intelligent and creative application of public policy, e-commerce could develop along a trajectory more closely aligned to sustainability. Here we identify how e-commerce could support urban sustainability by revisiting the four scenarios presented in Chapter 2. Although these are not explicitly focused on urban sustainability issues, it is possible to draw out some assumptions about the type of city that might exist within each scenario.

In each scenario we outline the vision of a possible urban future that is implied for e-commerce and sustainability. The scenarios enable us to build an understanding of the challenges involved in shaping e-commerce to support sustainability at the urban level. They are best understood as windows that provide different views of the city under various sets of institutional, social and economic conditions.

The city of CyberSpace

Deregulation rules the day. Global economic integration is pursued with increasing vigour, and cities find themselves the sometimes-unwilling subjects of intense competition with their counterparts elsewhere. As with any competition, there are winners and losers.

The drive to decrease costs is all-pervasive. E-commerce is used simply as a tool for increasing the efficiency and competitiveness of business, with little attention being paid to its wider social and environmental implications. Urban governance and public services, increasingly privatized, turn to e-commerce applications as a way of reducing costs. State provision of education, health and welfare declines and levels of service vary according to the user's ability to pay.

Notable too is the restructuring of the urban service sector following the rapid expansion of e-commerce in finance, retail logistics, entertainment, education and the health sector. Routine consumer purchases become increasingly automated as intelligent intermediaries source least-cost goods and services, and the retail sector shifts its emphasis towards demonstration and servicing. Again, it is the wealthy who benefit, as premium services are targeted at them, while the less affluent have access to a far lower level of services.

It is not only social concerns that suffer. The environment does too, for this is a highly transport-intensive, hyper-mobile future in which e-commerce stimulates the growth of urban freight and global logistics. Transport use grows, supported as it is by low energy prices. Cars, by now zero emission, remain the most popular means of transport through the use of ever-more-effective telematics, and this boosts the effective capacity of the road network and offsets congestion problems. Rapid growth of freight and air transport, again driven by e-commerce, requires major investments in transport infrastructure and telematics. Some significant gains in efficiency are stimulated by the development of B2B e-commerce in the urban economy, but this is against a background of increasingly intense competition as markets become more transparent and business seeks out the cheapest goods and services.

The city of DigitalIslands

In this scenario, economic instability and political problems over economic integration lead to a reassertion of national regulation and a slowing or even reversal of globalization.

Cities become less international in outlook, and focus instead on servicing markets at the national level. Social polarization continues, as the search for efficiency gains and cost reduction favours premium customers and bypasses those on lower incomes. The affluent enjoy increasingly automated routine services, and are targeted by a limited number of trusted national brands. For the less affluent, intermediaries support the development of buyers' clubs for those who seek bulk discounts but are excluded from home delivery because of the low value of individual purchases.

Socio-economic differences between and within cities are exacerbated. This is a world in which high levels of growth in core regions and pockets of affluence associated with e-commerce and the new economy coexist – probably unhappily – with 'black holes' of deprivation, in which services are mediated by charities and voluntary groups.

The environment fares badly, as this is a heavily car-dependent future with weak planning controls, except in privileged enclaves that defend their own environmental and economic interests. Public transport infrastructure receives little investment. Congestion continues to increase, although the use of telematics increases road capacity for the affluent. Road freight increases but there is lower growth in air freight due to reduced levels of international business. In summary, this is a socially and spatially segregated city with high-value enclaves connected to one another through smart hi-tech highways.

The city of CyberSociety

In this scenario, social and ecological values play a much larger role in shaping international integration and economic management. Cities support radical economic, social and technological transformation within more managed global trading systems, which are designed to reconcile growth with equity, fair trade and the environment. E-commerce applications are harnessed for explicit social and environmental goals at an urban level.

Within the e-economy, networks are more open and some form of universal internet access is applied through global regulation. There is selective migration of services to e-commerce. Rapid growth in B2C e-commerce coincides with high levels of investment in sustainable transport infrastructure. B2B e-commerce is used to reduce environmental impacts through improved supply-chain and life-cycle management. Internet conferencing and virtual reality tools are used to reduce business travel.

Government makes extensive use of the web in participative policy making and service delivery. Social and environmental drivers shape innovation, research and development. Rapid technological change and high levels of investment in public transport decouple the linkage between economic growth and transport/energy intensity. In summary, this scenario sees the dissemination of clean technologies, the reorientation of the transport network, and the creation of new social contexts for alternatives to the use of the private car.

The city of NetworkedCommunities

This scenario envisages a world characterized by communitarian values at a local and regional level. Dissatisfaction with the process of globalization leads to a renewed emphasis on local governance, with increasing stress on self-reliance and autonomy at a local level.

Powerful metropolitan regions develop but maintain strong links with other cities both nationally and globally, largely through ICTs. E-commerce is used to support and strengthen communities and smaller, localized markets. Production–consumption relations are managed through web-based technologies that facilitate local exchange.

There is a limited migration of services to e-commerce, as local markets already provide most services. Internet technology is used to support local coops, e-barter and e-LETS. E-government focuses on the universal provision of information, health and education services. Reduced levels of transport result from declining trade, lower demand for mobility and higher energy costs. There is also greater emphasis on reducing the need for travel, through car sharing, traffic management, planning measures and sustainable home deliveries. In summary, this vision strongly reflects the localist and self-reliant policies often contained within urban Local Agenda 21 strategies.

Scenario-based planning

The scenarios are useful conceptual devices that develop particular configurations of social and economic change, and then describe the type of city that would exist within that wider context. However, like any technique of conceptualization, they have their limits. They are neither forecasts nor predictions in any formal sense. Nor are they futures that can simply be selected in terms of which is the most desirable. However, used with due caution, the scenarios can tell us three things.

1   The first is the multiplicity of pathways along which e-commerce could develop at an urban level. The scenarios illustrate how particular configurations of social organization and regulation can shape

the objectives and direction of e-commerce, its use by business and government, and its impact on low-income users and the physical environment.

2   At the same time, these different pathways of e-commerce development coexist with varied visions of urban sustainability, each of which is simultaneously created and supported by particular ICT applications.

3   Finally, these scenarios are not mutually exclusive alternatives, but different pathways that coexist alongside each other. The challenge for policy is to slow down the negative trajectories and accelerate the positive, to bring e-commerce and wider urban sustainability objectives into better balance.

The e-commerce challenge to sustainable cities

In our view, e-commerce is a major challenge to the development of more sustainable cities and regions. Although the dominant rhetoric tends to focus on the environmental potential of ICTs, it is only that: potential. Over-confident perspectives ignore well-researched empirical evidence that ICTs tend to have a more complex, synergistic relationship with the physical environment.

The challenge for urban policy is to develop a new understanding of the role of ICTs within the changing physical fabric of contemporary cities. As the market begins to mesh and interweave building and transport networks with ICT infrastructure, so urban policy needs to keep pace through the parallel planning of electronic interconnections, physical places, and transportation networks.

Policy makers have not found a way of looking at planning, transportation and ICTs in an integrated fashion. Even in the urban white paper published in November 2000, discussion of sustainability, planning, transport and ICTs remain disconnected from one another.[21] A fuller understanding of the urban significance of ICTs will require three shifts in our conventional understanding of the city:

1   a move away from one-way, linear conceptions of how technology impacts upon cities;

2   a recognition of the complex, subtle and contradictory relations between ICT-based and face to face interactions within and between cities; and

3   a realization that physical movement and ICTs, interpersonal and electronic interchanges, affect one another in complex feedback loops.

Urban and regional ICT policy needs to be based on three principles. First, strategies for embedding ICT networks into government, libraries, schools and working life need to engage much more directly with the place-based lives of the individuals, groups and organizations who will use them, if they are to contribute more to the UK's urban life. Second, conventional planning initiatives such as development plans, district plans and transportation strategies need to incorporate ICTs within the planning process. They can no longer concentrate exclusively on face to face interactions and physical transport flows, while ignoring the whole realm of electronically-mediated communication and exchange. Finally, there needs to be a more critical engagement between urban planners and the e-commerce and telecoms industries. A new style of planning is needed: one which brings together different stakeholders to collaborate in the creation of digital cities, recognizes the active role of ICTs in the construction of physical and electronic spaces, and acknowledges that, even in the new economy, 'the power of place will still prevail…. Sometimes we will use networks to avoid going places. But sometimes, still, we will go places to network.'[22]

Notes and references

1   Kraemer, K L (1982) 'Telecommunications/Transportation Substitution and Energy Conservation, Part 1', *Telecommunications Policy*, March, pp39–99

2   Romm, J (1999) *The Internet Economy and Global Warming*, The Center for Energy and Climate Solutions, Version 1.00, December; http://www.cool-companies.org/ecom/index.cfm

3   ibid

4   Hakes, J E (2000) 'The Potential Impacts of Computers and the Internet on Electricity Consumption', Energy Information Administration, Department of Energy, February 2

5   Mokhtarian, P L (1996) 'The Information Highway: Just Because We're On it Doesn't Mean We Know Where We're Going', *The Journal of World Transport Policy and Practice*, Vol 2, No 1, pp34–42

6   Mokhtarian, P L, Handy, S L, and Saloman, I (1995) 'Methodological Issues in the Estimation of Travel, Energy and Air Quality Impacts of Telecommuting', *Transportation Research* 29A(4), pp282–303

7   Gillespie, A (1999) 'The Changing Employment Geography of Britain', in Breheny, M (ed) *The People: Where Will They Work?*, TCPA, London

8   DETR (2000) *Our Towns and Cities: The Future – Delivering an Urban Renaissance*, London, November

9   Fitzpatrick, T (1997) 'A Tale of Tall Cities', *The Guardian*, February 6

10   Borja, J and Castells, M (1997) *Local and Global: The Management of Cities in the Information Age*, Earthscan, London, p158
11   Graham, S and Marvin, S (2000) 'Urban Planning and the Technological Future of Cities', in Wheeler, J, Aoyama, Y, and Warf, B (eds) *Cities in the Telecommunications Age: The Fracturing of Geographies*, Routledge, New York and London
12   Hajer, M and Zonneveld, W (2000) 'Spatial Planning in the Network Society – Rethinking the Principles of Planning in The Netherlands', *European Planning Studies*, Vol 8, No 3, pp337–355
13   Retail and Consumer Services Foresight Panel (2000) *Clicks and Mortar: The new store fronts*, DTI, London
14   Dabinett, G and Booth, C (2000) 'Perspectives on Spatial Planning and Information and Communications Technology (ICT)', State of the Art Working Paper 1, SPECTRE Project, CRESR, Sheffield Hallam University
15   Government Office for the South East (2000) *Draft Regional Planning Guidance for the South East* (RPG9), Guildford; March
16   South West Regional Planning Conference (1999) *Draft Regional Planning Guidance for the South West*, Taunton; August
17   Association of North East Councils (1999) *Draft Regional Planning Guidance for the North East*, Newcastle; December
18   Regional Assembly for Yorkshire and Humberside (1999) *Advancing Together: Towards a Spatial Strategy, Draft Regional Planning Guidance*, Wakefield; October
19   East Midlands Regional Local Government Association (1999) *Draft Regional Planning Guidance for the Spatial Development of the East Midlands*, Melton Mowbray; November
20   Mitchell, W J (1995) *City of Bits: Space, Place and the Infobahn*, MIT Press, Cambridge
21   DETR, op cit
22   Mitchell, op cit

Response

by Peter Hall

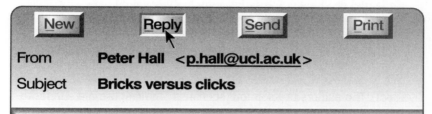

From   **Peter Hall   <p.hall@ucl.ac.uk>**

Subject   **Bricks versus clicks**

The first point is that no one really knows anything about all this; neither the academic commentators, nor the hapless entrepreneurs who (as ever in history) have hopelessly oversold the new technologies to gullible investors. We can say that e-commerce is changing the world, and will continue to change it. How much, and in which ways, is extremely difficult to gauge.

The second point is that the chapter rightly focuses on the impacts on urban function and urban form. There is no firm evidence at all that the digital economy will cause cities to empty out or disappear. Key texts by the chief evangelists of the digital economy both end with that conclusion.[1] In this sense, the authors of Bricks versus Clicks are simply repeating the conventional wisdom. The reasons are evident. First, the production side of the new economy is highly networked and highly agglomerated, as the classic example of Silicon Valley classically shows. Secondly, consumption is also agglomerated, because a high-income, high-consumption economy depends very much on direct personal experience, even shared experience. This is why shopping malls and rock concerts and theme parks and package holidays continue to flourish. Indeed, e-commerce may encourage face to face commerce: CD purchasers may go to a concert to see the original, and web surfers may go to look at the product in the mall.

Here, it is important – but also extremely difficult –- to distinguish carefully between influences and time periods. Decentralization of people and jobs and services did not begin with the digital economy, or even with Thatcherism. The first out-of-town (more accurately edge-of-town) stores opened in the early 1960s; Sainsbury opened their first superstore in Peterborough at the start of the 1970s. True, Thatcherite policies from 1979 onwards gave the process a boost, but it was already well under way. Nor is the networked economy, with its space of flows, a new phenomenon of the 1990s; it was alive and well in Victorian London and Birmingham, as Alfred Marshall discovered in the 1890s. What is new is its relative resurgence, after its partial eclipse in the era of Fordism from the 1920s to the 1980s. But the precise point, already underlined, is that invariably the network economy was and is spatially-bounded. Toyota outside

Derby draws on just-in-time suppliers, but the majority of these are in the adjacent West Midlands nearby. And the decaying high streets of smaller towns (not all of them, but some) were in trouble long before the digital economy; larger town centres are a bigger threat to them, far more than e-commerce.

So trends roll on, in the long term, with surprising consistency. And so far, there is little evidence that e-commerce has affected them much. This poses the question: do we have to worry? What is all the fuss about? The authors develop four scenarios. The first two are supposed to represent trends, the second pair to represent the injection of policy. My problem is understanding how some of the reactions would actually come about. For instance, in scenario two, economic instability and problems with economic integration lead to more national regulation and a slowing decline in or even reversal of globalization. Maybe, but how? Perhaps between the EU and North America. But within the EU? And what about the WTO? Likewise, in scenario three, 'Cities support radical economic, social and technological transformation within more managed global trading systems, which are designed to reconcile growth with equity, fair trade and the environment.' Very laudable, but it sounds rather like the local economic policies of the early 1980s. Which cities are ever going to do this, with what powers and what resources? How would they seek to assert themselves against the forces of globalization? The same problem occurs with redoubled force in scenario four, which implies a total transformation of values and power structures.

The authors issue a disclaimer: these scenarios 'are neither forecasts nor predictions in any formal sense. Nor are they futures that can simply be selected in terms of which is the most desirable.' But, if they are none of the above, then it is difficult – at least for this reviewer – to see what purpose they serve. Scenario building always presents the same problem: it essentially involves writing history backwards with the benefit of hindsight, in that it requires that we trace out a logically consistent and plausible set of processes and their interactions. And then, if we are interested in policy, it means that we have to inject just so much variation, of the right kind, as would be plausible in the concrete historical circumstances. If politics is the art of the possible, then scenario building is the art of predicting the possible. My problem is that some of these scenarios seem to go right outside those bounds, unless the authors are logically assuming a cataclysm of 1930s proportions. And they are nowhere asserting that. ∎

1   Gates, W (1995) *The Road Ahead*, Viking, London; Mitchell, W J (1995) *City of Bits: Space, Place, and the Infobahn*, MIT Press, Cambridge, Mass

Index